# The Doings of Hamish and Dougal

# The Doings of Hamish and Dougal

## You'll Have Had Your Tea?

By
Barry Cryer and Graeme Garden

preface

Published by Preface 2008

10 9 8 7 6 5 4 3 2

First published in Great Britain in 2008 by Preface Publishing
1 Queen Anne's Gate
London SW1H 9BT

An imprint of The Random House Group Limited

www.rbooks.co.uk
www.prefacepublishing.co.uk

Addresses for companies within The Random House Group Limited
can be found at www.randomhouse.co.uk

The Random House Group Limited Reg. No. 954009

A CIP catalogue record for this book is available from the British Library

ISBN 978 1 84809 023 1

The Random House Group Limited supports The Forest Stewardship Council
(FSC), the leading international forest certification organisation. All our titles
that are printed on Greenpeace-approved FSC-certified paper carry the FSC
logo. Our paper procurement policy can be found at
www.rbooks.co.uk/environment

Printed and bound in Great Britain by Clays Ltd, St Ives PLC

# CONTENTS

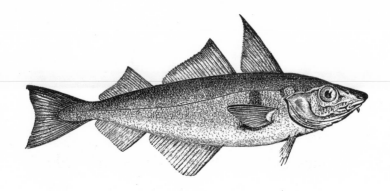

# FIRST SERIES

# THE MUSICAL EVENING

| | |
|---|---|
| *Band plays* | *Sig tune up and under* |
| Announcer | *You'll Have Had Your Tea. The doings of Hamish and Dougal. Today: 'The Musical Evening'* |
| *Band plays* | *Sig tune up and oot* |
| | *Door opens* |
| DOUGAL | Ah, Hamish! |
| HAMISH | Dougal! |
| DOUGAL | You'll have had your tea. |
| HAMISH | No, as a matter of fact … |
| DOUGAL | What a pity. I've just finished mine. |
| HAMISH | And mine too by the looks of it. |
| DOUGAL | But I'm looking forward to your company later on. |
| HAMISH | How would that be, Dougal? |
| DOUGAL | Oh Hamish, I'm having a musical evening. |
| HAMISH | Aye, well I'm the same after a baked bean supper. |
| DOUGAL | No no, man. An entertainment. Jings what fun we'll have. There'll be high jinks in the Glen, and no mistake. |
| HAMISH | I don't doubt it. But look here! Look here! Will I bring a bottle? |

*Old soldier Cpl Mungo MacDuff tucks into his liquorice bagpipes with gusto. Yum yum!*

| | |
|---|---|
| DOUGAL | Bring a bottle, aye! |
| HAMISH | Very well, I'll bring a bottle, as long as you fill it right up this time. But I'm bursting to know: what on earth have you laid on? |
| DOUGAL | I dinna ken, but it's stained the back of my kilt. |
| HAMISH | No no, the entertainment? |
| DOUGAL | A rare treat, Hamish. Did you ever see the Edinburgh Tattoo? |
| HAMISH | Well, I glimpsed it once when you were changing your sporran. |
| DOUGAL | No no, I'm talking about the great national spectacle. |
| HAMISH | So am I. |
| DOUGAL | Well, tonight's revelry will outdo even that. Young Bobby McTavish will be playing the bagpipes. |
| HAMISH | And will that be before or after the music? |
| DOUGAL | Instead of. |
| HAMISH | Oh I see. An economical alternative. |
| DOUGAL | And what a player, eh? The things he gets out of those pipes. |
| HAMISH | Right enough. I've seen him drag a rabbit out of those pipes. And no just the one! |
| DOUGAL | Well he was infested with the rabbits, poor lad. |
| HAMISH | I heard he had to shove a ferret up his chanter. |
| DOUGAL | It brings tears to the eyes. |
| HAMISH | Aye, you always had a soft spot for the ferrets. |
| DOUGAL | And do you know, I still have. But what am I thinking of? Come away in, man, and rest your weary feet. Pull up a chair: there's one in the cellar. ***Baa!*** |
| HAMISH | Glory be! What was that? |
| DOUGAL | Oh, I'm in the middle of making a haggis! |
| HAMISH | Well that's handy, I've just been to the baker's. Could you fancy a bannock cake? |
| DOUGAL | That I could, old friend! But would I respect it in the morning? |
| HAMISH | That's what you've got to ask yourself … |
| DOUGAL | Aye, aye, true … |
| MRS NAUGHTIE | Will I away and mash the neeps? |
| DOUGAL | Michty me! What on earth was that? |
| HAMISH | That was Mrs Naughtie herself. |
| DOUGAL | Oh but you're a fine one with the mimicry, Hamish … |
| MRS NAUGHTIE | No, it's really me! |

| | |
|---|---|
| DOUGAL | There you go again, ye wee scamp! Can ye do Anne Robinson? |
| MRS NAUGHTIE | It's me! The real Mrs Naughtie. |
| DOUGAL | Mrs Naughtie! You've missed a grand display of the impersonator's art just now. Hamish has you off to a tee. But where the devil are you, you wilful minx of a cleaning lady stroke housekeeper? |
| MRS NAUGHTIE | I'm over here – concealing myself behind this tussock. |
| DOUGAL | Whatever would you be doing that for, woman? |
| MRS NAUGHTIE | I'm just out of the bath. |
| HAMISH | Glory be! Is it September already? |
| MRS NAUGHTIE | I was drying myself behind the tussock. |
| HAMISH | Very wise – you dinna want to get a rash. |
| DOUGAL | Towel down briskly, Mrs Naughtie, and bundle yourself into your bloomers. Then be about your business – this place is a tip, and tonight I shall be entertaining. |
| MRS NAUGHTIE | That'll be a change. |
| DOUGAL | The parlour's a shambles. Look! There's a moose caught in the trap. |
| MRS NAUGHTIE | Oh me! Has it tangled its poor wee antlers in the mechanism? |
| DOUGAL | No no! It's a wee sleekit cowerin' tim'rous beastie … |
| MRS NAUGHTIE | Oh a moose! I thought you said 'caribou'! |
| HAMISH | Ach! What are you thinking, woman? A moose looks nothing like a caribou. |
| MRS NAUGHTIE | Neither does a walrus. |
| | ***Honk honk slap slap*** |
| MRS NAUGHTIE | See? |
| DOUGAL | You ken, that walrus reminds me of the old Beatles song … |
| HAMISH | Oh aye … |
| BOTH SING | We all live in a yellow submarine, a yellow submarine, a yellow submarine … |
| | *[**Musicians, walrus and audience join in, round and round**]* |
| | ***Banging at the door*** |
| HAMISH | Who's that banging at the door? |
| MRS NAUGHTIE | It's me – I want to get out! I've got to do my shopping list for tonight. Let's see, I'll need … a pencil, and paper … |
| DOUGAL | Well write it down, woman – you'll only forget. Write it down! |

| | |
|---|---|
| MRS NAUGHTIE | How will I write it down? |
| HAMISH | Oh wait – I've got a felt-tip and a yellow sticky. |
| DOUGAL | But you keep smiling. |
| HAMISH | Every day's a bonus. |
| MRS NAUGHTIE | Now, how many are expected tonight? |
| DOUGAL | Well I'm hoping for a big turnout. |
| HAMISH | You'd better get that over before the party starts. So who's been invited? |
| DOUGAL | Well let's see … There's the vicar … |
| HAMISH | The Reverend Hush … |
| DOUGAL | Angus the Sporran Mender, Elbows McKenzie the Vet, the Crankies … |
| HAMISH | Mr and Mrs Crankie, yes … |
| DOUGAL | Tim the Butcher. Tom the Baker, and Tam the Flasher. And of course the Carburettor twins, and Carol Smillie. |
| HAMISH | Oh my! |
| DOUGAL | Aye! Those are just a few of those who've said they couldn't make it. |
| HAMISH | Is Fingers McToot, the church organist, is he coming? |
| DOUGAL | No – he had a nasty blow-out on the Hymn 25. It made his ankle swell up to the size of a golf ball. |
| HAMISH | What about Mr McLeish from Dyno-Rod? |
| DOUGAL | He's pulled out. Damn his eyes!!! |
| HAMISH | So who is going to be here? |
| DOUGAL | Well, there'll be me … and er, you … |
| HAMISH | Well I have'nae confirmed, you know … |
| DOUGAL | Well, I'm not too sure about turning up myself … |
| HAMISH | Oh go on, you know you'll enjoy it. |
| DOUGAL | Do you think so? Who's coming? |
| HAMISH | Mrs Naughtie. |
| MRS NAUGHTIE | Hello! |
| HAMISH | Oh, I didn't see you there behind the walrus. What are you doing woman? |
| MRS NAUGHTIE | I was just turning some milk. |
| DOUGAL | Oh, I like a woman with a hint of mystery. Now away to the shops with you! |
| MRS NAUGHTIE | Here I go! |
| | ***Harley Davidson roars off*** |
| HAMISH | Sounds like that walrus needs a service. |
| DOUGAL | Well she's the woman for that. And I'm glad to see she's wearing a pelmet. |
| HAMISH | Aye, if she crashes it'll be curtains. |

| | |
|---|---|
| DOUGAL | You're too deep for me, old friend. |
| | ***Cuckoo clock bong! Cuckoo! [Once]*** |
| HAMISH | Bless me, is that the time? |
| DOUGAL | It is. Twenty past five. Come along, we must hurry up to the Big Hoose. I'm inviting the Laird, and we ought to deliver his invitation in person. |
| HAMISH | Then we'd better hurry! |
| *Band plays* | ***Hurry sting*** |
| DOUGAL | You're right. We'd better hurry. Come on! |
| | ***Fast running footsteps break into tap, then back into running*** |
| | ***Howling wind*** |
| HAMISH | Well, here we are at the front door of the Laird's Big Hoose … |
| DOUGAL | Should I pull this? |
| HAMISH | No, he might be looking. Throw this tombstone up at the window. |
| DOUGAL | Right! Hup! |
| | ***Mighty glass crash*** |
| HAMISH | Oh, you just don't know your own strength. |
| | ***Sash window opens*** |
| LAIRD | I've told you kids before about throwing tombstones! Oh, it's you. Be off with you before I give you a taste of lead. I'll count to three, then I'll make you suck these toy soldiers. |
| DOUGAL | Hello, your Lairdship. It's me, Dougal … and Hamish. |
| HAMISH | What? |
| LAIRD | Dougal! |
| DOUGAL | Yes. |
| LAIRD | And Hamish! |
| HAMISH | What? |
| LAIRD | Come away in, Dougal. And Hamish. |
| HAMISH | What??? |
| | ***Door opens and closes*** |
| | ***Wind effect out*** |
| LAIRD | Now then, what do you fancy? Brandy and snifter? |
| DOUGAL | Oh, I should say so. |
| | ***Two dogs yap*** |
| LAIRD | Down, Brandy. Down, Snifter. Now how about a drink? |
| DOUGAL | I'll just have a wee nip. |
| | ***Yap*** |

*Two wee contestants in the Etiquette and Deportment competition discreetly pass wind.*

| | |
|---|---|
| DOUGAL | Ooohooch! |
| LAIRD | Brandy! Snifter! Go to your baskets. It's time for your weaving. I had hoped for a son, you know. |
| | ***Pop. Drinks pouring*** |
| LAIRD | Say when … |
| HAMISH | Well, I'm free on Friday after six … |
| LAIRD | You're on. Now what's this all about? |
| DOUGAL | Well, you remember last week I ran into you in the supermarket? |
| LAIRD | Yes. You don't expect to see a tractor in there. |
| DOUGAL | It was on special offer. And I mentioned to you on the way to the hospital I'd be having a musical evening. Well, it's finally come up. |
| LAIRD | Ah. It's finally come up, has it? |
| DOUGAL | Yes, it's finally come up, and tonight's the night! |
| LAIRD | Well, count me in! |
| HAMISH & DOUGAL | A one two three four … |
| LAIRD [AND ALL] SING | We all live in a yellow submarine etc … |
| | ***Fade out*** |
| DOUGAL | It's party time! |
| ***Pipe Band plays*** | ***The Hokey Cokey!*** |
| | ***Establish and under. Music to come out at end of first or second chorus*** |

*Hoorah! Haggis Day celebrations get off to a flying start!*

| | |
|---|---|
| DOUGAL | *[Over music]* Hamish! How are you getting on with the meeting and greeting? |
| HAMISH | I've done what you said. Taken all the guests' coats and put them in the bedroom. Now, where shall I put all these coats? |
| DOUGAL | Oh! Come away downstairs, everybody. The entertainment's about to begin. |
| | **Small crowd murmur** |
| DOUGAL | Now then, I see you've all got a drink. |
| HAMISH | Could we not have one each? |
| DOUGAL | Oh very well, you hell-raiser you! Mrs Naughtie! Where have you been? |
| MRS NAUGHTIE | I've been getting ready for my dance. |
| HAMISH | Great heaven, woman, what's that you're wearing? |
| MRS NAUGHTIE | It's a surgical basque. And do you like the fishnets? |
| HAMISH | Very nice, but you might have taken the herring out first. And is that an ostrich feather? |
| MRS NAUGHTIE | No. |
| HAMISH | Oh. |
| DOUGAL | Order please, ladies and gentlemen! |
| HAMISH | One drink each, you tightarse … |
| DOUGAL | Now we're all having a grand time. We've enjoyed the Taggart brothers and their rendition of duelling bagpipes. |
| HAMISH | Three times. |
| DOUGAL | It's time now for Mrs Naughtie's party piece. Oh, what is it you'll be doing, Mrs N? |
| MRS NAUGHTIE | It's the dance of the seven voles. |
| DOUGAL | The dance of the seven … do you not mean seven veils? |
| MRS NAUGHTIE | No. That's what the man in the pet shop said. |
| DOUGAL | The pet shop. Is that where you got that ostrich feather? |
| MRS NAUGHTIE | No. |
| DOUGAL | Mrs Naughtie and the dance of the seven voles! |
| *Band plays* | *Exotic eastern instrumental of 'Yellow Submarine'* |
| CROWD | One! *[music builds]* Two! |
| HAMISH | Oh my goodness! I'm seeing Mrs Naughtie in a new light. |
| DOUGAL | It was a free gift with the Land Rover. |
| CROWD | Three! |
| HAMISH | Oh, the exotic wee temptress! Look at those beads. |
| DOUGAL | I know, I've never seen her sweat so much. |

| | |
|---|---|
| CROWD | Four! |
| DOUGAL | The voles seem to be enjoying it right enough. |
| HAMISH | For them it's a night out. |
| DOUGAL | How does she get those voles twirling in opposite directions like that? |
| HAMISH | Oh hello! Where's that wee rascal going? |
| CROWD | Five! |
| LAIRD | Give it some, Mrs Naughtie. Get 'em out for the Laird! |
| HAMISH & DOUGAL | Shhhh!!!! |
| CROWD | Six! |
| DOUGAL | Oh, would you believe it? She's standing on her head! |
| HAMISH | No no, it's somebody else's heid. |
| DOUGAL | It's the man from the *Daily Record*. He's looking for a scoop. |
| HAMISH | Aye, those voles are getting over excited. |
| DOUGAL | And they're not the only ones! |
| CROWD | Seven! |
| | *Crowd applause and cheers* |
| HAMISH | I've never seen anything like that in my life. What a tease! The seven voles – and one by one she put them on! |
| DOUGAL | Thank you, Mrs Naughtie. Mrs Naughtie will be signing your sausage rolls at the kitchen door later on. But now, his Lairdship has kindly consented to favour us with a wee song. |
| HAMISH | Hurrah. |
| DOUGAL | Well, your Lairdship, I know you've been rummaging through your repertoire. So, if you're comfy now … |
| LAIRD | Yes. And tonight, Dougal, I am going to be Atomic Kitten. |
| HAMISH | Ho ho! And will you sing us a song first? |
| LAIRD | I'm rather spoilt for choice, when one considers their cornucopia of chart entries. Those girls really are the dog's ballcocks. |
| HAMISH | Oh, so that's what they are. |
| LAIRD | My first thought was 'I Want Your Love'. |
| MRS NAUGHTIE | Ooooh jings! |
| HAMISH | I think you'll find he was talking to me, Mrs Naughtie. |
| LAIRD | 'See Ya', 'Whole Again', 'Right Now'. |
| HAMISH | I think he's talking to you this time, Mrs Naughtie. |
| LAIRD | So many to choose from. But I'm going to plump for 'Eternal Flame', their cover of the original version by |

|  | the Bangles. This is by way of my tribute to Natasha, Liz, and of course in those days Kerry, but just to show there's no hard feelings, I'd like to dedicate this number to Brian of Westlife. |
| DOUGAL | Oh, we're with the Halifax, but there you are. Ladies and gentlemen, accompanied by my good friend Hamish on the silent banjo, myself on the virginals, with Mrs Naughtie at the bellows, please welcome McCoist the McCoist of McCoist of that ilk, and his rendition of Atomic Ballcock's 'Eternal Phlegm'. Take it away, my sweet Laird! |
| *Band plays* | *Version of 'Eternal Flame'* |
| THE LAIRD SINGS | 'Eternal Flame' |
| *Band plays* | *Segue into 'Yellow Submarine'. Fade out* |
| HAMISH & DOUGAL | *Clearing up – hoovering* |
| HAMISH | Well, Dougal, that was a night to remember. |
| DOUGAL | What was? |
| HAMISH | Last night. |
| DOUGAL | Oh. Oh! My heid feels like the bottom of a Turkish wrestler's birdcage. |
| HAMISH | Well you did give the Famous Grouse a bashing last night. It was all it could do to fly out of the window. Now help me tidy up. |
|  | *Hoovering out* |
| DOUGAL | Jings! There's a pair of boots here. |
| HAMISH | Oh, they'll be the Laird's. |
| DOUGAL | That's just as well – he's still in them. Good morning, sir! |
| LAIRD | *[Waking]* Pot of tea for two and the *Daily Telegraph* this is my niece you understand. |
| HAMISH | And look at poor Mrs Naughtie leaning out of the window. |
| DOUGAL | That's a hell of a hangover. |
| HAMISH | Good morning, hen. |
| DOUGAL | She can't hear you. |
| HAMISH | No, there's a hen on the mantelpiece. And – oh! – who's done this in the ashtray? |
| DOUGAL | In the shape of the Taj Mahal. You've got to admire the workmanship. |
| HAMISH | You're not thinking of keeping it, are you? |
| DOUGAL | No no no! Mind you if we stamped it 'A wee gift from the sub continent' we could sell it at the trinket shop. |

| | |
|---|---|
| HAMISH | Always thinking! Always ahead of the game! |
| | *Cluck cluck cluck* |
| HAMISH | Oh, Mrs Naughtie's awake. |
| DOUGAL | GOOD MORNING! |
| HAMISH | Good morning, I said I see Mrs Naughtie's awake. |
| MRS NAUGHTIE | Oh … has anybody seen my wig? |
| DOUGAL | It's on your heid. |
| MRS NAUGHTIE | Oh, I knew I'd put it somewhere safe. Does my heid look big in this? |
| LAIRD | Now I really must be getting home. |
| HAMISH | Of course, your Lairdship. Thank you for gracing our wee gathering. |
| DOUGAL | And you can't leave without your going home present. |
| HAMISH | Here you are. |
| LAIRD | How frightfully kind. What is it? |
| DOUGAL | It's a gift from the sub continent. |
| ALL | Goodbye. |
| *Band plays* | *Play out music* |
| Announcer | *'You'll Have Had Your Tea', the doings of Hamish and Dougal, was written and performed by Barry Cryer and Graeme Garden, with Alison Steadman as Mrs Naughtie and Jeremy Hardy as the Laird. The producer was Jon Naismith.* |

*THE END*

*The Piping Ramblers negotiate
an unexpected obstacle.*

# THE MURDER MYSTERY

| | |
|---|---|
| *Band plays* | *Sig tune up and under* |
| Announcer | *You'll Have Had Your Tea. The doings of Hamish and Dougal* |
| *Band plays* | *Sig tune up and oot* |
| | *Loud garage music* |
| HAMISH | Dougal! |
| DOUGAL | Hamish! I'm very surprised to find you here. |
| HAMISH | Oh, I just dropped in to pick up my pension and a book of stamps. What about you? |
| DOUGAL | Oh, I just dropped in to ask them to turn down the music. |
| | *Music out* |
| DOUGAL | Thank you, Mrs McAlister. |
| MRS MCALISTER | Any time, big boy. We only had it on to get rid of the mice. And speaking of mice, I wonder if you could do me a favour. |
| DOUGAL | Any time, big boy. |
| MRS MCALISTER | I beg your pardon? |
| DOUGAL | I'm sorry, I thought you were standing up. |
| MRS MCALISTER | And well you might! Now look here, this letter has arrived for your cleaning lady, Mrs Naughtie. Perhaps you gents could deliver it for us, as we can't seem to find her … |
| HAMISH | Find her what? |
| MRS MCALISTER | Find her full stop. |
| HAMISH | I didn't know she'd lost it. |
| MRS MCALISTER | Lost her what? |
| HAMISH | Exactly. |
| DOUGAL | Mrs McAlister, do you mean you can't ascertain Mrs Naughtie's whereabouts? |
| MRS MCALISTER | And I don't know where she is either. |
| HAMISH | We can't help you there. We'd like to know what's become of her – we haven't seen her since she popped out last Tuesday. |
| DOUGAL | Aye, we averted our eyes, and when we looked round again, she was gone. |
| | *Dramatic chords* |
| DOUGAL | Now that's my kind of music, Mrs McAlister. |
| HAMISH | But it's very worrying. Our houses are in a terrible |

*Mlle Olga Fellini offers her clients a free drink with their massage!*

|  | mess since she went. The dust on the picture rail is knee deep. |
|---|---|
| DOUGAL | My bedroom looks like it's been hit by a bomb. |
| HAMISH | Mind you, it's looked like that ever since it was hit by that bomb. |
| DOUGAL | Nevertheless, I simply can't go on without a cleaning lady. |
| HAMISH | I've got a pile of filthy laundry. |
| DOUGAL | No, it has to be a cleaning lady. |
| MRS MCALISTER | Well, if you ask me, you're better off without her. |
| HAMISH | Why, what can you mean, Mrs M? |
| MRS MCALISTER | Come under the counter for a moment, and I'll tell you. |
| HAMISH & DOUGAL | *[Muffled echo]* Unf! Ooof! Etc! Right. |
| DOUGAL | You were saying? |
| MRS MCALISTER | *[Muffled echo]* Well, I'm not one to talk. |
| HAMISH & DOUGAL | Oh. Unf! Ooof! Etc. |
| DOUGAL | Well that was a waste of time. |
| MRS MCALISTER | But I will say this. Mrs Naughtie is no better than she ought to be. That woman is a man-eater. |
| HAMISH | I can assure you she draws the line at that. |
| MRS MCALISTER | I've said enough. |
| HAMISH | Very well. How much do I owe you? |
| MRS MCALISTER | My lips are sealed. |
| HAMISH | Well, it serves you right for licking those self-adhesive stamps. I'll bid you good day! |
| *Band plays* | *Linking sting* |
|  | *Knock on door* |
| HAMISH | Go away. |
| *Band plays* | *Exactly the same linking sting* |
|  | *Knock on door* |
| HAMISH | Oh, come in, you persistent bugger! |
| DOUGAL | No, I won't. |
| *Band plays* | *Exactly the same linking sting* |
|  | *Knock on door* |
|  | *Door opens* |
| HAMISH | Dougal! |
| DOUGAL | Hamish. |
| HAMISH | You'll have had your tea … |
| DOUGAL | Well no, I … |
| HAMISH | You took your time coming in. |

| | |
|---|---|
| DOUGAL | There was a queue. |
| HAMISH | Well, come back later. |
| | ***Door shuts*** |
| ***Band plays*** | ***Exactly the same linking sting*** |
| | ***Knock on door*** |
| | ***Door opens*** |
| HAMISH | Still no news of Mrs Naughtie? |
| DOUGAL | Apparently she was sighted … |
| HAMISH | Yes …? |
| DOUGAL | In a divorce case in 1972. |
| HAMISH | The McAlister case. It's all come flooding back. |
| DOUGAL | Oh, I'm sorry to hear it. Will I get you the rubber pouffe? |
| HAMISH | No, the case, man. Doris McAlister, and her husband the GP … |
| DOUGAL | Very small man … they were known as the wee Doc and his wife. |
| HAMISH | I remember. About five foot three, bald head, bushy ginger beard … |
| DOUGAL | She hasn't changed a bit. |
| HAMISH | A credit to the Post Office, and their employment policy. |
| DOUGAL | You remember her husband. Cruel eyes and a moustache like thunder. |
| HAMISH | Name of Duncan. |
| DOUGAL | That's right. He called his moustache Duncan. |
| HAMISH | And he disappeared in mysterious circumstances during the court case. |
| DOUGAL | And Mrs Naughtie – or Nurse Naughtie as she was then, and we must now think of her – was named as the other woman. |
| HAMISH | I'd never have thought she had it in her. |
| DOUGAL | Oh, she did, they had photographs. I ordered six of the large ones and one for my wallet. Look. |
| HAMISH | Jings! Has it been touched up? |
| DOUGAL | Hard to tell from this angle. |
| HAMISH | It's very fuzzy. What aperture were they using? |
| DOUGAL | Your guess is as good as mine. |
| HAMISH | Oh me! That's never Mrs Naughtie, is it? |
| DOUGAL | No, that's the settee. That's her on the wardrobe. |
| HAMISH | I recognise the hat. But where's he? |

'Hame thochts frae abroad!'

A snapshot of the wee village of Scotland, Papua New Guinea.

| | |
|---|---|
| DOUGAL | He's peeping out of the wardrobe. |
| HAMISH | As well he might. Is that a sink plunger? |
| DOUGAL | Oh aye, that's a sink plunger all right – I always keep one in my wallet. |
| HAMISH | Better safe than sorry. So Mrs Naughtie was old Dr McAlister's nurse. |
| DOUGAL | Yes – and I remember there was talk at the time that she'd persuaded him to change his will, making her the sole beneficiary. |
| HAMISH | And that's when all the mysterious accidents began to happen … |
| | *Flashback link* |
| MRS NAUGHTIE | Here's your tea, Doctor. |
| DOCTOR | Oh thank you, Nurse Naughtie. I didn't expect you back from the pest-control suppliers so soon. |
| MRS NAUGHTIE | Will you take a little white powder in your tea? |
| DOCTOR | Oh, I don't know. Is it odourless and tasteless? |
| MRS NAUGHTIE | Oh yes, completely undetectable. |
| DOCTOR | In that case, two spoons for me please. |
| | *Ambulance* |
| MRS NAUGHTIE | Doctor! Whatever are you doing at the top of that very long ladder? |
| DOCTOR | Would you mind holding it for me, Nurse Naughtie? |
| MRS NAUGHTIE | All right, but I'll wait till you come down. |
| DOCTOR | I'm just applying an antique effect crackle glaze to the chimney pots. |
| MRS NAUGHTIE | Well, you be careful. I'll just be opening the morning post with this chainsaw, in my usual carefree manner. |
| DOCTOR | Right ho! |
| | *Chainsaw* |
| | *Ambulance* |
| DOCTOR | I'll be away on my house calls, Nurse Naughtie. The Laird's set fire to his wooden leg. He was almost burnt to the ground. |
| MRS NAUGHTIE | Not again! But before you drive off, I'll just finish polishing these brake linings. There! |
| DOCTOR | You think of everything. Bye bye. |
| | *Car drives off, getting faster and faster, fades* |
| | *Ambulance* |
| | *River* |
| DOCTOR | Oh, you can't beat the peace and quiet of a day's |

| | fishing here on the river, can you, Nurse Naughtie? |
| | ***Burst of machine-gun fire*** |
| Mrs Naughtie | Well, it's never done that before. |
| | ***Ambulance*** |
| | ***Flashback out*** |
| Hamish | A bizarre series of incidents, and no mistake. |
| Dougal | You remember the police tried to finger Mrs Naughtie. |
| Hamish | Just boyish high spirits. |
| Dougal | To this day, tongues wag in the post office. |
| Hamish | And they're not just licking the stamps. |
| Dougal | It's my belief the poor woman has run away from all the hurtful gossip. |
| Hamish | Where can she be? |
| Dougal | There's only one place she can be. Tonight, Hamish, we go camping on the moors … |
| Hamish | That seems a bit callous when we should be looking for Mrs Naughtie. But whatever you say … |
| ***Band plays*** | ***Linking sting*** |
| | ***Wind howls bleakly*** |
| Dougal | Hamish, stop making that silly noise. |
| Hamish | *[Stops making wind noise]* Sorry. |
| Dougal | It's not clever and it's not funny. |
| Hamish | It's much in demand at parties. |
| Dougal | Oh yes? Like when you pull your trouser pockets out and do an impression of an elephant? Well, this isn't the Freemasons' ladies' night. |
| Hamish | Oh, very well. It's just so quiet out here on the moor. |
| Dougal | Aye. Camping out at night on the moors. Look up, Hamish, and tell me what you see. |
| Hamish | I see a clear night sky with a full moon and all the stars are shining, each one in its place, which tells me God's in his heaven and all's well with the world. |
| Dougal | Hamish, you're a dickhead. We're in a tent. It's impossible to see the stars at all. |
| Hamish | Oh, so it is. Unless, of course, somebody were to steal the tent. |
| Dougal | Steal the tent? Ho ho, that would be the funniest joke in the world. Ho ho! |
| Hamish | Ho ho ho! |
| | ***Ho-o-o-o-o-owl!*** |

*Miss Walsh, the Glen Exterminator, deals expertly with an unwelcome infestation of chickens.*

| | |
|---|---|
| DOUGAL | What was that? |
| HAMISH | I'll take a peep. |
| | *Z-i-i-i-i-i-i-i-i-p!!!* |
| DOUGAL | Well? |
| HAMISH | No, nothing out of the ordinary. |
| DOUGAL | Good. Now let's look outside the tent. |
| | *Flaps opened* |
| DOUGAL | Oh michty me! Look over there! |
| HAMISH | It's a large glow-in-the-dark dog. |
| DOUGAL | No wait! I recognise the hat! It's Mrs Naughtie. |
| HAMISH | Disguised as a large glow-in-the-dark dog! |
| DOUGAL | No. |
| | *Ho-o-o-o-o-owl!* |
| HAMISH | Mrs Naughtie! Don't move. Stay exactly where you are. |
| MRS NAUGHTIE | Why? |
| HAMISH | I want to remember you like this, always. |
| DOUGAL | Come away home with us, woman. |
| MRS NAUGHTIE | No! It's the gossip! The gossip! I've had it up to here. |
| HAMISH | Aye. That's what they're saying. |
| DOUGAL | But we're not at home to Mrs Tittle-Tattle. Come away home and I'll put the kettle on. |
| HAMISH | You know that always makes you laugh. And if it's elephant impressions you're after … |
| DOUGAL | You dare and it's no more buns for you, my lad! But look here! The fog's coming doon, Hamish. Come on – and beware of the quick-sands. |
| HAMISH | After you, Mrs Naughtie. |
| MRS NAUGHTIE | Right you are. |
| | *Hideous bubbling* |
| MRS NAUGHTIE | Oh. Beg pardon. |
| *Band plays* | *Linking sting* |
| MRS NAUGHTIE | Where are we? I canna see a thing. |
| HAMISH | It looks like pea soup. |
| DOUGAL | That's as may be. Zip up your kilt and let's press on. |
| HAMISH | Look! Look there ahead of us – it's the Laird's Big Hoose … |
| DOUGAL | He'll revive us with a hot toddy and a blazing row. |
| HAMISH | Hello, that's strange. Parked in the Laird's driveway – it's Mrs McAlister's rollerblades. |
| MRS NAUGHTIE | Mrs McAlister! It's all falling into place. |

| | |
|---|---|
| **DOUGAL** | Well, that's a matter of opinion. |
| **HAMISH** | I'll knock at the door. |
| | ***Doorbell*** |
| **DOUGAL** | Close. |
| | ***Sash window opens*** |
| **LAIRD** | Who's there? If that's Carol Vorderman, I can explain everything. |
| **HAMISH** | It's us. |
| **LAIRD** | Oh, you'd better come in. |
| ***Pipe band plays*** | ***Link*** |
| **LAIRD** | That'll be all, Drum Major. |
| **MAJOR** | Thank you, sir. Fall oot! |
| | ***March off*** |
| | ***Door opens*** |
| **LAIRD** | Come along in, you three. |
| | ***Yap yap yap yap!*** |
| **LAIRD** | Down, Brandy! Down, Snifter! You've met my daughters, haven't you? |
| **HAMISH** | Hello, girls! |
| | ***Yap yap yap!*** |
| **LAIRD** | I had hoped for a son, you know … |
| ***Band plays*** | ***Time passing link*** |
| **HAMISH** | *[Fading in]* And there you have it, your Lairdship. |
| **LAIRD** | Well, that is extraordinary. You'd swear it was an elephant. Now, what are you doing here? |
| **DOUGAL** | Well, it's a long story. *[Fading out]* It all started many years ago, when, as you'll recall, Dr McAlister disappeared in curious … |
| **LAIRD** | Speak up! I can't hear you. |
| **DOUGAL** | We're here to unravel the mystery. |
| **LAIRD** | What? At this time of night? |
| | ***Clock – bong*** |
| **MRS McALISTER** | Oooh! |
| | ***Clock – bong*** |
| **MRS McALISTER** | Oooh! |
| | ***Clock – bong*** |
| **MRS McALISTER** | Oooh! |
| | ***Clock – bong*** |
| **MRS McALISTER** | Oooh! |
| | ***Clock – bong*** |
| **MRS McALISTER** | Oooh! |
| | ***Clock – bong*** |

| | |
|---|---|
| MRS MCALISTER | Oooh! |
| | *Clock – bong* |
| MRS MCALISTER | Oooh! |
| | *Clock – bong* |
| MRS MCALISTER | Oooh! |
| | *Clock – bong* |
| MRS MCALISTER | Oooh! Etc. |
| HAMISH | That's a bonny clock you've got there. |
| LAIRD | Yes. It's a traditional Bavarian yelping clock. Been in the family for most of the afternoon. |
| | ***Bong, clock falls apart*** |
| MRS MCALISTER | Ouch! |
| HAMISH | Mrs McAlister! |
| MRS MCALISTER | Oh. Hello, everybody. I was just, er … waiting for a bus. |
| HAMISH | You'll have a long wait in this fog. |
| LAIRD | Perhaps I can explain. Mrs McAlister here is by way of being my current squeeze. But I see you know each other. |
| DOUGAL | I'll say we do. |
| HAMISH | Go on then. |
| DOUGAL | We do! I won't ask what Mrs McAlister was doing inside your clock. I think we've all got a pretty good idea. |
| MRS MCALISTER | Oooh! Is that an elephant? |
| LAIRD | No, it's a little party piece I've just learned. |
| HAMISH | Your Lairdship, we believe Mrs McAlister was behind her husband's mysterious disappearance. |
| DOUGAL | And she spread the rumours that Mrs Naughtie was to blame. |
| HAMISH | Well, Mrs Naughtie's here now to have it out with her, face to face. |
| MRS NAUGHTIE | Och no, I don't think that'll be necessary. |
| HAMISH | Go on, you two get stuck in. |
| MRS NAUGHTIE | No, I couldn't, really. |
| DOUGAL | You say your piece, and let Mrs McAlister explain herself if she can. |
| MRS NAUGHTIE | Well … this isn't going to be easy … but here goes. Mrs McAlister … |
| MRS MCALISTER | What? |
| MRS NAUGHTIE | You've made my life a misery. |

| | |
|---|---|
| MRS MCALISTER | How can you say that? |
| MRS NAUGHTIE | It isn't easy. Look at me when I'm talking to you! You, who have besmirched my good name. Explain yourself. |
| MRS MCALISTER | I would if I could get a word in edgeways … |
| MRS NAUGHTIE | Let's hear what really happened to Dr McAlister. |
| MRS MCALISTER | He tried to end it all behind the kirk. I found him hanging by the cloisters. |
| MRS NAUGHTIE | An unusual way out for a medical man. |
| MRS MCALISTER | Be that as it may, I cut him down but he left me. Last I heard he was living with a pole dancer in the Kyle of Bute. I can't remember his name. |
| MRS NAUGHTIE | Dr McAlister. |
| MRS MCALISTER | That's it. |
| LAIRD | Yes, I admit I am Dr McAlister. I took on the identity of the Laird, my identical twin sister, to escape Mrs Naughtie's attentions. Money changed hands … shallow grave … secret passage … birthmark … you know the sort of stuff. Well, there you have it. Mystery solved. Drum Major! |
| | *Pipe music: 'Viva Espana!' [Fade out]* |
| DOUGAL | Well Hamish, a most happy outcome. Bottoms up! |
| HAMISH | Is it? Oh, sorry, I didn't check in the mirror. Well, here's mud in your eye. |
| | *Splat* |
| DOUGAL | Ooch! Right, down the hatch. |
| | *Clatter down steps and thuds* |
| BOTH | Yell! |
| HAMISH | Well, after that I think we need a drink. |
| DOUGAL | Mrs Naughtie! Bring us a dram. Mrs Naughtie! Where is the woman? |
| HAMISH | Come to think of it, I haven't seen her for the last two days. |
| DOUGAL | Don't tell me she's disappeared again! |
| | *Door opens [she has her own key]* |
| MRS NAUGHTIE | Here I am! |
| DOUGAL | Where have you been, you we spannock? |
| MRS NAUGHTIE | I've been away doing the shopping. |
| HAMISH | And it's taken you two days? |
| MRS NAUGHTIE | Oh, there was a terrible queue at the tattoo parlour. |
| DOUGAL | Well, at last we're back to normal, and no more |

|              |                                                                 |
|--------------|-----------------------------------------------------------------|
|              | mysteries, let's hope.                                          |
| HAMISH       | There's one thing I don't understand, Inspector.                |
| INSPECTOR    | Yes, sir? What's that?                                          |
| HAMISH       | What are you doing here?                                         |
| *Band plays* | *Play out music*                                                |
| *Announcer*  | *'You'll Have Had Your Tea', the doings of Hamish and Dougal, was written and performed by Barry Cryer and Graeme Garden, with Alison Steadman as Mrs McAlister and Mrs Naughtie and Jeremy Hardy as the Laird. The producer was Jon Naismith.* |

*THE END*

*A braw smile from Morag Kelsey (28) the village schoolmistress, much admired for her tits.*

# FOLK OF THE GLEN

## HAMISH

Hamish is well-named, being in so many ways reminiscent of cured pork. For some time he has been a regular fixture at the Big Hoose, having spent many a year dangling beside the front door as a novelty bell-pull. In the warmer weather he undertakes many odd jobs around the estate: milking the grouse, polishing salmon, digging for porridge and some even odder jobs.

For me, running a big house like the Big Hoose is an ongoing nightmare, with so many things just waiting to go wrong and cause a problem that needs immediate attention. However, over the years I have developed a sort of system for coping with emergencies. For example, when the electricity fails I can always rely on Hamish to come and jam his thumb into the fusebox to keep the current running until the electrician arrives. When the great fireplace starts smoking due to a blocked chimney, it's Hamish who will come round and deal with the obstruction, usually by removing the chimney-boy who has got stuck up there. And whenever the drains are blocked my first action is to send for Hamish, and sure enough he will usually own up.

Like many a fellow countryman, Hamish is fond of a dram. Indeed it was Hamish who explained to me the first time I poured him a glass of whisky that a dram is the imperial measure equivalent to the Continental litre. Amusing company at the best of times, two or three drams will loosen his tongue and sometimes other parts. A fine figure of a man and the owner of a glorious singing voice once joined forces and kicked Hamish out of the pub.

I recall Hamish once said to me 'Well your Lairdship, you're a fine man to work for and a boon to the Glen.' I told him to shut his noise and remember his place before sending him on his way with a well-aimed boot to the kilt. But he didn't mind. That's the sort of man he is.

*A young Hamish and Dougal take a break from their gamekeeping duties across the Glen from the Nurses' Hostel.*

# ROMANCE IN THE GLEN

| | |
|---|---|
| *Band plays* | *Sig tune up and under* |
| *Announcer* | *You'll Have Had Your Tea. The doings of Hamish and Dougal* |
| *Band plays* | *Sig tune up and oot* |
| | *Door opens* |
| DOUGAL | Ah, Hamish! |
| HAMISH | Dougal! You'll have had your tea … |
| DOUGAL | Well, I wouldn't say no to a cuppie … |
| HAMISH | Oh dear – just when I've run out. I haven't a leaf in the hoose. Goodbye. |
| DOUGAL | Well, a coffee would be fine. |
| HAMISH | Oooh! Coffee, is it? Coffee! His lordship fancies a coffee, does he? I'd better tug my forelock and fill the catheter. |
| DOUGAL | Fill the catheter? |
| HAMISH | Well, I presume your lordship desires a full cup. |
| DOUGAL | What's got into you, man? |
| HAMISH | Nothing. |
| DOUGAL | Hamish old friend, what the devil's the matter with you? |

*Mary Niven checks this season's crop of Ladies' Hats.*

| | |
|---|---|
| HAMISH | Not a thing! |
| DOUGAL | You've been acting very strangely lately. We've all seen you, mooning about the village. |
| HAMISH | My kilt got stuck in my belt. |
| DOUGAL | Nevertheless, Mrs McAlister had to ask you to move away from her hot cross bun display. |
| HAMISH | Aye, that's typical, always coming out with a funny crack. |
| DOUGAL | That's what Mrs McAlister said. |
| HAMISH | Look, if you'll excuse me, I have to get on with unpacking my new hat. |
| DOUGAL | Oh, a new hat, is it? What was wrong with the old one? |
| HAMISH | If it's any of your business, the feather was bent. |
| DOUGAL | Is that all? And what's wrong with Big Tam the feather-straightener? |
| HAMISH | Big Tam? I wouldn't trust that man with a pipe-cleaner. |
| DOUGAL | But gee whiz, Hamish! Now I look at you – what's all this? A new hat, calfskin gloves, the ceremonial sporran complete with antlers and the eyes that move? And, unless I'm very much mistaken, you've sponged your kilt. |
| HAMISH | I've always been very particular about my appearance, as well you know – unlike some people with their tartan dungarees and hob nail sandals. |
| DOUGAL | If they were good enough for Mother they're good enough for me. But look here, this whole room has had a make over. Oh! This is new. |
| HAMISH | Aye. It's an escritoire. |
| DOUGAL | An escritoire, is it? Very wise – you don't want to be popping down to the bottom of the garden in the middle of the night. |
| HAMISH | Exactly. |
| DOUGAL | Aye, you never know when you might get the sudden urge to write a letter. |
| HAMISH | True. Of course I'm not one for writing letters. |
| DOUGAL | Oh really? Then what's this? |
| HAMISH | Give that here! |
| DOUGAL | Oh no no! Let's see, what does it say? 'My dearest darling blah blah blah … I shall never forget the first time I saw your blah blah blah … I long to blah blah blah … Yours in the hope that we |

blah blah blah … Affectionately blah blah blah.'
Well! This looks to me like it could be a love letter, if
it wasn't for all the blah blah blahs.

| | |
|---|---|
| HAMISH | Give me that! |
| BOTH | *Struggle!* |
| | *Rip!* |
| HAMISH | Oh! You've torn it! Right along the perforation. |
| DOUGAL | Aye, it may be soft, but it's not as strong as they make out. |
| HAMISH | You've ruined it, you clumsy gowk! |
| DOUGAL | No no, it's still perfectly usable. |
| HAMISH | No it is not! That was an anonymous love letter. |
| DOUGAL | Who to? |
| HAMISH | I told you, it was anonymous. |
| DOUGAL | Oho! Do I spy Cupid's dart? |
| HAMISH | Oh no, kilt stuck in the belt again. |
| | *Door opens* |
| MRS NAUGHTIE | Here we are. I've ironed your other sock. |
| DOUGAL | Mrs Naughtie, I believe this is for you. |
| MRS NAUGHTIE | Oh! Put it away! |
| HAMISH | Sorry! |
| DOUGAL | No no, I mean this paper. |
| | *Paper rustle* |
| MRS NAUGHTIE | Oh, how very thoughtful. Now off you go – I'm not using that escritoire with you two in the room. |
| HAMISH | Stop! That love letter is not intended for our resourceful treasure of a house keeper Mrs Naughtie here. |
| MRS NAUGHTIE | I should hope not. There was enough trouble when you hit on me in the scullery. |
| HAMISH | I've told you, woman – I was just trying to pick up a parsnip. |
| MRS NAUGHTIE | So it's writing love letters now, is it? This doesn't by any chance have anything at all to do with the new tenant at Capercillie Lodge? |
| HAMISH | Maybe … |
| DOUGAL | Ho ho! It's all coming out now! |
| HAMISH | Damn this belt! |
| DOUGAL | Come along, Mrs Naughtie – spit it out! |
| MRS NAUGHTIE | Very well. *[Spit]* |
| | *Ding!* |
| DOUGAL | Good shot. Have a goldfish. |

*At the village shop and pharmacy, Dod Galbraith dispenses free contraceptive advice.*

*At the village shop and pharmacy, Dod Galbraith dispenses free liquorice allsorts.*

| | |
|---|---|
| MRS NAUGHTIE | No thank you, I've just spat one out. |
| DOUGAL | A bizarre interlude, but let it not deflect us from our purpose. Who is this mysterious tenant of the Lodge? |
| HAMISH | Lady Caroline Fitz-Neatleigh. |
| DOUGAL | This has gone further than we thought. |
| MRS NAUGHTIE | Lady Caroline is a society beauty from Chelsea, no less. She's up for the fishing – and that's not all she's up for, by all accounts. |
| HAMISH | I'll never forget the first time I saw her – the wind blowing in her hair, sitting on top of Ben Affleck eating a picnic lunch. The moment I saw her, I felt something snap. |
| DOUGAL | You know I'd get rid of that belt if I were you. |
| HAMISH | Then as she ran down the mountainside, she caught her handbag on a thistle. I rushed to help her out of her clothes. When I came to, she was nowhere to be seen. She was behind me, with a rock. When I came to again, she was gone. |
| DOUGAL | Aye, that's often the way. But Hamish, old friend, whatever made you think that a sophisticated society beauty like Lady Caroline would give a second glance to a clapped-out, ignorant, clumsy, repulsive, unhygienic peasant like you, you ugly old bastard? |
| HAMISH | Oh I know you're just trying to make me feel better, but I must follow my dream … |
| *Band plays* | ***Link [possibly To Dream the Impossible Dream] River bank. Rustling in the bushes*** |
| DOUGAL | *[Whispering]* What can you see, Mrs Naughtie? |
| MRS NAUGHTIE | I can see the two of them on the river bank. Lady Caroline is casting a line across the current, and Mr Hamish is standing close beside her, murmuring into her ear, as she turns her head towards him, a smile playing about her rose-red lips. |
| DOUGAL | Good. That's exactly what I can see. But thank you for painting that vivid word picture for the benefit of those who may be listening. |
| MRS NAUGHTIE | Look, she appears to be admiring his flies. |
| DOUGAL | He ties them himself, you know. |
| MRS NAUGHTIE | Ever since he was a boy. |
| DOUGAL | Quick, pass me those binoculars. |
| MRS NAUGHTIE | I can't reach them. |
| DOUGAL | Damn. Hamish, can you reach the binoculars? |

| | |
|---|---|
| HAMISH | Here you are. Oh! Hello, you two. |
| MRS NAUGHTIE | I told you we were too close! |
| HAMISH | May I introduce my friend, Lady Caroline Fitz-Neatleigh? |
| LADY | How do you do? |
| DOUGAL | Hello, Lady Caroline. I believe this is your first time? |
| HAMISH | She soon got the hang of it. As soon as I took my tackle out, there was no stopping her. |
| LADY | Dear Hamish has been teaching me how to handle his rod. Or 'cock' as we call it in London society. |
| DOUGAL | Aye, that's Hamish for you. Well, I can see that you two young things want us to hang around for a bit. Mrs Naughtie, be so kind as to rustle us up a cup of tea and a plate of that sushi of yours. |
| MRS NAUGHTIE | No bother. Four teas coming up. |
| | *Door opens* |
| MRS NAUGHTIE | Good job I brought the kitchen with me, just in case! |
| | *Door shuts* |
| ALL | *Laughter* |
| | *Fade out* |
| *Band plays* | *Link* |
| | *Fade in* |
| ALL | *Laughter* |
| HAMISH | Well. It looks like she was lying about the tea. Back to the fishing. |
| LADY | Right ho! Here goes … |
| | *Fly cast* |
| DOUGAL | Oh dear, it seems to me we're having a little trouble with the casting. |
| LADY | Well, I'm doing my best. You told me I was only playing Mrs Naughtie. |
| HAMISH & DOUGAL | Whisht! Hrrhmph. Deary me … |
| | *Door opens* |
| MRS NAUGHTIE | Here we are – three cups of tea. |
| HAMISH | Only three? What about a cup for Lady Caroline? |
| MRS NAUGHTIE | Don't push it, sonny! |
| DOUGAL | Oh look! |
| | *Splash. Reel whizzes. Splashes* |
| HAMISH | Jings! It's a big one! |
| DOUGAL | Help her pull it out! |
| HAMISH | She's handling it like an old pro! |
| LADY | Oh, I do love it when you talk fishing. |

*Loving couple!*
*Jim and Jessie Toshack, photographed by their proud mum.*

| | |
|---|---|
| DOUGAL | All together now – heave! |
| | ***Splash squelch thump!*** |
| | ***Flap flap flap*** |
| DOUGAL | It's on the bank. What a monster! |
| LAIRD | Good afternoon. |
| HAMISH | Glory be – a talking fish! |
| LAIRD | It's me, the Laird. McCoist the McCoist of McCoist of that ilk. And who is this saucy little charmer? |
| DOUGAL | It's Hamish. |
| LAIRD | No no, of course I recognise that clapped-out, ignorant, clumsy, repulsive, unhygienic peasant's face, you ugly old bastard. |
| HAMISH | Then it's true … *[Weeps]* |
| LAIRD | I was referring to the lady. |
| DOUGAL | Oh. This is Lady Caroline Fitz-Neatleigh. Lady Caroline, this is the talking fish. |
| LADY | Charmed, I'm sure. |
| LAIRD | Forgive me if I don't get up. I was in the river having my morning dip – with chives – when suddenly you hauled me out. You must excuse the rubber suit. |
| LADY | Not at all. The waistcoat is charming. And may I say, the carnation is a delightful touch. |
| LAIRD | Yes. Well, it was either there or in the button hole. |
| HAMISH | Now, sir, let's help you to your feet so you can be on your way. |
| LAIRD | Thank you. Careful – this rubber suit has to go back in the morning. Lady Caroline, will you walk a little way with me? |
| LADY | I'd be glad to. |
| LAIRD | Goodbye, Hamish. Goodbye, Dougal. |
| HAMISH & DOUGAL | Goodbye, fish. |
| LAIRD | Come, my dear. |
| | ***Squeak squeak squeak squeak …*** |
| LADY | I'm terrible sorry, it's this new girdle. |
| LAIRD | Don't worry, I'll soon have that ripped off. |
| BOTH | ***Laugh lightly as the squeaking fades*** |
| HAMISH | Oh … Jings! |
| DOUGAL | What is it, old friend? |
| HAMISH | You can't know what it feels like when the love of your life goes off with a talking fish. |
| DOUGAL | Oh, but I do … |
| ***Band plays*** | ***Link into romantic background music*** |

| | |
|---|---|
| LADY | Oh your Lairdship! Wonderful place you have here. |
| LAIRD | Thank you. More chips? Salt and vinegar? |
| LADY | What kind of girl do you take me for? |
| LAIRD | I'm sorry. And please, call me Kylie. |
| LADY | Kylie. Is that your name? |
| LAIRD | Good God no. |
| LADY | What must you think of me? We've only known each other ten minutes, and already we're lying naked in front of an open fire. |
| LAIRD | Let me fetch you another brandy. |
| | ***Squeak squeak squeak squeak …*** |
| LADY | That girdle suits you, Kylie. |
| LAIRD | What girdle? |
| | ***They laugh, tinklingly*** |
| ***Band plays*** | ***Link*** |
| HAMISH | Oh, I can just imagine them now. Lying naked in front of a roaring fire, tucking in to plaice and chips. |
| DOUGAL | Surely not! |
| HAMISH | Oh yes. He tried that on with me, you know. But I wasn't having any of it! |
| DOUGAL | I should hope not. You're a haddock man if ever there was one. |
| HAMISH | Now please, leave me alone with my thoughts, and my pain. |
| DOUGAL | Are you sure you'll be all right? Because when you came in on that unicycle with an orange wig and a custard pie, I thought 'I hope he's not going to do anything silly …' |
| HAMISH | Oh cruel world. What's left for the likes of me? |
| | ***Door opens*** |
| LADY | Here we are, a nice bit of haddock for your tea. |
| HAMISH | Thank you … Mrs Naughtie. |
| MRS NAUGHTIE | Oh bum! Hoots! Here's a nice bit of haddock for your tea, the noo, by the way. |
| | ***Door opens*** |
| LAIRD | Haddock? What luck, my favourite. |
| | ***Squeak squeak squeak …*** |
| LAIRD | Mmm … rather chewy … |
| | ***More squeaks*** |
| HAMISH | You! I don't know how you dare show your face, and sit there chewing my haddock … |

| | |
|---|---|
| LAIRD | Calm yourself, Hamish. Calm Hamish, Dougal. I'm here to tell you you've had a lucky escape. |
| HAMISH | How so? |
| LAIRD | *[Mouth full]* This haddock's disgusting. Not only that, Lady Caroline so-called Fitz-Neatleigh has made fools of us all. |
| DOUGAL | What do you mean, Kylie? |
| LAIRD | My God, that's got round quickly. What I mean is, I discovered her true nature when I caught her rifling through my drawers. Luckily I wasn't wearing them at the time, and the rifle wasn't loaded. |
| DOUGAL | I knew it – I knew she was a common fortune-hunting tart the minute I heard that phoney accent! |
| MRS NAUGHTIE | Well thank you! |
| LAIRD | Yes, she was just after my money. I sent her packing when she confessed the only man she ever truly loved was Hamish. |
| HAMISH | She what …? |
| LAIRD | Yes, Hamish was her heart's desire. So I chased her off with the dogs. |
| DOUGAL | A happy conclusion for one and all. |
| HAMISH | Wait a minute! |
| DOUGAL | We won't be seeing her again – the trollop! |
| LAIRD | Hurrah! Now you're all invited up to the Big Hoose for plaice and chips in front of a roaring fire. |
| HAMISH | But … but! |
| DOUGAL | Come on, man, it'll do you good. Mrs Naughtie, put out that fire, then let's all put our clothes back on, and away up to the Big Hoose. |
| HAMISH | But … |
| DOUGAL | What are we waiting for? |
| LAIRD | That's the spirit. |
| DOUGAL | Lead on, fish! |
| | *All laugh* |
| | *Hamish still sadly going but … But …* |
| *Band plays* | *Sig and oot under credits* |

**THE END**

# NAUGHTIE BUT NICE!

Leaves from Mrs Naughtie's Recipe Book. Whether it's a banquet at the Big Hoose or a humble supper chez Hamish or even a simple candlelit picnic close by the Muckle Bog, you can be sure that Mrs Naughtie will have had a hand in it.

Here in her own words Mrs Naughtie shares the secrets of the very best of traditional Scots cooking!

# SCOTCH BROTH

A winter favourite that warms the belly on a cold frosty night taught me this recipe during one of his recent visits.

INGREDIENTS: Fresh vegetables, 1 potato (cubed), 1 carrot (squared), 1 neep (square root of), 1 onion (to the power of 10), 4oz of split peas (or 2oz of whole peas), lintels and pearl bailey, meat-flavoured tofu chunks, 1 bottle of cooking whisky, seasoning (in season).

METHOD: Shred the cabbage and put to one side. Beat the butter into a froth and put to the other side. Shell the peas mercilessly from high ground. Carefully pour the whisky into your Broth Cauldron through the hole at the top.

Phone Kylie's Karry-oot Kitchen for a Highland Take-away and while waiting for it to be delivered, drink the Scotch.

# THE SHOOTING PARTY

| | |
|---|---|
| *Band plays* | *Sig tune up and under* |
| *Announcer* | *You'll Have Had Your Tea. The doings of Hamish and Dougal* |
| *Band plays* | *Sig tune up and oot* |
| | *Howling wind, birdsong and footsteps approaching through the gorse* |
| HAMISH | Dougal! |
| DOUGAL | Hamish. You'll have had your tea … |
| HAMISH | No, as a matter of fact. I can't get the top off this thermos flask that Mrs Naughtie left out. |
| DOUGAL | Here, let me give it a twist. |
| | *Bzzzzzzzzzzzzzzz …* |
| DOUGAL | Oh Hamish! This is not a thermos. |
| HAMISH | Not a thermos? |
| | *Bzzz!* |
| DOUGAL | No. |
| HAMISH | You mean … it's a razor? |
| DOUGAL | A what? |
| HAMISH | A razor. You know full well Mrs Naughtie shaves her legs. |

*Eager sportsmen respond to the news that a grouse has been sighted.*

| | |
|---|---|
| DOUGAL | What? Hers as well? |
| HAMISH | Yes. You must have noticed that five o'clock shadow around her ankles. |
| DOUGAL | And there's me thinking she was wearing pop-socks. But this is no razor. |
| HAMISH | What is it then? |
| DOUGAL | If you ask me, old friend, I'd say it was a … *[Whisper Whisper]* … |
| HAMISH | A pie grater? |
| DOUGAL | Pie grater? No! Marital aid. |
| HAMISH | Well, if I can get the top off I'll have a glass of that. I'm parched. |
| LAIRD | Hello, you two! |
| HAMISH | It's the Laird! |
| DOUGAL | Quick, hide that thing! |
| HAMISH | Consider it hidden! |
| | *Bzzzzzzzzzzzzz …* |
| HAMISH | Jings! |
| LAIRD | What on earth are you doing with my Christmas present to Mrs Naughtie? |
| DOUGAL | Och, that was just our novelty thermos flask. |
| LAIRD | My mistake. Pity. I've got a pie here that badly needs grating. Hamish! |
| | *Bzz!* |
| HAMISH | YES? |
| LAIRD | You look full of the joys of spring. |
| HAMISH | You could say that … |
| | *Bz!* |
| HAMISH | Oo! |
| LAIRD | Now, I came up here to tell you: I'm having a shoot this afternoon. |
| DOUGAL | Whoa! Too much information! |
| LAIRD | The Glorious Twelfth. |
| DOUGAL | All in the one day? Have you tried hard-boiled eggs? |
| LAIRD | Yes, but I find them too easy to hit. Now look here, I fancy a bit of practice. Are you two at a loose end? |
| | *Bzz!* |
| HAMISH | I SHOULD SAY SO! |
| LAIRD | Good. So, Dougal, you can load my guns … |
| DOUGAL | Oh … you meant 'shoot'! Bang. |
| LAIRD | And Hamish, you will release the clays on the |

|  | command 'pull!' |
|---|---|
|  | *Bzz!* |
| HAMISH | OK! |
|  | *Gun loading* |
| DOUGAL | Your gun, your Lairdship. You've got one up the spout. |
|  | *Bzz!* |
|  | *Wee pause* |
| LAIRD | Hamish, you look as if you're about to say something? |
| HAMISH | NO …! |
| LAIRD | Very good then. Pull! |
|  | *Twang!* |
|  | *Whooshhhh!* |
|  | *Gunshot* |
|  | *Boom!* |
|  | *Crashing of pottery for ages* |
|  | *Pause* |
| LAIRD | They're not much of a challenge, these clay stags. |
| DOUGAL | No. We said the same thing about the clay salmon. |
| LAIRD | Don't bother me with your problems. Pull! |
|  | *Pop!* |
|  | *Bzzzzzzzzzzzzzzzzzzzz …* |
|  | *Gunshot* |
|  | *Crack boing tinkle tinkle* |
| HAMISH | Aah, that's better. But you know, in a way, I'll miss it … |
| *Band plays* | *Link* |
|  | *Kitchen noises. Pots clattering, pans boiling …* |
| MRS NAUGHTIE | *[Singing a cooking song]* 'If I knew you were coming I'd have boiled a neep, boiled a neep, boiled a neep … etc.' |
|  | *Door opens* |
| DOUGAL | Ah, Mrs Naughtie. There you are. |
| MRS NAUGHTIE | And where else would I be? |
| DOUGAL | But this is my bedroom. |
| MRS NAUGHTIE | The kitchen's full. I'm catering for the Laird's shooting party. He's inviting all the smart folk up from London, and a married couple from Milton Keynes. |
| HAMISH | So that's how many altogether? |
| MRS NAUGHTIE | About two thousand all told. And they'll all be gagging for pies. And by the way, has anybody seen my pie grater? |

*Grouse shooting the way it used to be.*

| | |
|---|---|
| HAMISH | No. |
| MRS NAUGHTIE | No matter. I could never see the point of it. |
| HAMISH | Neither could I. |
| MRS NAUGHTIE | Now away with the pair of you – I've got to butter my baps. |
| DOUGAL | Oh, many's the time I've watched you do that. |
| MRS NAUGHTIE | So it was you in the wardrobe! |
| DOUGAL | Among others. |
| MRS NAUGHTIE | Och! Will you just look at the time? It's over there by the parsley. |
| HAMISH | Jings, it's almost half past. |
| DOUGAL | Yes, we'd better get up to the moor for the afternoon's slaughter. |
| BOTH | Goodbye. |
| | ***Door closes.*** |
| ***Band plays*** | ***Jolly blood sports link*** |
| | ***Thunder, rain, howling wind*** |
| HAMISH | A grand day for it, your Lairdship. |
| LAIRD | Yes, but unfortunately we're stuck out here. |
| | ***Train toots*** |

*Hamish and Dougal in more carefree days, bargain-hunting in Aberdeen.*

|  | *Cars and motorbikes screech up* |
|  | *Helicopter lands* |
|  | *Etc.* |
| LAIRD | Ah, splendid – my smart guests from down south have arrived. |
| HAMISH & DOUGAL | 'Hellay' 'Waa Waa' 'Haa ha ha!' 'Ai I say!' etc, etc. |
| LAIRD | Come on, you two, stop taking the piss and go and greet them properly. |
| HAMISH | Sorry, your Lairdship. |
| LAIRD | And right on time, here's Mrs Naughtie, our catering queen! |
| MRS NAUGHTIE | I've got the hampers. |
| LAIRD | Have you tried hard-boiled eggs? I find that sometimes gets a laugh. |
| MRS NAUGHTIE | Here we are, two thousand ungrated pies, and a dozen clay salmon sandwiches. Now, who ordered the onion bhajee? |
| LAIRD | Ah, that was me. Pull. |
|  | *Twang* |
|  | *Whooosh* |
|  | *Gunshot* |
| MRS NAUGHTIE | Missed! |
| LAIRD | Yes, but look at it this way. That's another bhajee returned to the wild. |
| MRS NAUGHTIE | My brother was a bargee. |
| LAIRD | Now you're just being silly. *[To the crowd]* Now listen up, people – are you ready for some sport? |
|  | *Wembley crowd roar* |
| LAIRD | Good. Dougal, over to you. |
| DOUGAL | Good afternoon, ladies and gentlemen, and how are you today? I'm Dougal and I'll be your gillie. Kindly follow the piper to your shooting positions on the ridge. At fifteen hundred hours the Panzers will move in on the left flank, while the airborne division lays down a covering barrage. Enjoy your day. |
|  | *Piper leads off four thousand marching feet* |
|  | *Pause.* |
| DOUGAL | Right, your Lairdship, everybody's in position. |
|  | *Two people running* |
| HAMISH | Come along, you two, you're not in Milton Keynes now. |

| | |
|---|---|
| LAIRD | Now Hamish, you and Dougal will act as beaters. I want you to drive the birds towards the guns.<br>*[Oh, ho ho ... ]*<br>And when I say drive, I don't mean by car, I mean frighten the birds.<br>*[Oh, ho ho ... ]*<br>And when I say birds, I don't mean young ladies, I mean the grouse.<br>*[Oh, ho ho ... ]*<br>And when I say grouse, I mean crows, pigeons, rabbits, kittens, caterpillars, anything that moves. They're from London, they won't know the difference. |
| DOUGAL | Very good, sir. Hamish – commence beating.<br>*Beating bracken and gorse* |
| HAMISH & DOUGAL | Hup!<br>Boo!<br>Move along there, you grouses!<br>Look out – there's a lot of folk about with guns.<br>Fly for your lives! |
| HAMISH | Away they go!<br>*Wings flapping and grouse peeps [build]*<br>*Gunfire*<br>*Machine guns*<br>*Artillery*<br>*Tanks*<br>*Dive-bombers* |
| LAIRD | Right! That concludes the afternoon's sport. Now, if you all line up in alphabetical order with your vouchers, Mrs Naughtie has prepared a delicious picnic. |
| MRS NAUGHTIE | Yes, and as soon as I've eaten it, I'll be handing out the pies. And I'm delighted to see you've all brought your own graters.<br>*Wembley roar*<br>*Stampede* |
| DOUGAL | Well done, Mrs Naughtie. |
| HAMISH | You must be fair whackit. Sit ye doon and take the weight off your bannocks. |
| MRS NAUGHTIE | That I will. |
| DOUGAL | Don't sit on that! It's the clay pigeon launcher. |
| LAIRD | No, that's all right, as long as nobody shouts 'Pull!' |

|  |  |
|---|---|
|  | *Twang* |
|  | *Whoooooosssshhhhhh!* |
| MRS NAUGHTIE | Ooooooooooh! |
|  | *[Build as before]* |
|  | *Gunfire* |
|  | *Machine guns* |
|  | *Artillery* |
|  | *Tanks* |
|  | *Dive-bombers* |
| LAIRD | *[Over]* Hold your fire! Hold your fire! Hold your fire! |
|  | *Silence* |
|  | *Two shots* |
| LAIRD | That includes you too, Milton Keynes. |
| HAMISH | I daren't look. What happened? |
| DOUGAL | I don't believe it. As luck would have it, I've just found 50p in the bracken. |
| HAMISH | 50p? There'll be no speaking to you for a week. But what happened to Mrs Naughtie? |
| DOUGAL | I don't know – I wasn't looking. |
| MRS NAUGHTIE | *[Distant]* Ooooo … |
| HAMISH | There she goes – commencing her descent … |
| LAIRD | Mrs Naughtie, if you get to the Big Hoose before us, put the kettle on. |
| MRS NAUGHTIE | *[Distant]* No sooner said than … |
|  | *Enormous glass crash* |
| HAMISH | Thank God! The greenhouse broke her fall. |
| ALL | Hoorah! |
|  | *Crowd roar* |
| *Band plays* | *Link* |
|  | *Crowd singing 'You'll Never Walk Alone'* |
| LAIRD | Well, goodbye, you two thousand. Goodbye! |
|  | *Door shuts. Singing out* |
| LAIRD | I thought they'd never go. Well, Hamish, Dougal. Cheers. Good health. Bottoms up. |
| HAMISH & DOUGAL | Thank you. Bottoms up. Good health. Cheers. Etc, Etc. |
| LAIRD | Well, I don't know about you two, but I'm going to have a drink. |
|  | *Drinks trolley arrives* |
| MRS NAUGHTIE | Here we are. |
| LAIRD | Mrs Naughtie. What a day you've had. By the way, |

|  | thank you for mending the greenhouse. Oh, there's an ugly lump of putty on your nose. |
|---|---|
| MRS NAUGHTIE | No there isn't. |
| LAIRD | Oh, sorry. Well, look on the bright side – some people say warts are lucky. And may I say, you're a very, very lucky woman. |
| MRS NAUGHTIE | Why thank you, kind sir. |
| LAIRD | Now, if I'm any judge of character, you'll be in need of a stiff one. |
| MRS NAUGHTIE | You can read me like a book. |
| LAIRD | Yes – and I always like to peep at the end before I start. |
| MRS NAUGHTIE | I believe you're trying to get me tiddly. |
| LAIRD | I am if I can find it. |
|  | *They laugh* |
| DOUGAL | Ahem, will you be requiring us any further this evening, sir? |
| LAIRD | Oh, forgive me. The writers had quite forgotten you were here. What would you chaps say to a couple of large Teachers? |
| HAMISH | We cannae see the blackboard! |
| LAIRD | Correct. Now I'd like to propose a toast. To the ladies! |
| DOUGAL | OK. |
|  | *Scampering feet* |
|  | *Door opens and shuts* |
|  | *Loo flush, then echo acoustic for the scene* |
| LAIRD | *[Echo]* Right. Now we're all in here, I'd like to sing a little song. Best acoustics in the Big Hoose. Is the band here? |
| *Voice* | *Cubicle three.* |
| LAIRD | Then hit it! |
| *Laird and Band plays* | *'Little Red Rooster'* |
|  | *Fade out and mix to* |
|  | *Footsteps on gravel* |
|  | *Wind. Distant owl hoot* |
|  | *Soft moonlight* |
| DOUGAL | Well, the Laird looked very happy when we left. |
| HAMISH | Aye, singing away there – conducting with his other hand. |
| DOUGAL | Aye. It's Mrs Naughtie I feel sorry for. When we left, her cubicle still had engaged on it. |

| | |
|---|---|
| HAMISH | Incidentally, Dougal, did you notice how neat the graffiti was in that Ladies'? |
| DOUGAL | It would be. They've got both hands free. |
| HAMISH | Oh, I never thought of that. Often heard it, but never thought of it. |
| DOUGAL | Well, here's my front door. |
| HAMISH | What the hell's it doing out here? |
| DOUGAL | Oh, we'll worry about that in the morning. I'm going in. Goodnight. |
| | ***Door open and close*** |
| HAMISH | Goodnight. |
| | ***Sig credits and oot*** |

**THE END**

*Following recent floods, visitors are happy to pay up to £500 a week for the fishing on this stretch of the A9.*

*Aftermath of the explosion at the Auchtermuchty talcum factory.*

# SECOND SERIES

# FAME IDOL

| | |
|---|---|
| *Band plays* | *Sig tune up and under* |
| Announcer | *You'll Have Had Your Tea. The doings of Hamish and Dougal. Today, 'Fame Idol'* |
| *Band plays* | *Sig tune up and oot* |
| | *Sleepy lagoon* |
| | *Door opens* |
| HAMISH | Dougal! |
| DOUGAL | Hamish, you'll have had your tea ... |
| HAMISH | No ... but you're listening to the wireless. |
| DOUGAL | *Desert Island Discs*! It wouldn't be Sunday without it. **Click. Grams out** |
| HAMISH | Dougal! Why did you switch it off? |
| DOUGAL | Sue Lawley! |
| HAMISH | Oh ho! |
| DOUGAL | Oh ho indeed! You can't listen to that woman on the Sabbath. There's something of the nightie about her. |
| HAMISH | Oh aye, she's the bee's knees in the cat's pyjamas. Every time I hear her voice, my libido jumps up and shouts 'Game on!' |

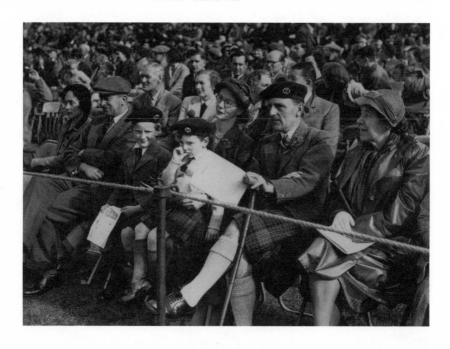

*The crowd goes wild!*

| | |
|---|---|
| DOUGAL | Well, she just has me reaching for the knob. Now, help yourself to the Sunday papers. |
| HAMISH | Thank you. Do you mind if I glance at your pull-out? |
| DOUGAL | Feel free. |
| HAMISH | Here we go, the same old rubbish every week. 'Ten ways to drive your man wild in bed.' |
| DOUGAL | Eat biscuits! |
| HAMISH | Ha ha ha! No, wait, that's not on the list. |
| DOUGAL | Oh look here! The search is on for talent in the Glens. '*Fey MacAdemy*. Trossachs Television is looking for up-and-coming stars of the future.' |
| HAMISH | That'll be the follow-up to their series to find talented dogs. |
| DOUGAL | *Pup Idol.* Or that one to find the laziest person in the world. |
| HAMISH | *Bone Idol.* But this is more of a talent competition. |
| DOUGAL | You ought to go in for that. |
| HAMISH | What? |
| DOUGAL | Oh, I remember that Burns Night when you did the ventriloquist act with the turnip. |
| HAMISH | Oh, that was just a bit of nonsense. |
| DOUGAL | Maybe, but you never saw that turnip move. And then there was that bit where you drank a whole pint of beer without drawing breath … then you went on and did the act. |
| HAMISH | Then I ate the turnip. |
| DOUGAL | There wasn't a dry eye in the house. |
| HAMISH | But what about you, old friend? You should go on. |
| DOUGAL | Ach, what would I do? |
| HAMISH | You could … put up a shelf. |
| DOUGAL | Aye, that's true … och, but they'll have hundreds of young hopefuls doing that … |
| HAMISH | Who dares wins! Come on, let's fill in the application form. Here we are: 'Can you sing, dance, put up shelves? We want to meet YOU!' |
| DOUGAL | Singing and dancing? Oh, we never thought of that. |
| HAMISH | Well, there you are. I've seen you cut a rug. |
| DOUGAL | I could do that. Or measure up some lino … |
| HAMISH | Wait a minute. Four and twenty virgins came down from Inverness! |
| DOUGAL | What page is that on? |

| | |
|---|---|
| HAMISH | No, no, we used to sing it at the needlework evenings. |
| DOUGAL | I think that would be a bit too post-watershed for their requirements. |
| HAMISH | We'd be in with a chance, though. There's nobody round here who can sing like us. |
| | *Maria Callas sings* **Tosca** |
| DOUGAL | Mrs Naughtie! Turn that radio off. |
| | *Out* |
| | *Door opens* |
| MRS NAUGHTIE | I haven't got a radio in here. |
| HAMISH | Then who was that singing? |
| MRS NAUGHTIE | I'm afraid that was me. I always enjoy a wee warble when I'm peeling the tatties. |
| DOUGAL | You? It sounded wonderful. Sing us some more. |
| MRS NAUGHTIE | *[Sings]* Four and twenty virgins came down … |
| DOUGAL | No no! What you were singing before. |
| MRS NAUGHTIE | Oh, you mean this? |
| | *Callas again for a couple of bars, then out* |
| HAMISH | Mrs Naughtie, we are going to enter you! |
| MRS NAUGHTIE | Well, let me finish the potatoes first. |
| DOUGAL | No. There is to be a nationwide talent contest throughout the Trossachs, which you are bound to win. |
| HAMISH | You'd be a celebrity. Fame, wealth, a life of glamour. |
| MRS NAUGHTIE | Been there, done that. |
| HAMISH | This is more than you just winning first prize for a porridge arrangement in the shape of a well-known body part, with red rosette and free salt for a month. |
| DOUGAL | You'd be right up there with Nasty Nick and Maureen from *Driving School* … |
| MRS NAUGHTIE | It's tempting, I'll admit … |
| HAMISH | Then consider yourself entered. |
| DOUGAL | Let's fill in the form. Full name? |
| MRS NAUGHTIE | Margaret Morag Beyonce Naughtie. |
| DOUGAL | Now, do forgive me asking this: age? |
| MRS NAUGHTIE | Twenty-nine? |
| DOUGAL | Stop fooling about! |
| MRS NAUGHTIE | Sixty-two. |
| DOUGAL | I said stop fooling about! |
| MRS NAUGHTIE | Oh, all right. Thirty-one. |
| DOUGAL | That's more like it. |

*Pipe Major Alec Rifkind and his pony*
*Fochabers Lassie execute the pas de deux from Swan Lake.*

| | |
|---|---|
| HAMISH | Now, the rest of your details … |
| MRS NAUGHTIE | Flat … 38B. |
| HAMISH | Well, which? |
| MRS NAUGHTIE | No that's my address. Flat 38B, Peegee Wood House, Sidney Green Street, Peterlaurie. |
| DOUGAL | Type of act? Well, after what we witnessed in the kitchen … |
| HAMISH | Peeling potatoes. |
| DOUGAL | Don't be stupid! Singing! While peeling potatoes … |
| HAMISH | Distinguishing features? |
| MRS NAUGHTIE | I have a wee tattoo on my birthmark. |
| HAMISH | Please enclose. |
| | ***Rip*** |
| DOUGAL | There we are, all done and dusted. |
| MRS NAUGHTIE | Oh, I'm so excited! |
| | ***'I Feel Pretty'!*** |
| DOUGAL | Ooh, shut the door. |
| HAMISH | It goes right through you. |
| DOUGAL | Like fingernails on a blackboard! |

| | |
|---|---|
| **BOTH** | Ugh! Ohh! Ooooh! etc. |
| | ***Door shuts*** |
| | ***Out*** |
| ***Band plays*** | ***Link*** |
| | ***Rattling locks and chains, big door creaks open*** |
| **LAIRD** | Everything all right in here? |
| **HAMISH** | Oh fine, your Lairdship. |
| **DOUGAL** | It's very kind of you to lend us your rehearsal room here in the Big Hoose. |
| **LAIRD** | That's all right, I'm not using it this afternoon. I've pushed the bed to the wall to give you a bit more room. I'll just move these out of your way. |
| | ***Rattling chains, goat bleats*** |
| **HAMISH** | We were just admiring these photographs. |
| **LAIRD** | Oh, just a few family snaps. That's my aunt Nancy. |
| **HAMISH** | Oh, she takes a bikini very well. The bottom half anyway. |
| **DOUGAL** | Who are all the gentlemen with her? |
| **LAIRD** | Uncles. |
| **DOUGAL** | A very close family by the look of it. |
| **LAIRD** | Yes. Might I enquire what you're rehearsing in here? |
| **HAMISH** | We're rehearsing our turns for the TV talent show. |
| **LAIRD** | Good grief, that turnip just spoke! |
| **DOUGAL** | That was Hamish! You should see his singing sprouts. |
| **HAMISH** | Aye, they're a cauliflower tribute band. |
| **LAIRD** | Most impressive. And what do you do, Dougal? |
| **DOUGAL** | My party piece is an impression of Macauley Culkin. |
| **HAMISH** | Show him, Dougal, do it now. |
| **DOUGAL** | *[Clears throat]* |
| **HAMISH** | You won't believe this, your Lairdship. |
| | ***Hammering*** |
| **LAIRD** | Astounding! That's exactly how Macauley Culkin would put up a shelf. |
| **HAMISH** | It's as if he was in the room. |
| **LAIRD** | Well, this all sounds the most jolly fun. I've half a mind to enter myself. |
| **HAMISH** | A clever trick if you can do it. |
| **LAIRD** | Can you keep that turnip quiet? |
| **DOUGAL** | But look here, your Lairdship, you must have a hidden talent up your sleeve? |
| **LAIRD** | Well, I had a little party piece that used to go down |

|  |  |
|---|---|
|  | well in the mess. And she taught me an entertaining little turn. |
| HAMISH | Well, let's see it! |
| LAIRD | Oh no no no no … |
| HAMISH | Oh come on! |
| LAIRD | No no no no no no … |
| HAMISH | Oh that's a pity. |
| LAIRD | Well, if you insist … here we go. Just hold that would you? |
| DOUGAL | My pleasure. |
| LAIRD | Right. *[Groans and straining]*. Ah! |
| DOUGAL & HAMISH | *[Applause]* Bravo! |
| LAIRD | On second thoughts, there might be ladies present. *Loud zzzzzip!* |
| DOUGAL | Oh, pity. |
| LAIRD | No, I shall just have to sing a song. Goodbye. *Door slams* |
| HAMISH | Oh jings! You remember the last time he sang? |
| DOUGAL | Aye, at Jimmy's funeral. |
| HAMISH | It started off as his wedding. |
| DOUGAL | What a day that was. |
| HAMISH | I get goosebumps now, every time I hear the 'Birdy Song'. |
| DOUGAL | Normally he'd be no contest, but knowing the Laird he'll be up to some mischief to make sure he wins. |
| HAMISH | Aye, he'll be bribing the judges or having singing lessons … |
| DOUGAL | Aye, the sneaky devil. We'd better rethink our act. Wait a minute – it's staring us in the face. |
| LAIRD | *[Off]* No, it's all right, it's a two-way mirror. |
| DOUGAL | I think we had better continue this discussion in private. Come on – we're off home. |
| *Band plays* | *Link* |
|  | *Rattling tea tray* |
| MRS NAUGHTIE | There we are. Shall I be mother? |
| DOUGAL | There's no time for all that. Just pour the tea. *Tea pouring* |
| DOUGAL | Two lumps for me please. *Splish, splish* |
| HAMISH | Just the one for me. *Massive sploosh!!!* |

# ARBROATH PATCHES

A popular treat, now that smokies are no longer permitted in the workplace.

INGREDIENTS: 1 box of fresh Arbroaths (1 per person), 1 small pint of cooking water, a knob of parsley.

METHOD: Gut, flay, bone and fillet the Arbroaths. Slap them around a bit too, if you're in that kind of mood. Cook, drain, press and apply to the upper arm.

| | |
|---|---|
| HAMISH | I don't like it too sweet. |
| DOUGAL | Now, how are we going to ensure that we beat the Laird and win the contest? |
| HAMISH | We could kill him. |
| DOUGAL | No, we'd get caught, like last time. |
| HAMISH | True. |
| MRS NAUGHTIE | Well if you ask me, why don't we all join forces, and form a singing group? We could have backing from the village band, the Sporranaires, and the WI dance group, Hot Broth. |
| DOUGAL | Yes, well, nobody did ask you, Mrs Naughtie. Nevertheless, you could be on to something. |
| HAMISH | We could all do that song you sing at throwing-out time. |
| MRS NAUGHTIE | At the pub? |
| HAMISH | At wherever he sings it. |
| DOUGAL | Oh aye! 'Whackit on the Dram!' Mrs Naughtie, you are a housekeeper. Be about your business. |
| MRS NAUGHTIE | I'm on my way. |
| | ***Exits singing the Habanera from* Carmen** |
| DOUGAL | Oh, nails on a blackboard! |
| HAMISH | Jelly on a plate. |
| DOUGAL | What? |
| HAMISH | Just joining in. Cheese on toast. |
| DOUGAL | Stop it! We've got to assemble our super-group. I'll get on to Big Tam the Window Dresser. He plays the banjo like an angel. |
| HAMISH | Molly McLuskey from the pet shop! Her accordion can bring tears to your eyes. |
| DOUGAL | And hers if she's not careful. |
| HAMISH | She's a big lass. |
| DOUGAL | Then we'll have Mad Meg on buckets … |
| HAMISH | Always a crowd pleaser … |
| DOUGAL | Plus the Sporranaires and Hot Broth – we've cracked it. |
| LAIRD | *[Off]* Damn and blast! I shall have to raise my game. |
| DOUGAL | Hamish, was it your idea to bring that two-way mirror home with us? |
| HAMISH | I'm sorry. I think I misunderstood the principle. |
| DOUGAL | Well, come on, man, we must prepare for the talent show. |
| HAMISH | When does it start? |

| | |
|---|---|
| **DOUGAL** | In about three seconds. Come on! |
| | *Whoosh!* |
| **Band plays** | *Link* |
| | *Crowd murmur* |
| | *Skaters waltz* |
| **DOUGAL** | So far so good. This magician is no competition. |
| **HAMISH** | No. Sawing a turnip in half, indeed! He's toast! |
| **DOUGAL** | And the judges weren't impressed with that first act. |
| **HAMISH** | Dainty Miss Chalmers, the Pride of Arbroath? |
| **DOUGAL** | Aye. What's so clever about doing that with a couple of lemons? |
| **HAMISH** | Her mother used to do it with coconuts! |
| | *Lukewarm applause* |
| **DOUGAL** | Right, who's up next? |
| **HAMISH** | It's a novelty act. 'Balloon-O: TV's balloon man.' |
| **DOUGAL** | What does he do? |
| **HAMISH** | See for yourself. He takes that poodle, and twists it into the shape of a balloon. |
| | *Balloon squeaks and poodle yaps and whimpers* |
| | *Bang!* |
| **DOUGAL** | He could do with some practice. |

*The laird on 'Ketamine' enjoys a leap over some mad people.*

| | |
|---|---|
| HAMISH | And a more robust poodle. |
| DOUGAL | And is it right, the Highland dancers have pulled out? |
| HAMISH | Aye. Lack of preparation. At the rehearsal, I had to lay out all the swords on the ground for them myself. |
| DOUGAL | That'll have given them a bit of a surprise. |
| HAMISH | That it did. Especially as they'd lost their boots. |
| DOUGAL | So there's only one more act, then it's us. |
| HAMISH | Who do we follow? |
| DOUGAL | It's Mad Mick McMurtry, the Motorcycle Maniac, and the Wall of Death! |
| | ***Motorbike revving, then accelerates off. Crash!!!*** |
| DOUGAL | Oh. I thought there'd be more to it than that. |
| HAMISH | We're home and dry. Funny there's been no sign of the Laird. |
| DOUGAL | I dare say he pulled out when he saw what he was up against. |
| HAMISH | Not for the first time. |
| MRS NAUGHTIE | Oh Mr Hamish, Mr Dougal! Disaster! I'm so nervous I've completely lost my voice. |
| DOUGAL | Now, where on earth is Mrs Naughtie? |
| MRS NAUGHTIE | I'm right here! What are we going to do? |
| HAMISH | *[Calling for her]* Mrs Naughtie? |
| DOUGAL | Mrs Naughtie! |
| | ***Slap!*** |
| HAMISH | Ouch! Mrs Naughtie. There you are. I've found her. |
| DOUGAL | Where is she? |
| MRS NAUGHTIE | I'm right here in front of you, and I can't sing because I've lost my voice. |
| DOUGAL | Well, don't just stand there mouthing silently. We've got some singing to do. |
| HAMISH | I think Mrs Naughtie has lost her voice. Either that, or we've both gone deaf. |
| DOUGAL | Hamish!? |
| HAMISH | I'm here. |
| DOUGAL | So you are. For a minute I thought I'd lost my sense of smell. Now come on, we've got to sort out Mrs Naughtie's voice. |
| HAMISH | I've heard that a sudden shock will often do the trick. |
| DOUGAL | Right. Plug her in. |
| | ***Zap! Electric crackle*** |
| | ***High C*** |

| | |
|---|---|
| **Dougal** | Right, we're in business. Everybody ready? |
| *Band plays* | ***No*** |
| **Dougal** | Then away we go! |

| | |
|---|---|
| *Band plays and All* | Wackit on the dram |
| | There's a wackit on the dram, |
| | And a hooley doon the noo, |
| | There's a snicket in the drappet |
| | Where the midden slotters coo, |
| | There's a wishty washty winky in the muckle buckers' moo |
| | |
| | Hi ho for the open road. |
| | |
| | ***1st verse Hamish and Dougal*** |
| | ***2nd verse Mrs Naughtie operatic*** |
| | ***3rd verse the Laird*** |
| | ***4th verse all*** |
| | ***Big finish*** |
| | |
| **Laird** | Thank you. Thank you so much. Please show our appreciation for my backing group – Hamish and Dougal, Mrs Naughtie, Big Tam, Miss McLuskey, the Sporranaires and the dear ladies of Hot Broth, not forgetting Mad Meg on buckets. |
| | ***Bucket clang*** |
| **Laird** | Ow! I couldn't have done it without them. Well, I hope you enjoyed my little number, and I'm sure I can count on you in the phone-in voting. |
| | ***Phone rings. Pick up*** |
| **Laird** | Hello? Oh too kind. Thank you so much. |
| | ***Phone down*** |
| **Laird** | Apparently I've won. All together now – one more time! |
| *Band plays and All* | ***'Wackit on the Dram'*** |
| | ***Fade …*** |
| | ***Chink of glasses*** |
| **Mrs Naughtie** | Well, I expect you two could do with a stiff one. |
| **Hamish** | There's no time for all that, woman. Just get us a drink. |
| | ***Clink clink*** |
| **Mrs Naughtie** | There we are. You drink those while I put my clothes on. |

| | |
|---|---|
| DOUGAL | Well, cheers, old friend. The Laird has defeated us once again. |
| HAMISH | Who'd have thought he would hijack our entry and claim it as his own? |
| DOUGAL | And not only that, win the competition. |
| HAMISH | A fly-away safari in Dundee, if you please. |
| DOUGAL | Hamish, a toast. To the Laird. Damn his eyes! |
| HAMISH | The two-faced cheating conniving snivelling back-stabbing evil son-of-a-bitch bastard! |
| LAIRD | *[Off]* I heard that! |
| DOUGAL | Hamish, I thought I told you to get rid of that two-way mirror. |
| HAMISH | Oh Jings! I've done it again. Goodbye. |
| LAIRD | *[Off]* Toodle-oo! |
| ***Band plays*** | ***Sig and oot under credits*** |

**THE END**

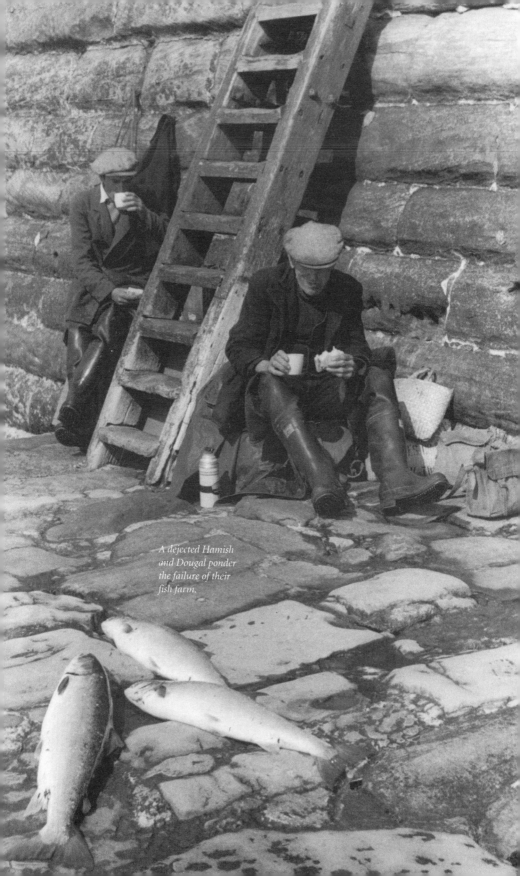

A dejected Hamish
and Dougal ponder
the failure of their
fish farm.

# FOLK OF THE GLEN

## DOUGAL

Dougal comes from a long line of Highlanders who tend to loiter round the back door of the Big Hoose on soup day. His lugubrious face rarely cracks into a smile or even a grin, but he is noted for his impish sense of smell. He is what the locals round here describe as 'canny'. Ask him to do a job, no matter how arduous, and he will as like as not reply 'Oh I canny do that!' and then vanish into the heather as mysteriously as he came.

Dougal is the outdoor type, as anyone who has spent time with him in an enclosed space will verify. He has served as Occasional Assistant Under Deputy Gillie on the estate for the best part of the last ten years (i.e. that sunny afternoon in 2003). He is a keen sportsman, and I once marvelled at the sight of him playing a 20lb salmon for over half an hour, in fact until I told him to take off the fish costume, get out of the river and stop messing about. In the grouse season he is one of my regular beaters, a task which he undertakes with gusto and to great effect while everyone else is out shooting on the moors.

On the long winter's evenings a group of neighbours will often make their way to Dougal's modest dwelling, intent on a sociable evening round the fire with brimming glasses, tales of long ago and a few of the old songs. The moment these fun-seeking visitors arrive, Dougal will get out his trusty bagpipes and that usually gets rid of them. Nevertheless, Dougal is noted in the Glen for his tireless work for charity; he is famed far and wide for his Highland Cattle Sanctuary, where he gives a home to 'clapped-oot old coos' in the big meadow between the abattoir and Dougal's Pie Shoppe. Sport of any kind is Dougal's passion. He is captain of the village Australian Rules netball team, and on the soccer pitch he can play in any position, be it on one leg, on all fours, or even missionary. In the winter he is our champion at the curling, and helps out with tints and perms as well.

# THE FITNESS CLUB

| | |
|---|---|
| *Band plays* | *Sig tune up and under* |
| Announcer | *You'll Have Had Your Tea. The doings of Hamish and Dougal. Today, 'The Fitness Club'* |
| *Band plays* | *Sig tune up and oot* |
| DOUGAL | *[Straining, puffing and panting]* |
| | *Door opens* |
| HAMISH | Dougal …! |
| DOUGAL | Hamish … you'll hahhh … you'll hhhh … had your … phwooof … |
| HAMISH | I've not had my tea, since you ask. |
| DOUGAL | Hhhhphwww … youllhavehadyourtea. |
| HAMISH | Och, it's a waste of time talking to you, riding that exercise bicycle standing on your head. |
| DOUGAL | Ooff! Whoof! |
| | *Frantic pedalling, bicycle bell* |
| HAMISH | For goodness' sake, man, your kilt's fallen over your eyes. You don't know where you're going! |
| DOUGAL | Well, keep out of the way – I can't see a thing. |
| HAMISH | I wish I could say the same! |
| DOUGAL | I'm trying to keep in shape. |
| HAMISH | I can see that. And so can the crowd at the window. |
| DOUGAL | Are they still there? Well, don't just stand there, man, get outside and pass round the hat. Oops! |
| | *Clatter crash clang thump tink crash boing crash!* |
| | *[Sparse polite distant applause from the window]* |
| HAMISH | Oh the crowd liked that. Are you all right? |
| DOUGAL | Never better. My body is a temple. |
| HAMISH | Aye, so is the Parthenon, and look at the state of that. |
| DOUGAL | Wheesht! Now pass me those weights. |
| HAMISH | I didn't know Players were still making them. |
| DOUGAL | If you're going to be unhelpful, just stand over there and shut your trap. I've got to do a hundred pop-ups before lunch. |
| HAMISH | Pop-ups? What are pop-ups? |
| DOUGAL | They're the same as press-ups, but you don't use your hands. Now stand back! |
| HAMISH | Gladly! |
| DOUGAL | One, two, three, four … |
| | *Fade out* |
| *Band plays* | *Time passing link* |

PC Donald McIllivray draws the crowd's attention to an unexpected total eclipse of the sun.

| | |
|---|---|
| DOUGAL | *[Fading in]* Up down, up down, ninety-nine, a hundred! Whew! |
| MRS NAUGHTIE | Oh, don't stop now! |
| DOUGAL | Mrs Naughtie! I didn't see you there. |
| MRS NAUGHTIE | Oh, I've been standing here for ten minutes. I was doing this sculpture of you. I'm making it out of pastry. |
| HAMISH | It's very lifelike. |
| MRS NAUGHTIE | Thank you. I'll just put this cherry on the top. There! Five more minutes, I'd have done the rest of him. |
| CROWD | Ooooh! |
| | *Polite applause* |
| DOUGAL | Away home with you! I'd pull the curtains if I had the strength. Now where was I? Let's look at my regime chart. Abs, pecs, quads … tick tick tick tick tick. What does that mean? Oh, buy a stopwatch. Good. Time to go jogging. |
| HAMISH | Oh, not again. Last time you took that up you spent a month jogging five miles a day. |
| DOUGAL | Your point being? |
| HAMISH | You finished up in Dundee! |
| DOUGAL | Hamish. Why don't you boil your head? |
| MRS NAUGHTIE | Because I do the cooking in this house! Talking of which, I've brought your midday power snack. |
| DOUGAL | It'll have to wait. I'm away to the top of Muckle Brae, and back again. Goodbye! |
| | *Door opens* |
| | *Six footsteps* |
| DOUGAL | Return to Muckle Brae, please. |
| | *Bus bell, ding ding* |
| | *Bus drives off* |
| MRS NAUGHTIE | All this good food going to waste |
| HAMISH | Oh Mrs Naughtie, I wouldn't mind toying with one of your baps. |
| MRS NAUGHTIE | In your dreams, Buster. You can have a bite of Mr Dougal's diet. One dry crispbread, half a carrot, a chocolate fudge cake and lard pudding with clotted cream and eight pints of lager. |
| HAMISH | A curious menu. |
| MRS NAUGHTIE | It's the Vegas diet. |
| HAMISH | Oh, Las Vegas? |
| MRS NAUGHTIE | No, Johnny. Tuck in. |

| | |
|---|---|
| HAMISH | No thank you, I have a Pot Noodle in my sporran. |
| MRS NAUGHTIE | So you have. And a couple of plums for afters. |
| HAMISH | Yes. Sorry about that. Away you go, boys. But look here, I'm awfy worried about Dougal. What is this fitness mania that seems to have him in its thrall? |
| MRS NAUGHTIE | Well, his head's been full of silly nonsense ever since he joined the health club. |
| HAMISH | That old place in the High Street that used to be the Conservative Party Headquarters? |
| MRS NAUGHTIE | You remember they had the squatters? |
| HAMISH | I'm not surprised when they saw the election results. |
| MRS NAUGHTIE | Well, now it's the Bonny Body Fitness and Tanning Studio. All the smart set's going there. |
| HAMISH | Ah, now it all falls into place! I saw Mrs McAlister in the post office tearing up telephone directories with a face like a tandoori chicken! |
| MRS NAUGHTIE | And that leotard does her no favours! She looks like a haggis in a catapult! |
| HAMISH | Please, not when I'm eating … But why has Dougal got himself involved? |
| MRS NAUGHTIE | Then you obviously haven't met the proprietress – his personal trainer? Miss Monika Diesel! Hmph! She's set the women's tongues wagging, I can tell you. |
| HAMISH | Well, I'm not one to listen to gossip. So piss off. |
| MRS NAUGHTIE | Fair enough. |
| *Band plays* | *Link* |
| | *Into Bavarian-style jolly march* |
| MONIKA | Attention class! Step to the side. Step to the side. Step to the side. Will you step to the side? Thank you very much, I thought I'd never get in. |
| DOUGAL | Good afternoon, Fräulein Diesel. |
| MONIKA | Ah, Herr Dougal. How are your pop-ups? |
| DOUGAL | Not as bad as they look. |
| MONIKA | You appear to be bursting with good health. |
| DOUGAL | Aye, that'll be the Spandex kilt. But look here, what do you think of my six-pack? |
| MONIKA | To me it still looks like two packets of three. But keep up the good work, and one day you might even be fit enough to appeal to a woman like me! Ha ha ha! |
| DOUGAL | Jings, you're so enigmatic. |
| MONIKA | Now go over there with the rest of the girls. |
| DOUGAL | Yes, miss. |

| | |
|---|---|
| *Band plays* | *Link* |
| | *The moors, wind howling etc.* |
| | *Two twelve-bore gunshots* |
| LAIRD | Bang on target, what? Hamish? Why so glum? |
| HAMISH | You've just shot me, twice. |
| LAIRD | Don't take on so. It's nothing a roll of Sellotape and a squirt of WD40 won't cure. But you've been moping about the moors all day with a face like a badly stowed hammock. What's up? |
| HAMISH | Well, your Lairdship, it's Dougal. |
| LAIRD | Oh, not the old trouble again? |
| HAMISH | No no. I've had the carpet cleaned and changed the locks. But does 'Monika Diesel' ring any bells? |
| LAIRD | No, the vicar's nephews do all that. |
| HAMISH | No no, big strapping blonde woman – runs the fitness club. |
| LAIRD | Oo-er! Wait a minute, I think I did read something about her in *Big Fit Babes* magazine. I get it for the gardening notes. |
| HAMISH | Well, Dougal is obsessed with her, and he's gone mad on the fitness kick. If he keeps it up, it'll kill him. |
| LAIRD | Well, that's your problem. Now, I can't stand here all day talking. I'm off to the fitness club. |
| *Band plays* | *Bavarian link and under* |
| MONIKA | Come along, ladies, pick those feet up. I don't know who they belong to, but they've been there since last night. Now, everybody on the floor, legs crossed, hands on heads, elbows on chins. Very good. Now, class, carry on doing something funny. Herr Dougal and I will have a session on the rowing machine. |
| | *Squeaky rowing noises* |
| DOUGAL | Oh, I don't know if can keep this up. |
| MONIKA | Don't worry, big boy. I have an outboard motor. |
| | *Outboard motor starts, and continues under* |
| MONIKA | You Scottish men fascinate me. |
| DOUGAL | I've got a stamp collection. |
| MONIKA | How fascinating! On top you seem so cold, and yet underneath I feel there is something warm and soft. |
| DOUGAL | Jings, the top's come off my thermos of porridge again. |
| MONIKA | Damn your porridge! I'm a woman! Can't you see what I'm trying to say? |

*Jock Stewart and Jimmy Kyle please the crowd with their display in the Men's Tango final.*

*Allan Murchison, outright winner of the 'Guess the Weight of the Balloon' competition.*

| | |
|---|---|
| LAIRD | Hello, mind if I join you? |
| DOUGAL | Oh, your Lairdship. Don't just stand there, sir. Go away. |
| LAIRD | Coming aboard. The McCoist of McCoist of McCoist of that ilk, at your service. |
| DOUGAL | Careful, sir, you'll capsize the rowing machine. |
| LAIRD | Hello, and who is this attractive lady? |
| MONIKA | I am Monika Diesel, the owner. |
| LAIRD | Charmed. I just popped in here looking for my new mistress. And I believe I have found her. |
| MONIKA | Oh, you are a dirty old man! |
| DOUGAL | So am I! |
| MONIKA | What a lucky girl I am – to have two dirty old men fighting for my affection. |
| LAIRD | We must settle this like dirty old gentlemen. |
| | ***Smack! Bird screech!*** |
| DOUGAL | Ooch! You just slapped me in the face with a gannet! |
| LAIRD | Yes, it's the nearest I've got to a gauntlet. |
| MONIKA | A challenge to a duel! How romantic! |
| ***Band plays*** | ***Link*** |
| HAMISH | A duel? |
| DOUGAL | Aye, tomorrow at dawn the Laird has challenged me to a full MacAthlon! |
| HAMISH | A MacAthlon? Is that where the first leg is swimming the length of Loch Crankie …? |
| DOUGAL | And the second leg's cycling up and down Ben Kingsley while tossing the caber … |
| HAMISH | And the third leg is running the length of Glen Close … |
| DOUGAL | And all to the tune of 'Scotland the Brave'! |
| HAMISH | Jings! Will you be up to it? |
| DOUGAL | Not the night before a MacAthlon. |
| HAMISH | But are you having misgivings? |
| DOUGAL | Not the night before a MacAthlon! |
| HAMISH | Well, I'll be right behind you. |
| HAMISH & DOUGAL | Not the night before a MacAthlon!!! |
| HAMISH | But look here, do you think you can pull it off? |
| DOUGAL | *[Pause]* Yes. |
| HAMISH | What? |
| DOUGAL | I was browsing in Wee Sandy's Sporting Accessories and Surgical Goods Outlet. |
| HAMISH | What did you get? |
| DOUGAL | Well, apart from my regular order, I found these! |

| | |
|---|---|
| HAMISH | A pair of apparently unremarkable running pumps? |
| DOUGAL | So you may think, but these are Triumph of the Trossachs Turbo-Thrust Trainers. |
| HAMISH | I like the kitten heels. |
| DOUGAL | Thank you. And look, they're pneumatic. This wee valve controls the air pressure. |
| | *Phwwrrsssssssssssssss!* |
| HAMISH | Ah … You were saying, that wee valve controls the air pressure? |
| DOUGAL | Not only that, they have wee sidelights, indicators, a CD player, beverage holder, go-faster stripes and 40 gigabytes of memory. |
| HAMISH | What will they think of next? |
| DOUGAL | I got you a pair of nose-hair clippers, while I was in. |
| HAMISH | Oh, thank you. Now I can start my collection. |
| DOUGAL | *[Going off]* Right, I'll be off then, goodbye. |
| HAMISH | Hmmmm … If Dougal wins this MaCathlon, he'll become embroiled with that Teutonic Diesel woman. And that way inevitably lies disaster!!!!! I must do everything in my power to thwart his endeavours. He must not win! |
| DOUGAL | I said 'I'll be off then, goodbye'. |
| HAMISH | Right then, goodbye … |
| *Band plays* | *Link* |
| | *Exterior atmos. Crowd atmos.* |
| LAIRD | Well, Dougal … |
| DOUGAL | Well your Lairdship. May the best man win. |
| LAIRD | That's very kind of you. |
| DOUGAL | Your Lairdship, I feel I should warn you that I shall be wearing a pair of Triumph of the Trossachs Turbo-Thrust Trainers. |
| LAIRD | And I, as you can see, am wearing my ostrich costume. And if you look under the tail … you'll get a fat lip. Let battle commence! |
| HAMISH | Right, Mrs Naughtie, have you got the starting pistol? |
| MRS NAUGHTIE | Starting pistol? Oh, I must have misheard. I got this in Big Wullie's Novelty Shop. |
| HAMISH | Oh I see. Well, near enough. Start the race. |
| MRS NAUGHTIE | On your marks, get set … |
| | *Loud raspberry* |
| | *Crowd cheer* |
| HAMISH | They're away! |

|  |  |
|---|---|
| | *Splash splash!!* |
| **Band plays** | *'Scotland the Brave'* |
| | *Rhythmic splashing* |
| HAMISH | Loch Crankie has never seen the likes of this! |
| MRS NAUGHTIE | I just hope they don't get wet. The forecast was changeable … |
| HAMISH | Oh no – Dougal's forging ahead! The Laird's sinking! Weighed down by the feathers! |
| MRS NAUGHTIE | He's struggling out of the ostrich costume! |
| HAMISH | And now he's struggling into the rhinoceros costume! That'll give him the edge. |
| | *Splashing* |
| | *Crowd noise* |
| HAMISH | That's the loch done in double quick time. Now on to the bicycles. |
| **Band plays** | *'Scotland the Brave'* |
| | *Rhythmic cycling* |
| | *Bicycle bells tring tring!* |
| MRS NAUGHTIE | Well, I've never seen a rhinoceros riding a bicycle before! |
| HAMISH | I hope it gets out of the way before the Laird comes along. That would be too confusing! |
| MRS NAUGHTIE | They've nearly reached the summit. |
| HAMISH | Now they're free-wheeling down the rocky path. Oh, they'll be glad to see the bottom of Ben Kingsley. |
| MRS NAUGHTIE | And who wouldn't! |
| | *Bicycles discarded* |
| | *Crowd noise* |
| HAMISH | They're neck and neck! Now all they've got to do is knock off Glen Close … |
| MRS NAUGHTIE | Do you have Mr Dougal's running pumps ready? |
| HAMISH | I have them here. |
| LAIRD | Ah, those look a fine pair of running pumps. Mind if I try them on? |
| MRS NAUGHTIE | Certainly not! |
| HAMISH | No, of course you can. Here, I'll just make this minor adjustment … |
| | *Crank boing ting ting ting* |
| LAIRD | Thank you. Away I go. |
| | *Footsteps getting faster and faster* |
| | *Whoosh disappearing* |
| **Band plays** | *'Chariots of Fire'* |

| | |
|---|---|
| DOUGAL | Hamish … |
| HAMISH | Yes, Dougal? |
| DOUGAL | Did you give the Laird my Turbo-Thrust Trainers? |
| HAMISH | I did. |
| DOUGAL | And were they cranked up to the fastest top speed setting? |
| HAMISH | By the look of things, yes. |
| DOUGAL | And is that the Laird winning the race and disappearing over the horizon hotly pursued by Ms Monika Diesel in her Mercedes-Benz moon boots? |
| HAMISH | Aye. They'll be in Wolverhampton by now. |
| DOUGAL | How could you do this to me? |
| HAMISH | It was for your own good. Believe me, I've saved you from a world of pain. |
| MRS NAUGHTIE | Oh, come away home, the pair of you. I've got a bap for each of you, and a denouement in the oven. |
| HAMISH | Well, that gets my vote. |
| DOUGAL | Mine too. |
| BOTH | Goodbye. |
| *Band plays* | *Sig and oot under credits* |
| *Announcer* | *'You'll Have Had Your Tea', the doings of Hamish and Dougal, was written and performed by Barry Cryer and Graeme Garden, with Alison Steadman as Mrs Naughtie and Monika and Jeremy Hardy as the Laird. The producer was Jon Naismith* |

*THE END*

*Australian visitor Bruce McBruce delights the crowd with the size of his didgeridoo.*

# FOLK OF THE GLEN

## MRS NAUGHTIE

My eye was first drawn to Mrs Naughtie when I spied her one day bending over a stove. I was impressed at once and even more so when I saw her casually straightening the stove up again. It was a skill I was to see her put to good use more than once in the future, not least when Big Tam the Roadmender's steamroller struck Dinny McKay's prize boulder. For the last seventeen years she has put her strength and ingenuity at my disposal as part-time housekeeper and undergroom at my gracious home, the Big Hoose.

Margaret Morag Beyonce Naughtie was born and raised in the village, one of eighteen sisters who at one time were famed as Scotland's premier female vocal musical group – the Skirls. The fifteen sisters who couldn't sing formed a successful ladies Rugby Union team and lifted the Highland Grand Slam Trophy in 1964, the year before they were made to return it.

Mrs Naughtie is famed for her mop of bright red hair, which she bought at a sale of work and often uses to sluice the marble floor of my indoor sitting room at the Big Hoose. Her own hair is now silver grey with a streak of brown over her right ear behind which she keeps her Crunchie bar.

As a housekeeper/cleaning lady she has no equal. She is particularly keen on providing what she considers a balanced diet. Her typical shock tactic is to fill a skip with bread, pizzas, burgers, butter, cheese, lard, deep-frying oil, baps, nougat, chocolate, chips, and all manner of junk. She will then indicate the disgusting skipload of stuff and declare 'This is what you will eat in a single year!' She will then leave you to work your way through it.

Wise, witty, compassionate, charming, free-thinking, well informed and quick-witted – not her! Yet you won't find a more popular woman in the Glen. I know, for I have tried.

*Villagers diligently follow the score during Mrs Naughtie's Shostakovich recital.*

# THE POISON PEN LETTERS

| | |
|---|---|
| *Band plays* | *Sig tune up and under* |
| *Announcer* | *You'll Have Had Your Tea. The doings of Hamish and Dougal. Today, 'The Poison Pen Letters'* |
| *Band plays* | *Sig tune up and oot* |
| | *Door opens* |
| HAMISH | Dougal! |
| DOUGAL | Hamish, you'll have had your tea … |
| HAMISH | Well, yes and no … |
| DOUGAL | An enigmatic reply, old friend. What do you mean? |
| HAMISH | I was raising it to my lips when the telephone went. |
| DOUGAL | No! |
| HAMISH | Aye. And if I find out who took it, then I'll know who's responsible and no mistake. But that's not the half of it. I went to get my morning post and I found this on the doormat. |
| DOUGAL | Well don't bring it round here – go and scrape it off into the bin! |

*Jimmy the Tree Hermit receives some welcome news.*

| | |
|---|---|
| HAMISH | Oh, I thought you'd be interested. |
| DOUGAL | No. And wash your hands while you're at it. |
| | ***Running water into bowl and hand washing noises*** |
| DOUGAL | Hello! There's something else on your doormat. |
| HAMISH | Oh really? |
| DOUGAL | Aye, it's a letter. It's addressed 'To Whom It May Concern'. |
| HAMISH | Aye, that's me all right. |
| DOUGAL | Well, aren't you going to … haud on, just your hands! |
| HAMISH | Oh, you know me, I could never resist the sight of a loofa. |
| DOUGAL | That may well be, but there isn't room in this sink for both of us. |
| HAMISH | Self, self, self. |
| | ***Getting out of the sink, splashing and dishes clattering*** |
| DOUGAL | Ah that's better. Pass me the wee rubber duck. |
| HAMISH | No, I'm going to see who's written me this letter. |
| | ***Rip*** |
| HAMISH | Oh. |
| | ***Rustling paper*** |
| HAMISH | Oh!! |
| | ***Furious rustling paper*** |
| DOUGAL | When you've quite finished towelling yourself down with the *Arboath Herald*, will you open the letter, man? |
| HAMISH | Och, I've got newsprint all over me. Oh, I see local man steals poultry … |
| DOUGAL | Stop reading your leg and open the letter. |
| HAMISH | Very well. |
| | ***Rip*** |
| HAMISH | Oh. Green ink. |
| DOUGAL | Oh, so it's a green ink letter, is it? |
| HAMISH | It is. |
| DOUGAL | Oh. Looks very attractive. What does it say? |
| HAMISH | Right. Where are my glasses? |
| DOUGAL | Where you left them – on the end of your … |
| HAMISH | Ah yes. |
| DOUGAL | Why do you keep them there? |
| HAMISH | Well, even in the dark, I can always put my hand on them. |
| DOUGAL | What does it say? |

| | |
|---|---|
| HAMISH | Well, it never complains. Oh, the letter … let's see. 'Dear To Who It May Concern, It is my unpleasant duty to inform you that certain persons in this village are less than the whited sepulchres they would have us believe.' |
| DOUGAL | What are they on about? The Whited-Sepulchres moved out three weeks ago. |
| HAMISH | Lovely family. Mind you, Marjorie could be a bit of a handful in her cups. |
| DOUGAL | Aye, a big lass, but very free and easy. But read on, old friend. |
| HAMISH | 'For instance, at 1407 hours on Wednesday last, a certain person was observed outside the post office mounting a bicycle without the consent of its owner.' |
| DOUGAL | Och, that'll be Bikey Bob the Saddle Fiend up to his old tricks. |
| HAMISH | 'It was not, as you might expect, Bikey Bob, but an erstwhile upstanding pillar of the community. I will mention no names, suffice it to say that the perpetrator lives at the Big Hoose.' |
| DOUGAL | Oh, here's a mystery. Who lives at the Big Hoose with the Laird? |
| HAMISH | Nobody. |
| DOUGAL | Exactly! |
| HAMISH | You're right, it is a mystery. |
| DOUGAL | Is there any more? |
| HAMISH | 'Yours sincerely, a friend. PS: more will be revealed in my next letter.' *Scratching noise* |
| DOUGAL | What's that? |
| HAMISH | Something coming through the letterbox … *Letterbox opens, thud on doormat* |
| HAMISH | Look there, on the doormat. |
| DOUGAL | Jings! That's an agile dog. |
| HAMISH | And there next to it … another letter! |
| DOUGAL | It's addressed to Theo Cupier. |
| HAMISH | Theo Cupier? He's not the occupier. |
| DOUGAL | Not at this address! I'd better open it. *Rip, rustling paper* |
| DOUGAL | Och, you've had the best of this *Arbroath Herald*. There's only the sports section left. |

| | |
|---|---|
| HAMISH | Well, you can dry that on the kitchen towel. |
| DOUGAL | Now what's in this letter? |
| | *Rip* |
| DOUGAL | Oh! Look at that! |
| HAMISH | What? |
| DOUGAL | Zero per cent APR over three years. Tempting. But here's another letter – and it's in green ink! |
| | *Rip* |
| HAMISH | Let me see that. |
| DOUGAL | No, read the letter. |
| HAMISH | Right. 'As I was saying, this village is a sink of iniquity. Further to my last letter I can reveal that a certain housekeeper is not all she appears to be, leading as she does a double life as a nocturnal pole dancer at the Caber Tossing Society's night club, Splinters.' |
| DOUGAL | A housekeeper? |
| HAMISH | I wonder if our Mrs Naughtie knows her … |
| DOUGAL | Mrs Naughtie, our housekeeper, you mean? Oh, I can't imagine her writhing round a pole. |
| HAMISH | Well, you remember her lodger, Mr Benardczyk from Gdansk? |
| DOUGAL | There was talk at the time. |
| HAMISH | Aye, there was. Couldn't understand a word of it. |
| DOUGAL | Well, there's only one way to solve the mystery of these letters. To the post office! |
| *Band plays* | *Link ['I'm Going To Sit Right Down and Write Myself a Letter']* |
| | *Shop door opens* |
| DOUGAL | Well, here we are at the post office. |
| HAMISH | Why did you say that? |
| DOUGAL | Well, it doesn't do any harm. |
| MRS MCALISTER | *Having hysterics.* |
| HAMISH | Mrs McAlister! Whatever is it? |
| MRS MCALISTER | I'll be fine if you two cover yourselves up. |
| HAMISH | Oh. Two copies of the *Arbroath Herald* please. |
| MRS MCALISTER | I've only got the *Falkirk Bugle* left. |
| DOUGAL | At the risk of looking complete idiots, we'll take those. |
| MRS MCALISTER | There you are. You'll find the newsprint doesn't come off and it's a softer texture. |
| | *Rustling papers* |

| | |
|---|---|
| DOUGAL | Very kind but that's not why we're here. We have received communications this morning of a distinctly unsavoury nature. |
| HAMISH | Have any other letters passed through the post office written in green ink? |
| MRS MCALISTER | No, not one. I was steaming open the letters this morning and there wasn't one in green ink. |
| HAMISH | Steaming open the letters? |
| MRS MCALISTER | Well what happened was, I happened to leave a pile of letters next to the kettle, and a few of them just flew open … eventually. |
| HAMISH | And none in green ink? |
| MRS MCALISTER | Not one. Except … |
| DOUGAL | Except? |
| MRS MCALISTER | Except this one to me! |
| | ***Rustling paper*** |
| HAMISH | Oh, I'm sorry. This *Falkirk Bugle* just hasn't got the staying power. |
| MRS MCALISTER | Of course I didn't believe the dreadful things they say in the letter. Not about Mr Dougal here. |
| DOUGAL | What about me? |
| MRS MCALISTER | About you worrying the sheep. |
| DOUGAL | Me? I have never worried a sheep in my life! |
| MRS MCALISTER | It says here you do – whenever the moon is full … |
| DOUGAL | Ah well, you didn't mention the full moon … hem hem … |
| HAMISH | Where have these letters come from? What's the postmark? |
| MRS MCALISTER | There isn't one. |
| DOUGAL | There isn't one on the letters we got either. |
| HAMISH | Then these letters must have been delivered by … magic! |
| DOUGAL | Yes. Or … by hand! |
| HAMISH | Well, all right, I suppose that's a possibility. |
| | ***Van draws up ouside and toots horn*** |
| MRS MCALISTER | Oh, there's the second post. I'd better get the kettle on. |
| HAMISH & DOUGAL | Goodbye. |
| | ***Door shuts*** |
| | ***Shop door opens and shuts*** |
| HAMISH | Mrs Naughtie! You've just missed Mrs McAlister. |

# SHORTBREAD FANCIES

The perfect accompaniment to Afternoon Tea or Morning Sickness.

1 – Lay out half a dozen assorted shortbreads.
2 – Fancy them.

*The Laird's first wife, Pussy, in fancy dress, stuffed and mounted on a regular basis.*

| | |
|---|---|
| MRS NAUGHTIE | That's a relief. |
| DOUGAL | Why so? |
| MRS NAUGHTIE | This green-ink letter accuses our postmistress of … oh, I can't say it. |
| DOUGAL | Why not? |
| MRS NAUGHTIE | It's a foreign word. |
| DOUGAL | Let me see. Oh! And you'd think butter wouldn't melt in her mouth. |
| HAMISH | You mean she's behind the spate of butter-melting that's plagued the village? |
| DOUGAL | Well, that's one mystery solved. |
| MRS NAUGHTIE | But not the mystery of who's sending these letters. |
| | ***Shop door opens*** |
| LAIRD | Good morning! |
| HAMISH | Your Lairdship! What brings you to the post office? |
| LAIRD | I was just passing on my way to deliver these green-ink letters by hand. |
| ALL | Letters by hand? |
| LAIRD | Yes, there's one for each of you. |
| ALL | One for each of us? |
| LAIRD | Are you going to stop that? |
| ALL | Yes. |
| LAIRD | Good. There you are, and there's one for Mrs McAlister. |
| MRS NAUGHTIE | She's not here just now. I'll take that for her. |
| LAIRD | Pity. If what my letter said about her is true, I could have availed myself of her special services. Never mind, I dare say the fishing net and custard will keep. Now, I must be on my way … |
| DOUGAL | Not so fast, your Lairdship. I think you have some explaining to do. |
| LAIRD | How dare you? Are you suggesting I have something to do with this plague of poison pen letters that has torn apart our little community? |
| HAMISH | You seem to know a lot about it. |
| LAIRD | Only what I've read in the *Falkirk Bugle*. Mind if I turn over? |
| HAMISH | Please yourself. |
| | ***Paper rustle*** |
| LAIRD | Mm. Soft. No more *Arbroath Herald* for me! |
| DOUGAL | Never mind all that. Why are you delivering all these green-ink letters? |

| | |
|---|---|
| LAIRD | Oh, that's easily explained. |
| DOUGAL | Well, I'm glad to hear it. Sorry to have troubled you. |
| MRS NAUGHTIE | No wait. I'd like to hear his story. |
| LAIRD | Very well, Mrs N. Once upon a time … no no, just having a laugh. The fact is I found this pile of post at the Big Hoose this morning, with a note saying 'please deliver these green ink letters by hand. Ta very much, a friend.' I am simply following orders. |
| MRS NAUGHTIE | But if you didn't write the letters, who did? |
| LAIRD | I should have thought that was obvious, Trixie. These foul documents contain dreadful allegations against me and you, Mrs McAlister and Dougal. But there is one among us whose reputation remains unsullied. |
| HAMISH | That would be me, I'm happy to say. |
| LAIRD | Exactly. There is the author of these poison missives! |
| DOUGAL | Hamish!? |
| HAMISH | But … but … |
| LAIRD | I'll get the police. *[Calls]* PC World. PC World! Where in the world …? PC World! |
| PC WORLD | Aye, sir? |
| LAIRD | Arrest this man. |
| PC WORLD | Aye, sir. |
| HAMISH | Wait! Surely the perpetrator would name him or herself in the letters to divert suspicion. |
| LAIRD | True, but too late. Lock him up. |
| | ***Door opens*** |
| MRS MCALISTER | What's going on? |
| MRS NAUGHTIE | Don't ask me. Please. |
| MRS MCALISTER | Hamish, thank goodness you're still here. That bottle of green ink you ordered. It has just arrived. |
| HAMISH | Nooooooooooooooooooooooo! |
| ***Band plays*** | ***Dramatic sting*** |
| | ***Crowded courtroom murmur. Gavel raps*** |
| LAIRD | Hamish, oh Hamish. You stand accused of uttering a malicious document, and common slander. Are you guilty or not guilty? |
| HAMISH | Well, that's not for me to say. |
| LAIRD | Did you do it or not? |
| HAMISH | That's for me to know and you to find out. |
| LAIRD | Dougal, you appear for the defendant. How does he plead? |

| | |
|---|---|
| **DOUGAL** | Not very well by the sound of it. |
| **LAIRD** | I'll enter a plea of not guilty then. |
| **HAMISH** | Good. I'll be on my way. |
| **LAIRD** | I haven't tried you yet. |
| **HAMISH** | And you're not going to, Sonny Jim! |
| **LAIRD** | Dougal, is your client going to take the stand? |
| **DOUGAL** | Well, he's a light-fingered wee tinker, I wouldn't put it past him. |
| **HAMISH** | Well, a fine friend you are! |
| **DOUGAL** | Your Lairdship, I would like to call Mrs McAlister. |
| **LAIRD** | Well I've got her number, if that's any use. |
| **DOUGAL** | No, she's here. Over there, chatting to Mrs Naughtie. |
| **LAIRD** | I wish we could hear what they're saying. |
| **MRS NAUGHTIE** | Well you can't. |
| **DOUGAL** | Mrs McAlister, you have told us a customer made a regular purchase of one bottle of green ink per week at your post office store. Can you see that person in court? |
| **MRS McALISTER** | No. |
| **DOUGAL** | No further questions. |
| **LAIRD** | Dougal, would you be so kind as to remove that bucket from Mrs McAlister's head, please? |
| **DOUGAL** | Oh very well. |
| | ***Bucket removed*** |
| **ALL** | ***Gasp!*** |
| **LAIRD** | That isn't Mrs McAlister. |
| **DOUGAL** | No, it's Meg the mad bucket-woman. What are you doing, Meg? Away with you. Coming in here with your silly bucketing, you must be mad … |
| **LAIRD** | Nice try, Dougal. Call your next witness. |
| **DOUGAL** | Call the handwriting expert. |
| **LAIRD** | You are a handwriting expert? |
| **EXPERT** | You'll have to speak up, I'm very short-sighted. |
| **LAIRD** | You have examined the letters. Have you come to any conclusion? |
| **EXPERT** | Who said that? |
| **LAIRD** | Oh, this is ridiculous. You're turning this courtroom into a circus. Dougal, get off that trapeze and call a proper witness. |
| **DOUGAL** | Certainly. |
| ***Band plays*** | ***Drum roll and cymbal. Flourish*** |

| | |
|---|---|
| **DOUGAL** | Hop-la! |
| **LAIRD** | Nice dismount. |
| **DOUGAL** | I call Hamish to the stand. |
| **HAMISH** | Here I am, ladies and gentlemen. Oh, you're a lovely crowd. What do you get if you cross a caber and a lettuce? A salad that tosses itself. No, but seriously. |
| **LAIRD** | Be quiet. |
| **HAMISH** | Hello, a heckler. |
| **LAIRD** | These are very serious charges … |
| **HAMISH** | Serious charges? I got my gas bill this morning … |
| **LAIRD** | Never mind your gas bill … |
| **HAMISH** | Never mind your gas bill, he says! I do that, I'll end up in court. Speaking of which, have you ever noticed … |
| **LAIRD** | STOP IT! |
| | *Gavel: rap rap rap!* |
| **HAMISH** | Ooh, that hurt. |
| **LAIRD** | And there's plenty more where that came from. |
| | *Gavel: rap rap rap rap rap rap raprapraprap rap!!!* |
| **LAIRD** | Anybody else want a go? |
| | *Bucket clang!* |
| **LAIRD** | Not you, Mad Meg. |
| **DOUGAL** | Your Lairdship, surely the facts in this case are perfectly plain. My client is clearly guilty as sin. Sorry, Hamish, I told you to hire a professional. |
| **LAIRD** | Quite right. Hamish, you are found guilty of the most heinous crime ever to have been brought before this bench. You will be taken from this place to that place, and there you will serve your sentence of life imprisonment, or community service, whichever shall be the longer. Take him down. |
| | *Scuffle thud clang!* |
| **LAIRD** | Not you, Mad Meg. |
| **HAMISH** | Huh! Community service he says! After all the 'community service' I've done for you! |
| **LAIRD** | I'm sure I don't know what you mean. |
| **HAMISH** | I think you do. Every week buying a bottle of green ink for you at the post office, then delivering all your letters by hand to save on the stamps, and passing on all the wee bits of tittle-tattle and gossip from around the Glen, plus being up at all hours peeping in through bedroom windows and listening at keyholes … |

|  | *Gavel: rap rap rap!* |
|---|---|
| HAMISH | Ouch! |
| LAIRD | Case dismissed. You leave this court without a stain on your kilt. |
| ALL | HOORAY!!! |
| DOUGAL | Well done, old friend. |
| HAMISH | I'm only sorry that the true identity of the poison-pen fiend will remain for ever a mystery. |
| DOUGAL | Who cares? Bring on the elephants! |
| *Band plays* | *Circus music* |
|  | *Trumpeting, thundering feet, buckety clangs* |
| ALL | *Wild cheering!* |
| *Band plays* | *Segue into sig and oot under credits* |

*THE END*

# THE VAMPIRE OF THE GLEN

| | |
|---|---|
| *Band plays* | *Sig tune up and under* |
| *Announcer* | *You'll Have Had Your Tea. The doings of Hamish and Dougal. Today, 'The Vampire of the Glen'* |
| *Band plays* | *Sig tune up and oot* |
| | *Outdoor atmos. Door opens* |
| LAIRD | Hamish! Dougal! You'll have had your tea. |
| HAMISH & DOUGAL | Well no, as a matter of fact … |
| LAIRD | Splendid. Then you can get straight to work. You'll be digging over my allotment. |
| HAMISH | And it's the very day for it. Sunny and mild, with a light breeze to lift the kilt. |
| DOUGAL | It's a day with allotment written all over it. |
| HAMISH | Lead us to it! |
| LAIRD | Follow me. |
| | *Indoor footsteps. Door creak* |
| | *Footsteps descend stone staircase* |
| | *[Echo on voices]* |

*The Iron Stag, where stalkers can practice their marksmanship by shooting at one of the wee dogs released by the Laird*

| | |
|---|---|
| HAMISH & DOUGAL | Oh. Oooh. |
| | *Footsteps stop. Dripping water* |
| DOUGAL | Your Lairdship, is your allotment down here? |
| LAIRD | Good Lord no! It's down here. |
| | *Door creak. More footsteps descending stone stairs.* |
| | *Footsteps stop. Lock and key screech, bolts and* |
| | *chains released, door creaks open & Dripping water* |
| | *and rat squeaks* |
| LAIRD | Here we are. |
| HAMISH | An underground allotment. That's a novelty. |
| LAIRD | Been here for years. Originally it was an underground roof garden, but we thought that was silly, so we turned it into an allotment. |
| DOUGAL | Well, it's a bit obvious but it seems to have worked. |
| | *Rat squeak* |
| HAMISH | Oh jings! Look at that enormous rat! |
| LAIRD | Don't worry. McTaggart will take care of him. |
| DOUGAL | Who's McTaggart? |
| LAIRD | That absolutely gigantic rat over there. |
| | *Loud rat squeaks* |
| | *Flurry and squeaking of many rats* |
| LAIRD | That was unexpected. |
| DOUGAL | Aye. Who'd have thought fifteen even more absolutely gigantic rats would have jumped out and overpowered McTaggart? |
| LAIRD | Yes. Well, I'll leave you to it. You'll find spades and forks over there in the potting shed, just behind the old oak tree. |
| HAMISH | The tree by the duck pond? |
| LAIRD | No, that big one across the lawn. |
| HAMISH | Oh yes, I couldn't see it for the greenhouse. |
| LAIRD | I need you to dig out a bed for my sprouts. Just here, about … oh … six feet deep, big enough to take a small oddly shaped wardrobe. |
| HAMISH | Dougal, he's beginning to frighten me. |
| LAIRD | Well, better get a move on, the forecast said rain. See you later. |
| HAMISH | You're not going to leave us down here in the dark? |
| LAIRD | Oh all right, I'll leave you this flaming torch, and a spare bloody battery. Goodbye. |
| | *Door closes, footsteps recede* |
| DOUGAL | What the fff … |

| | |
|---|---|
| **HAMISH** | What was that all about? |
| **DOUGAL** | Hamish – are you thinking what I'm thinking? |
| **HAMISH** | No. |
| **DOUGAL** | Does that coffin-shaped wardrobe remind you of anything? |
| **HAMISH** | Oh yes. A coffin-shaped sideboard. |
| **DOUGAL** | Exactly. Well, whatever it is, let's dig a grave-shaped hole for it, and get out of here. |
| **HAMISH** | Right! And the sooner the quicker! |
| | *Digging* |
| ***Band plays*** | *Link* |
| | *Clatter of tea things, tea pouring* |
| **MRS NAUGHTIE** | Here we are, a cup of tea and a meringue? |
| **DOUGAL** | No you're not, that's a cup of tea all right. |
| **HAMISH** | Two lumps, Mrs Naughtie. |
| **MRS NAUGHTIE** | It's rude to point. |
| **HAMISH** | Sorry. Oh Mrs N, you won't believe what's just happened to us. We were both knocked down by Joe Salmonella's ice-cream van coming out of the public baths. |
| **DOUGAL** | Why he can't use a car wash like everyone else I do not know. |
| **MRS NAUGHTIE** | Where the devil have you been, coming home covered in dust and cobwebs? |
| **HAMISH** | The car wash, but it doesn't seem to have shifted the worst of it. |
| **DOUGAL** | You see we've been digging in the Laird's underground allotment. |
| **MRS NAUGHTIE** | I've heard tell of this. Mrs McAlister claims he took her down there once and showed her his prize hollyhocks. She was very disappointed. She wanted to see his genitalia. |
| **HAMISH** | Well, some you win, some you lose. |
| **DOUGAL** | It was most disturbing. He had us digging a grave-shaped hole for a coffin-shaped wardrobe. |
| **MRS NAUGHTIE** | Jings. |
| **DOUGAL** | You may well say jings, Mrs Naughtie. For all the time we were digging, there were strange noises. |
| **HAMISH** | Well, I was very nervous. |
| **DOUGAL** | As was I. And Hamish, did you notice that portrait? |
| **HAMISH** | I'll never forget it! |
| **DOUGAL** | Good, then you can remind me what it looked like. |

# MACARONI CHEESE

Here's a tasty and convenient snack that can be slipped into a handbag or pocket and carried about until no longer edible.

INGREDIENTS: 1 packet of Pasta Tubelets, manufactured by the MacAroni family of Dunoon. 1 handful of milk, 2 slices of streaky bread, 1 small pot of flour, 1 pat of mustard, 1 pint of water (free-range organic if you can get it). A generous grating of cheese. The cheese should be chosen according to taste and availability. Gloucestershire, Leicestershire, Chestershire and Cheddarshire are traditionally used, but there is nothing to stop you using a Camembert or Buffalo Mozzarella or even Goat's Cheese if you don't mind the way it turns out. Scotland's own traditional cheese, Gordonzola, was made by monks in the 16th century, so is probably past its best.

METHOD: Cook the pastas in the usual way, and remove from the spit when the skins have gone crispy. Boil the water, stirring in the milk and adding a pinch of carrot to taste. Finely chop the flour and add to the pan, stirring occasionally. Mix all the ingredients and simmer for 30 minutes. Spread the mixture on toast and put in a cupboard when cool.

| | |
|---|---|
| **HAMISH** | An ancient picture of a man who was the very embodiment of evil. And the eyes! Those eyes! They followed us round the room, out the door and all the way home. |
| **MRS NAUGHTIE** | From your description, that can only be one man. The Laird's ancient ancestor – Count Cardula the Cad. |
| *Band plays* | *Dramatic accordion chord* |
| **DOUGAL** | Count Cardula – the accordion player? |
| **MRS NAUGHTIE** | Legend has it he was noted for his cruelty. |
| **HAMISH** | What did he do? |
| **MRS NAUGHTIE** | He played the accordion. |
| **DOUGAL** | The fiend! |
| **MRS NAUGHTIE** | And they do say he can still be heard on a winter's night when the moon is full and the tide is high and somebody puts on an accordion record. |
| **HAMISH** | Oh, the hairs on the back of my neck need trimming. Sorry, I was miles away. |
| **DOUGAL** | Well, heaven knows what the Laird is up to, but one thing I do know – none of us will sleep tonight. |
| **MRS NAUGHTIE** | Not again! You and your elbows ... |
| **DOUGAL** | It's Hamish, always grabbing the duvet. |
| **MRS NAUGHTIE** | That wasn't the duvet! |
| **HAMISH & DOUGAL** | Oh ... |
| *Band plays* | *Link* |
| | *Clap of thunder* |
| **LAIRD** | Ooooh! Is there no end to this torment? |
| *Band plays* | *Weedy accordion noise* |
| **LAIRD** | Nooo! Begone! Leave me in peace. |
| *Band plays* | *Silly accordion noise* |
| **LAIRD** | Shall I have no rest? |
| **DOUGAL** | Stop hogging the duvet! |
| **LAIRD** | It's him and his elbows! |
| **MRS NAUGHTIE** | Get some sleep! And that isn't the duvet, by the way! |
| **HAMISH** | And those aren't my elbows! |
| **ALL** | Oh ... |
| *Band plays* | *Accordion noises* |
| **LAIRD** | Noooo! |
| | *Thunderclap* |
| **LAIRD** | Agh! Oh. Thank goodness, it was only a dream. |
| **DOUGAL** | Aye, now can we all get some sleep? |
| **ALL** | Goodnight. |

| | |
|---|---|
| *Band plays* | *Link* |
| | ***Supermarket atmos*** |
| HAMISH | Dougal! |
| DOUGAL | Hamish. I didn't see you behind the cooked meat counter. |
| HAMISH | That's because I'm over here. |
| DOUGAL | So you are. Stocking up? |
| HAMISH | Yes, I'd better. These garters are perished. |
| DOUGAL | I've just popped in for a loaf of bread. |
| HAMISH | Then it's your lucky day – look, buy one get one free. |
| DOUGAL | But I only need the one loaf. |
| HAMISH | Well, take the free one. |
| DOUGAL | Good thinking. |
| HAMISH | Any news of the Laird since he disappeared last week? |
| DOUGAL | Oh Hamish, to all intents and purposes, the Laird has vanished from the face of the earth! |
| LAIRD | Hello, you two. |
| DOUGAL | Your Lairdship! This is a surprise. |
| LAIRD | That's very kind of you. I'll open it later. |
| DOUGAL | Oh. Well, there goes the free loaf. |
| LAIRD | Now, I feel I owe you some explanation for the events of the other evening. Well, here it is. |
| | ***Paper rustle*** |
| HAMISH & DOUGAL | *[Muttered reading]* |
| | 'P.T.O.' |
| | ***Rustle*** |
| HAMISH & DOUGAL | *[Muttered reading]* |
| | 'P.S.' |
| | ***Mutters*** |
| HAMISH | Well, that all makes perfect sense. |
| DOUGAL | Oh yes, we should have realised. |
| HAMISH | Everything all right now, your Lairdship? |
| LAIRD | Oh yes. The shepherd was very understanding. |
| HAMISH | Good. As long as you didn't have to grease his palm. |
| LAIRD | No, he seemed to be getting on quite well without. |
| DOUGAL | There's just one thing I don't understand. Why did you get us to bury a coffin-shaped wardrobe in your underground allotment? |
| LAIRD | Ah – whatever my reason, it had nothing at all to do with the curse that has blighted my family since the days of evil Count Cardula the Cad, and the tragedy |

*A brace of lassies arrive for a day's work as fence-posts.*

and suffering he has brought on the house of
McCoist, so put all such thoughts out of your minds
at once.
'Bad boy! I told you never to talk to strangers!'
Sorry, Mother, it won't happen again.
'Take me back to the Big Hoose before anyone notices
you're doing both voices.'
Coming, Mother! Good afternoon.

| | |
|---|---|
| **HAMISH** | Well, that's cleared that up. |
| **DOUGAL** | What? |
| **HAMISH** | This ointment I was just putting on. What did the Laird want? |
| **DOUGAL** | I don't know. But I can tell you what does concern me. Have you noticed anything odd about Mrs Naughtie recently? |
| **HAMISH** | No. |
| **DOUGAL** | Well, take a look, she's here in the trolley. |
| **HAMISH** | So she is. And there's me thinking you'd bought a new central heating boiler. |
| **DOUGAL** | Look, man, look at her neck. |
| **HAMISH** | Double jings! Puncture marks! |
| **DOUGAL** | Like two inverted commas. |
| **HAMISH** | Punctuation marks! |
| **DOUGAL** | You know what this means? |
| **HAMISH** | Direct speech! |
| **DOUGAL** | Correct. But also the mark of the vampire! |
| ***Band plays*** | ***Dramatic chord*** |
| **HAMISH** | This supermarket muzak gets more intrusive by the day. |
| **DOUGAL** | Luckily for Mrs Naughtie, I know exactly what to do. We must drive a stake through her heart and cut her head off. |
| **HAMISH** | Right ho! |
| **MRS NAUGHTIE** | You'll do no such thing. I wear these marks upon my neck with pride, for they are love tokens from Willie the Kleen-e-zee Man, who pops in once a month to lay out his hardware on the kitchen table. |
| **HAMISH** | You let him bite you? |
| **MRS NAUGHTIE** | Well, it was either that or buy another shammy and sponge for the car. |
| **HAMISH** | Fair enough. |

| | |
|---|---|
| DOUGAL | That's as may be, but the Laird still has some questions to answer. Come on – to the Big Hoose. |
| HAMISH | Aye. We'll be on our way as soon as you've put your trolley through the check-oot. |
| MRS NAUGHTIE | It's just as well I'm on special offer this week. |
| *Band plays* | *Link* |
| ALL | *[Murmur of conversation]* |
| LAIRD | May I say what a pleasure it is to have you all here? It gets very … lonely in the Big Hoose. Now, can I fill your glasses? |
| HAMISH | This is no time for party tricks, your Lairdship. |
| DOUGAL | No. Once was impressive, but twice is just showing off. |
| HAMISH | We're here to find the truth about that coffin-shaped wardrobe in your cellar. |
| DOUGAL | And I must warn you, I've got a pointed stick. |
| LAIRD | Shall I get you a cushion? |
| HAMISH | And I have a crucifix and a bottle of holy whisky. |
| MRS NAUGHTIE | And, garlic being hard to come by in the Glen, I've a jar of pickled onions. |
| LAIRD | Very well, you deserve the truth. As you know I am a dapper character, and have long been proud of my coffin-shaped suits. |
| DOUGAL | Aye, your coffin-shaped suits are the talk of the launderette. |
| HAMISH | And I think I see where this is going … |
| LAIRD | Naturally I kept them in a specially made coffin-shaped wardrobe. |
| HAMISH | I was right. |
| LAIRD | However, as you may recall, three weeks ago last Thursday they suddenly went out of fashion. I could never wear them in public again. Filled with shame, I determined to get rid of them … you know the rest. |
| DOUGAL | Mystery solved! |
| HAMISH | I'll drink to that! |
| ALL | *[Laugh]* |
| LAIRD | Who's there? I can hear voices – who is it? Just a few chums, Mother. Well, get rid of them, you bad boy. |
| HAMISH | Dougal! The Laird! He's speaking in two voices. |
| DOUGAL | Aye, when he's a mind to show off, there's no stopping him. |

| | |
|---|---|
| LAIRD | Behave, Mother, or it's back to the cellar you go … You wouldn't dare. A boy's best friend is his mother. |
| DOUGAL | Aye, you're right there, Mrs Laird. |
| LAIRD | Oh hello, Mother Dougal, I didn't know you were here. |
| HAMISH | We're all here! |
| LAIRD | Mother Hamish! Will you take a dram? |
| HAMISH & DOUGAL | Oh aye, that'd be very nice, just the one, etc. |
| MRS NAUGHTIE | It's party time! |
| LAIRD | Grandpa Naughtie! The gang's all here! |
| ALL | Hooray! |
| | *Laughter …* |
| *Band plays* | *Screeching psycho accordion link* |
| | *Clap of thunder* |
| | *Howling wind* |
| | *Door creaks open* |
| | *Slow heavy footsteps* |
| LAIRD | Who's there? Who is it? Who comes to the Big Hoose at this time of night? Agh! Get away from me! No, not the teeth! Not the teeth! All right, I'll take another shammy and sponge for the car. Same time next month, Willie? Cheerioh. |
| *Band plays* | *Sig and oot under credits* |

**THE END**

# THE GREAT FLOOD OF 1957: TOLD IN PICTURES

*Shortly before the flood.*

*The search for Alistair Muir's £1 note, lost in the flood.*

*The bingo crowd hears of the flood.*

*'Where's my car?' Farmer Stuart McIver scans the Co-op car park for his Ford Popular.*

*Mick Niven flees the flood with the help of his dog and what was left of his flock.*

*Anxious dog-fanciers await the rising waters.*

*Hughie Nairn bravely tests the railway bridge, damaged by the flood.*

*The Reverend Hush and his lady wife read about the flood.*

*Jimmy Tunnock races against time to bring in his fences to safety before the flood.*

*Panic-stricken crowds flee the flood.*

*Desperation! Food runs low at the height of the flood.*

*Inspiration!*
*The makings*
*of a lovely pie!*

# THE MONSTER IN THE LOCH

| | |
|---|---|
| *Band plays* | *Sig tune up and under* |
| *Announcer* | *You'll Have Had Your Tea. The doings of Hamish and Dougal. Today, 'The Monster in the Loch'* |
| *Band plays* | *Sig tune up and oot* |
| | *Howling wind and rain. Rowing boat* |
| DOUGAL | [Appreciative drinking noises] |
| | *Slurp! Aaaaah! Slurp! Aaaaaaaaaaaaahh!!!!* |
| | *Rowing stops* |
| HAMISH | Dougal … |
| DOUGAL | Hamish? |
| HAMISH | By the sound of it, you'll have had your tea. |
| DOUGAL | No, I was just dropping a wee hint. |
| HAMISH | Oh, I knew I'd forgotten something. I left the thermos back on the shore. |
| DOUGAL | You great lummock! And I suppose you've forgotten |

*The Monster in the Loch!*
*Hoping to sight the monster, the Laird's gunnery sergeant aligns his new Peachy & Armstrong 5"*
*rapid-fire short cannon.*

|  |  |
|---|---|
|  | the anchovy toast and the Battenberg and the egg and cress sandwiches and the petit fours? |
| HAMISH | Oh no, I've eaten those. |
| DOUGAL | Right, that's it. We've been out here on the loch for six hours and never a fish. |
| HAMISH | Well, I had a tiddler. |
| DOUGAL | And that scared the fish away. |
| HAMISH | Let's give it one final cast. |
| DOUGAL | Very well. Here goes! |
|  | ***Whoosh twang zzzzzzzz splosh*** |
| DOUGAL | Ho ho! How's that for a cast? |
|  | *[Pause]* |
| HAMISH | *[Off]* Dougal, could you pull me back in please? |
| DOUGAL | You're supposed to let go of the hook. You do that every time. |
| HAMISH | Only since I had fishing lessons with Soaking Wet Tam, the gillie. |
|  | ***Splashing*** |
| DOUGAL | Oh very well, give me your … oh my God! Don't move! |
| HAMISH | What? What is it? |
| DOUGAL | What's that sticking up out of the water? |
| HAMISH | Oh, be fair, I am doing the backstroke. |
| DOUGAL | I've never seen anything like it. |
| HAMISH | Thank you. |
| DOUGAL | No, over there, behind you. |
| HAMISH | Behind me? Agh! What is it? |
| DOUGAL | Hamish. |
| HAMISH | Yes? |
| DOUGAL | I'm off. |
|  | ***Outboard motor starts up, and speeds off*** |
| HAMISH | Dougal! Don't forget me! |
| DOUGAL | *[Off]* I'll never forget you, old friend! Goodbye! |
| HAMISH | You can't leave me out here with this thing! Look at it – a great monster head on a great monster neck looming over me like a monstrous great monster of a monster! Wait a minute, you don't think this could be the … Aaaaagh! |
|  | ***Splashing, stops*** |
|  | ***Outboard returns and stops*** |
| DOUGAL | Hamish? Hamish! Sorry about that, call of nature. |

|  | Now where are you? Hamish, stop playing the giddy goat. I've got the tea! |
|  | ***Splashing as Hamish and monster emerge from the deep*** |
| HAMISH | *[Gargling]* Save me! |
| DOUGAL | Jings, look at the size of it! It's as big as a big tree trunk. |
| HAMISH | It's got me caught in its branch-shaped jaws! |
| DOUGAL | Watch out for its twig-shaped claws! |
| HAMISH | Hit it! |
| DOUGAL | Hit it with what? |
| HAMISH | Hit it with that harpoon gun. |
| DOUGAL | Right. Hup! Wait, I've got a better idea. Load, aim, keep your fingers out of the way, Hamish, and … fire! |
|  | ***Harpoon gun: bang, swish, thud!*** |
| DOUGAL | Got it! |
| HAMISH | Hooray. |
| DOUGAL | Now let's get this brute ashore. Fame and fortune beckon! |
|  | ***Outboard starts up and zooms off*** |
| DOUGAL | *[Sings]* |
|  | Hooray and up she rises, early in the morning … etc. |
|  | *[Fades]* |
|  | ***Pause*** |
|  | ***Feeble splashing*** |
| HAMISH | Dougal? Douga – a –a-a-al! *[Bubbling]* |
| ***Band plays*** | ***Link*** |
|  | ***Footsteps along the loch-side path*** |
| MRS NAUGHTIE | *[Humming to herself]* |
|  | ***Rustling of undergrowth*** |
| LAIRD | Good evening, Mrs Naughtie. |
| MRS NAUGHTIE | Oh, your Lairdship. I didn't expect to see you popping out of the undergrowth. |
| LAIRD | Oh, I often take a stroll in my undergrowth. And you, enjoying your evening constitutional? |
| MRS NAUGHTIE | Oh no, I had that before I came out. |
| LAIRD | And very good it was too, I'm sure. I believe I'll join you. I often walk this way. |
| MRS NAUGHTIE | Oh dear. I've got some talcum powder in my bag … |
| LAIRD | No need, I'm doing it on purpose. |
| MRS NAUGHTIE | Oh well, I suppose it's dark. |

| | |
|---|---|
| LAIRD | You don't mind if I accompany you? |
| MRS NAUGHTIE | Oh really, there's no need. |
| LAIRD | No matter. I'll leave the piano here. I always say the loch looks its best at night. The full moon shining on the water, the stars twinkling above, the glow from that enormous fire … |
| MRS NAUGHTIE | What's an enormous fire doing, glowing out here? |
| LAIRD | My thoughts exactly. Well, Mrs Naughtie, you know what we must do. |
| MRS NAUGHTIE | Indeed I do! |
| LAIRD | And as soon as we've finished, we'll go and investigate that enormous fire! |
| *Band plays* | *Link 'Come On, Baby, Light My Fire'* |
| | *Enormous fire roaring* |
| DOUGAL | What a blaze. Are your chestnuts roasted yet? |
| HAMISH | Aye, it's my own fault for standing too close to the fire. |
| DOUGAL | Well, who'd have thought it? That log-shaped monster turned out to be nothing more than a monster log. |
| HAMISH | Aye. But it makes a grand fire. |
| | *Rustling undergrowth* |
| LAIRD | Hamish, Dougal … |
| DOUGAL | Your Lairdship, Mrs Naughtie … |
| HAMISH | Oh Mrs Naughtie, er … the back of your skirt … it's tucked into the Laird's undergrowth. |
| MRS NAUGHTIE | That's how the youngsters are wearing them these days. |
| LAIRD | You two certainly have a grand bonfire on the go here. It's clearly visible from the other side of the loch, even when you're lying down. |
| MRS NAUGHTIE | Watch your tongue, tiger! |
| DOUGAL | There's an amusing story behind this bonfire, as it happens, your Lairdship. |
| LAIRD | Do tell. |
| DOUGAL | We were out fishing, and we accidentally harpooned this gigantic log. |
| HAMISH | And you won't believe this, but we thought it was the monster of the loch! |
| BOTH | Ha ha ha ha ha ha ha ha!!! |
| LAIRD | You fools! |
| DOUGAL | What? |

| | |
|---|---|
| LAIRD | It is the monster of the loch! |
| HAMISH | No, it's just a big log. |
| LAIRD | Do you realise what you've just done? Our entire tourist industry depends on idiots like you mistaking this old log for the monster. Now you've burnt it, we're completely cattle-trucked. |
| MRS NAUGHTIE | Language! |
| LAIRD | We can say goodbye to my monster boat trips, and my peculiar postcard range … |
| MRS NAUGHTIE | And my monster tea shoppe, not to mention my Highland fudge outlet. |
| HAMISH | Oh Dougal, he's right. You make a fair whack out of your furry monster dollies, and your Punch and Monster Show … |
| DOUGAL | As do you with your monster granite key-rings, and your famous monster lunch-box … |
| HAMISH | Not to mention your bumper stickers saying 'My boyfriend went to see the monster, and all he got me was this lousy Porsche … ' |
| DOUGAL | And your monster duvet cover and matching wheelbarrow cosy … |
| HAMISH | And my monster surgical appliance – though that one never really caught on. |
| DOUGAL | Well, I said the rustic wood finish was a mistake … |
| LAIRD | Shut it! The tourist season starts tomorrow. We've got to find a replacement for the monster. Mrs Naughtie, have you got a rubber suit? |
| MRS NAUGHTIE | You know I have. You brought it back from Monte Carlo. |
| LAIRD | Then put it on, it helps me think. As for you two, go back to your homes and await my orders. |
| *Band plays* | *Link* |
| LAIRD | And take that gramophone with you. |
| HAMISH | Yes, your Lairdship … |
| DOUGAL | Sorry sir, we're on our way. |
| *Band plays* | *Same link* |
| LAIRD | What did I just tell you? |
| DOUGAL | Sorry. We're off now. |
| *Band plays* | *Same link* |
| HAMISH | Forgot the gramophone, sorry. |
| *Band plays* | *Same link* |

*American monster-hunter Chuck Normanson in his submarine,*
*'Plunger' preparing for what was sadly to be his last dive.*

*The rescue party looking for Chuck after his last dive.*
*Many thought he should have taken the submarine with him.*

|  | *Knock at door* |
| HAMISH | Come in. |
|  | *Door opens* |
| DOUGAL | No tea for me, thank you. |
| HAMISH | And where have you been for the last week? |
| DOUGAL | In Singapore. That's the last time I go there for no apparent reason. Have I missed anything? |
| HAMISH | The place has been crawling with tourists, and there's an ugly mood afoot. |
| DOUGAL | I was afraid of this ... |
| HAMISH | You know the Laird's lunchtime picnic monster cruise round the loch in his wee boat the *Bunty*? |
| DOUGAL | Aye. |
| HAMISH | Well, last week they ran into trouble. |
| DOUGAL | Why, what happened? |
| HAMISH | The tourists mutinied, and cast the Laird adrift in an open sandwich. |
| DOUGAL | Mutiny on the *Bunty*? Whatever next? |
| HAMISH | It's in all the papers ... |
| DOUGAL | What's this? Mrs McAlister from the post office has been taken hostage by a coach party of Rotarians from Cheadle Hulme? They say they won't release her until they've seen the monster? |
| HAMISH | We put up a big sign by the loch, saying: 'Just because you can't find it, doesn't mean it isn't there.' |
| DOUGAL | Well, nobody's going to believe that, are they? Now, where's Mrs Naughtie? |
| HAMISH | Protesting for the Laird. I heard she lay down in the road for him. |
| DOUGAL | Not for the first time. |
| HAMISH | No no no, she laid herself down in front of the army tanks. |
| DOUGAL | Army tanks, here? |
| HAMISH | No, she had to go to Salisbury Plain. But it was a brave gesture. And a day out. |
| DOUGAL | Well, I hope she's brought us back some rock or a hat. |
| HAMISH | I'm sure of it. She's a good woman. |
| DOUGAL | Where is she now? |
| HAMISH | Over there getting the track-marks out of her tweed two-piece. |
| DOUGAL | Oh yes. I suppose lying down in front of a steamroller would do the trick. |

|  |  |
|---|---|
|  | ***Steamroller, clangs, crunch, hiss, clatter*** |
| DOUGAL | No, broke the steamroller. |
| HAMISH | Nice try, Mrs Naughtie! |
| MRS NAUGHTIE | Thank you. I should have remembered, it didn't work last time either. |
| DOUGAL | Have you any idea if his Lairdship is doing anything to avert this absent monster crisis? |
| MRS NAUGHTIE | ***Starts to cry*** |
| HAMISH | Oh dear, what can the matter be? |
| MRS NAUGHTIE | My dear Laird's locked in his laboratory. He's been there from Monday till Saturday, Nobody knew he was there. |
| *Band plays* | ***Chord!*** |
| HAMISH | Hey! Hands off our gramophone! |
| DOUGAL | What can he be up to? |
| MRS NAUGHTIE | All I know is, he was down to Big Tam's Video Emporium last week, and he took out *Frankenstein* and *Godzilla*. |
| DOUGAL | Big Tam's daughters? |
| MRS NAUGHTIE | No, no, videos. |
| HAMISH | Videos? Of Big Tam's daughters? |
| DOUGAL | It's a very popular line. |
| HAMISH | Aye? I'd take issue with the dubbing. |
| DOUGAL | Well, he's up to something, that's for sure. Come on, to the Big Hoose. |
| *Band plays* | ***Sinister link*** |
|  | ***Wind. Owl hooting.*** |
| DOUGAL | Hamish, stop doing that owl impression. |
| HAMISH | It calms my nerves. |
| DOUGAL | Well, do something else. |
| HAMISH | All right. Look, here comes Rover the sheepdog. Woof woof! Mind those cows, Rover. Moo. Moo, woof woof, moo! |
| MRS NAUGHTIE | I can do an impression of a burglar alarm. |
| DOUGAL | What? |
| MRS NAUGHTIE | Listen. |
|  | ***Burglar alarm*** |
| LAIRD | Who's there? |
| DOUGAL | Now you've done it. |
| HAMISH | It's me and Dougal and Mrs Naughtie, sir. |
| LAIRD | You'd better come in. But leave Rover and the cows out there with the owl. |

| | |
|---|---|
| **HAMISH** | Moo … |
| **DOUGAL** | Hamish! |
| **HAMISH** | Sorry. |
| | *Heavy door creaks open* |
| **DOUGAL** | Yes, very good Hamish. Open up. |
| | *Ordinary door opens* |
| **LAIRD** | Come in quickly and close the door behind you. |
| | *Door creak and booming slam* |
| **MRS NAUGHTIE** | That was me. Now, any requests? |
| **LAIRD** | How about a nice cup of tea? |
| **MRS NAUGHTIE** | Oh, that's a difficult one. |
| **LAIRD** | All right, what about a Zeppelin raid? |
| **DOUGAL** | Your Lairdship, that's not why we're here. There's a crisis in the Glen, and we want to know what you're doing about it. |
| **LAIRD** | That's a very good impression, Mrs Naughtie. Can you do Hamish? |
| **MRS NAUGHTIE** | Not till Tuesday after six. |
| **DOUGAL** | For goodness' sake!!! What is going on in this laboratory? |
| **LAIRD** | Very well – what do you think of this? |
| **DOUGAL** | That doesn't answer my question. |
| **LAIRD** | No, this! |
| **ALL** | *[Gasp!]* |
| *Band plays* | *Chord* |
| **HAMISH** | Whatever is it? |
| **LAIRD** | This is my … creature. |
| **MRS NAUGHTIE** | It's enormous. |
| **DOUGAL** | Over here, Mrs N. |
| **MRS NAUGHTIE** | Oh! That's the most horrible thing I've seen since the over-sixties Nude Motorcycle Display Team crashed in the middle of their human pyramid routine. |
| **LAIRD** | Creating this almost cost me my sanity. Fearful nights haunting the abattoir and mortuary, clandestine visits to Farmer McPhee's farm with his 'pick your own cow' pasture, hijacking the travelling giblet-monger, and dreadful hours spent in the circus graveyard. |
| **DOUGAL** | And this … thing is the result? |
| **LAIRD** | It is! Ha ha ha! |
| | *Crash of thunder* |
| **LAIRD** | The storm is raging – now for the final touch. Quick, |

*In search of the monster, the Laird baits his hook …*

before the lightning strikes – connect those wires, turn that handle, stand by the big switch … now, elements, do your thing!
***Crash of thunder***
***Sparks, fizzes, crackling, pops, click***

LAIRD     Right, now we've got the light on you can see it properly.

HAMISH     Jings – it looks like a … like a … like a … log.

LAIRD     It is a log. It's a very big log.

DOUGAL     It's identical to the other very big log.

LAIRD     Exactly. Don't think it was easy. Scraps of wood stolen from all those places I mentioned, painstakingly glued together, along with over five hundred spent matches.

DOUGAL     You know this very big log could fool the gullible tourists in precisely the same way as the other very big log fooled the gullible tourists.

LAIRD     I couldn't have put it better myself.

HAMISH     Your Lairdship, that's brilliant.

LAIRD     Yes, once again … the monster lives! Ha ha! And now …

*Proof at last! The Laird's sensitive detecting equipment locates a giant fishlike creature leaping from the loch! (Notice the curious almost finger-like structures on the creature's underside.)*

| | |
|---|---|
| ALL | To the loch!!! |
| *Band plays* | ***Dramatic link*** |
| | ***Wind, lapping water*** |
| DOUGAL | Well, here we are at the loch. |
| HAMISH | Why did you say that? |
| DOUGAL | I usually do. |
| LAIRD | Time for the launching. Mrs Naughtie, will you do the honours? |
| MRS NAUGHTIE | Of course, but let's get this launching over first. |
| DOUGAL | Have you got a bottle about our person? |
| MRS NAUGHTIE | Just by chance I do have a litre of industrial-strength crème de menthe. I carry it for medicinal purposes. |
| HAMISH | Aye, you're martyr to your bunions. |
| DOUGAL | But you keep smiling. |
| LAIRD | On with the launch! |
| MRS NAUGHTIE | I name this log *Monster of the Loch*. God bless it and |

|  | all who fall for it. Whee! |
|  | *Whistle clink* |
| HAMISH | Ooh! |
|  | *Whistle clink* |
| DOUGAL | Ooh! |
|  | *Whistle clink* |
| LAIRD | Ooh! |
|  | *Whistle clink* |
| MRS NAUGHTIE | Ooh! |
|  | *Whistle, crash tinkle!* |
| ALL | Hooray! |
|  | *Trundling rumble …* |
| LAIRD | There she goes! |
|  | *Splash bubbling* |
| HAMISH | We're back in business! |
| DOUGAL | That very big log would fool anybody! |
|  | *Massive splashing. Monster roar!* |
| HAMISH | What's going on now? |
| DOUGAL | What's that? |
| HAMISH | It's a great big scaly monster! It's attacking the very big log! |
| DOUGAL | Not attacking, Hamish. It's trying to mate with it. |
| LAIRD | Don't look, Mrs Naughtie. |
| MRS NAUGHTIE | It's trying to get its leg over. |
| HAMISH | That's not its leg! |
|  | *Great roar* |
| DOUGAL | Well that was quick. |
| MRS NAUGHTIE | Oh yes? Listen who's talking. |
|  | *Roaring, crunching, splashing* |
| HAMISH | What's it up to now? |
| DOUGAL | It's eating the very big log! It must be one of those creatures that eats its partner after mating. |
| LAIRD | Like a praying mantis? |
| DOUGAL | No thanks, I'm trying to cut down. |
|  | *[Crunch, gulp, swallow. Satisfied]* |
|  | 'Aaaaaah!' |
| LAIRD | The bastard's eaten my very big log! I'll teach him a lesson. |
|  | *Twelve bore. Both barrels* |
|  | *Monster howl, splashing, bubbles* |
| DOUGAL | Your Lairdship … |

| | |
|---|---|
| LAIRD | Yes? |
| DOUGAL | You know we started all this to fool the tourists into thinking there was a monster in the loch? |
| LAIRD | Yes. |
| DOUGAL | Well, we had a real monster all the time. |
| HAMISH | But you just shot it. |
| DOUGAL | And now we don't even have a very big log. |
| LAIRD | I take your point. Let me think. Ah, yes! Mrs Naughtie … |
| MRS NAUGHTIE | I know. I'll get the rubber suit. |
| *Band plays* | *Sig and oot under credits* |

**THE END**

*It's the Tall Ships race across the North Sea for the under-twelves, and the crew of the Cutty Remark are first over the finishing line, after an incident-packed voyage!*

With Big Tam
our Local Guide

(Not during pub opening hours)

S

No

e!'

or

ly

## DON'T MISS
# KIRSTY COHEN'S
# NAIL SALON

**She also has a range of
hammers and chisels.**

fe

If yo

**Book into the**
# Thistle McHilton

With Big Tam

## our Local Guide

(Not during pub opening hours)

No

SO

CALL IN AT

# THE HAGGIS AND LAPTOP

for a malt and a bottle of brown!

(Malt Loaf and HP Sauce, yummy!)

If you're lucky you might arrive during one of Mrs Naughtie's Funeral Teas!

## ALL WELCOME!

Guaranteed to bring a smile to every face!
People are dying to be there!

of

Th

n

Savour the nightlife at

TARTAN RHINO

# TRAPPED!

| | |
|---|---|
| *Band plays* | *Sig tune up and under* |
| *Announcer* | *You'll Have Had Your Tea. The doings of Hamish and Dougal. Today, 'Trapped!'* |
| *Band plays* | *Sig tune up and oot* |
| | *Traffic, street noise* |
| *Band plays* | *Hare Krishna [Voices, drums, bells]* |
| NEWS VENDOR | *Star, News* and *Standard!* |
| SELLER | Violets, lovely violets! |
| POLICEMAN | Move along there, you Pearly Kings and Queens. |
| PEARLY KING | God bless you, Constable! |
| SELLER | *[Sings]* Who will buy this beautiful morning? |
| POLICEMAN | Shut your face! |
| DOUGAL | Well, Hamish, here we are amid the bustle and hubbub of London's busy Oxford Street, on our very first visit to the nation's capital. |
| HAMISH | Why did you say that? |
| DOUGAL | Well, it doesn't do any harm. |
| HAMISH | Aye, better safe than sorry. |
| DOUGAL | Well, we can't stand around here blethering. Shall we commence our shopping spree? |

*A rare photo of Hamish and Dougal doing their well-loved hedgehog impressions.*

| | |
|---|---|
| HAMISH | Well, right off I'm going to buy some bigger shoes. |
| DOUGAL | Where are you going to get them? |
| HAMISH | That man over there's selling them. |
| MAN | *Big Issue, Big Issue!* |
| HAMISH | That's lucky, he's got a pair of bigger shoes. |
| DOUGAL | You stupid tumpsy! Come on, let's away into this well-known department store, here on London's busy Oxford Street. |
| HAMISH | I'm right behind you. |
| | ***Footsteps walking away*** |
| MAN | Bigger shoe! I've got size twelve in a wider fitting! Get your bigger shoe here! |
| | ***Door swish and department store interior atmos*** |
| DOUGAL | Come on, Hamish, keep up. |
| HAMISH | I'm doing my best. My old shoes are pinching me something terrible. |
| DOUGAL | You've got them on the wrong feet. |
| HAMISH | No I haven't. |
| DOUGAL | Yes you have – they're Mrs Naughtie's. |
| HAMISH | Well, I got dressed in a hurry. |
| DOUGAL | Never mind, they go very well with that negligee you're wearing. |
| LADY ASSISTANT | Good morning, sir, madam. |
| DOUGAL | Hello? |
| LADY ASSISTANT | Plaisir de la Nuit? |
| HAMISH | I don't mind if I do! |
| | ***Spray. Shhhhhhhhh! Shhhhhhhhhhhh! Shp!*** |
| HAMISH & DOUGAL | *[Coughing]* |
| HAMISH | What are you spraying us with, woman? |
| DOUGAL | Plaisir de la Nuit – that'll be some kind of perfume. |
| LADY ASSISTANT | No, it's Mace. I saw that look in your eye! |
| DOUGAL | Come along, Hamish, we've no time to exchange pleasantries with this over painted hussy. |
| LADY ASSISTANT | Well! I'm not very impressed with your husband's manners, madam. |
| HAMISH | Haud on – I'm rather taken with this Mace fragrance. It's an improvement on my habitual eau de toilette. |
| DOUGAL | Come away, Hamish. You'll wake up being sold in Tangiers. |
| HAMISH | Should we not get a little something for Mrs Naughtie? |

| | |
|---|---|
| DOUGAL | Such as what? |
| HAMISH | Aftershave? |
| DOUGAL | No! Terrible stuff. I don't know what these people see in it. |
| HAMISH | True. Mind you, down here they probably drink it with tonic. |
| DOUGAL | Let's get on with our shopping list. I have it here. Let me see: shortbread, sporran oil, one 'Le Creuset' haggis brick, and some more shortbread. |
| HAMISH | Oh, here's a guide to the store. First floor: soft furnishings and marquees … |
| DOUGAL | Fifth floor: children's ironmongery and chemical toilets … |
| HAMISH | Twenty-third floor: parachutes … |
| DOUGAL | Ah! There it is! Second floor: lingerie, car wash, fuel, and shortbread! |
| HAMISH | Then what are we waiting for? Second floor, here we come! |
| | *Running feet* |
| HAMISH | Dougal! Slow down! Oh, these old shoes are so tight, my verucca's jumped ship! |
| | *Fast limping feet fade …* |
| *Band plays* | *Ascending link* |
| DOUGAL | Help! Help! |
| HAMISH | Help! Help! |
| DOUGAL | Help! |
| HAMISH | It's no use, nobody can hear us. |
| DOUGAL | Don't be silly. This well-known store on London's busy Oxford Street is packed with customers. It's just a matter of time. |
| HAMISH | Help! We're stuck between floors! We're trapped! Help! |
| DOUGAL | Hamish, you're getting hysterical. |
| | *Slap! Slap! Slap! Slap!* |
| HAMISH | Well don't just stand there applauding, do something. |
| DOUGAL | Right. |
| | *Slap! Slap! Slap!* |
| HAMISH | Ouch! |
| DOUGAL | Now control yourself, or next time it's the face. |
| HAMISH | All right. I'll put my head between my knees. |
| DOUGAL | What good will that do? |

| | |
|---|---|
| HAMISH | Don't knock it till you've tried it. |
| DOUGAL | Carry on. All we can do is wait till somebody comes along and repairs the mechanism. *[Hums]* |
| HAMISH | I spy with my little eye, something beginning with P. |
| DOUGAL | Hamish, will you take your head out from between your knees? |
| HAMISH | Do you give up? |
| DOUGAL | Yes. |
| HAMISH | Pantihose! Oh, I did get dressed in a hurry … |
| DOUGAL | Come on, we've got to keep our spirits up. What was that poem Mrs Naughtie always says when things look grim? A lady from South Carolina, took a cruise on a great ocean liner … |
| HAMISH | Steady on, old friend … |
| DOUGAL | She said to the stoker … |
| HAMISH | I don't like the way this is going … |
| DOUGAL | A bit of a joker … |
| HAMISH | Leave it, leave it … |
| DOUGAL | It's high time you saw Indo-China. |
| HAMISH | Phew, that was a close one. I thought you were going to say v– |
| DOUGAL | For goodness' sake! What do you take me for? |
| HAMISH | Well, that's the way Mrs Naughtie tells it. You ask anybody in the Bible class. |
| DOUGAL | Jings, this is a fine way to end our trip to London. |
| HAMISH | Aye, it's been a disaster from start to finish. The coach trip down was dreadful. |
| DOUGAL | Big Tam fell asleep at the wheel. |
| HAMISH | Aye, I thought we'd never set off. |
| DOUGAL | Then five miles up the road he had a blowout. |
| HAMISH | We had to open all the windows. |
| DOUGAL | We had to abandon the coach. |
| HAMISH | And the train was no better. |
| DOUGAL | We had to change at Dundee and again at Edinburgh … |
| HAMISH | Just as well we had spare kilts. |
| DOUGAL | Mind you, it's our own fault for travelling in the buffet car. |
| HAMISH | Aye, they don't make trains like they used to. Every time we hit a leaf, the air was thick with cock-a-leekie. |
| DOUGAL | Then when we got to London, the Tube! Oh, the Tube was a nightmare! |

| | |
|---|---|
| **HAMISH** | Well I warned you not to have that colonic irrigation. |
| **DOUGAL** | Aye, I should have read the small print. But it's hard to read when your eyes are watering. |
| **HAMISH** | To be honest, I didn't even know that Starbucks were doing them. |
| **DOUGAL** | And the hotel! The hotel? Four stars indeed! |
| **HAMISH** | To be fair, you could see them through the hole in the roof. |
| **DOUGAL** | And now this. Trapped! Trapped! We're trapped! |
| | ***Slap! Slap! Slap!*** |
| **HAMISH** | Will you stop hitting me? |
| **DOUGAL** | Well, take your head out from between MY knees! |
| **HAMISH** | I spy … |
| **DOUGAL** | Stop it. Oh why did we ever leave the Glen? |
| **HAMISH** | Aye, that's where we belong. Down here we stick out like fish out of a square thumb. |
| **DOUGAL** | You're right there, old friend. Happy days in the Glen. Do you remember … the time when we went up to the Laird's laboratory because we thought he was creating a monster? |
| **HAMISH** | Oh yes … |
| ***Band plays*** | ***Flashback gliss*** |
| | ***Crash of thunder*** |
| **LAIRD** | Creating this almost cost me my sanity. |
| **DOUGAL** | And this … thing is the result? |
| **LAIRD** | It is! Ha ha ha! |
| | ***Crash of thunder*** |
| **LAIRD** | The storm is raging – now for the final touch. Quick, before the lightning strikes – connect those wires, turn that handle, stand by the big switch … now, elements, do your thing! |
| | ***Crash of thunder*** |
| | ***Sparks, fizzes, crackling, pops, click*** |
| **LAIRD** | Right, now we've got the light on you can see it properly. |
| **HAMISH** | Jings – it … just a minute. What's going on? What's all this about? |
| **DOUGAL** | It's a flashback, Hamish. It's what people get when they're trapped between floors. |
| **HAMISH** | You mean this isn't now, it's then? |
| **DOUGAL** | No, this is now, but that was then just now. |

# RUMBLEDETHUMPS

The inevitable accompaniment to any Scottish meal!

INGREDIENTS: ½ pint semi-skimmed milk of magnesia, 3 sun-dried bicarbonates of soda

METHOD: Seek medical advice if symptoms persist.

| | |
|---|---|
| HAMISH | So if that was now then, and this is then now, then this is now then. |
| DOUGAL | Yes. Now and then. Now then … |
| HAMISH | Ah, so people trapped between floors remember incidents from previous episodes of their lives. |
| DOUGAL | Yes. It's a well-known way of passing the time, and quite economical. |
| HAMISH | Can I have a go? |
| DOUGAL | Yes, why don't you share a fond clip from the past? |
| HAMISH | Right, here goes. Ho ho, I'll never forget that time, ho ho ho, that time when Ross and Chandler gave a surprise party for Rachel, but Monica let the cat out of the bag when Joey and Phoebe … |
| DOUGAL | Haud on, haud on! |
| HAMISH | What? |
| DOUGAL | You haven't got the hang of this, have you? They're supposed to be our own past episodes you're remembering. |
| HAMISH | Oh, I see. Right. Do you remember that night we were watching *Friends* on TV, and Ross and Chandler gave a surprise party for Rachel … |
| DOUGAL | No no no! |
| HAMISH | But it was funny, because Monica let the cat out of the bag … |
| | *Slap! Slap! Slap!* |
| HAMISH | … when Joey and Phoebe … |
| | *Slap!* |
| HAMISH | Can we not play another game? |
| DOUGAL | No. Think of something amusing that happened to US! |
| HAMISH | Right … Oh! Ha ha ha! Yes! Ho ho ho, I've got it! |
| DOUGAL | Good. |
| HAMISH | Bigger shoe! *Big Issue*! Ho ho, that was funny. |
| DOUGAL | Yes. |
| HAMISH | Mind you not as funny as the time when Ross and Chandler gave a surprise party for Rachel, but Monica let the cat out of the bag when Joey and Phoebe … |
| DOUGAL | Help! Help! |
| HAMISH | Help! |
| | *Banging on steel panel* |
| MRS NAUGHTIE | [*Off*] Mr Hamish? Mr Dougal? Is that you? |

| | |
|---|---|
| DOUGAL | Mrs Naughtie! |
| MRS NAUGHTIE | Where are you? |
| HAMISH | We're stuck between floors. |
| DOUGAL | Here, on this escalator. |
| MRS NAUGHTIE | On the escalator? Oh yes, I can see you now. |
| HAMISH | We've been here for hours. |
| DOUGAL | Waiting for somebody to get the thing moving. |
| HAMISH | But that's enough about us. What are you doing here, Mrs Naughtie? |
| MRS NAUGHTIE | I came down to see my son James. He's been working here as a doorman since things went belly-up at the BBC. |
| HAMISH | He's lucky to have the work. I heard his pal John Humphrys got a job at the Listening Bank, but he didn't last the week. |
| DOUGAL | Fascinating, I'm sure, but are you going to rescue us? |
| HAMISH | The sooner the better. My claustrophobia's getting worse with all these people pushing past us on their way up. |
| ALL | 'Scuse me, |
| | Gangway! |
| | Move your arse. |
| | Violets, lovely violets. |
| | *Big Issue*! |
| HAMISH & DOUGAL | Help! Help! |
| MRS NAUGHTIE | Just keep calm, the pair of you. As you know, I used to be a midwife. So take deep breaths, put your heads between your knees, and whatever you do, don't push. |
| HAMISH | I spy with my little eye, something beginning with ... H. |
| DOUGAL | I thought you said the ointment was working a treat? |
| HAMISH | No, look! A Helicopter! |
| | ***Helicopter approaches*** |
| LAIRD | Hello down there! |
| DOUGAL | Your Lairdship. How did you get your helicopter into the store? |
| LAIRD | Oh, they know me here. So, what seems to be the problem? |
| HAMISH | No problem, the ointment worked a treat. |
| MRS NAUGHTIE | Your Lairdship, they're stuck on a broken-down escalator between floors. |

*Business as usual for these busy air traffic controllers at the Glen Airport.*

| | |
|---|---|
| LAIRD | How awful. I have an idea. Mrs Naughtie, strap yourself into this leather and nylon harness. |
| MRS NAUGHTIE | I'm not falling for that one again. |
| LAIRD | Get into the harness, then I can winch you down to pluck Hamish and Dougal from the jaws of doom. |
| MRS NAUGHTIE | Very well. |
| | ***Straps and buckles being fastened*** |
| MRS NAUGHTIE | I'm ready. |
| LAIRD | Ha ha, she falls for it every time! Now where's my webcam? |
| DOUGAL | Your Lairdship! |
| LAIRD | Oh all right, party pooper. Here we go – winching Mrs Naughtie into position now! |
| | ***Helicopter up, and winch noises*** |
| MRS NAUGHTIE | Oooooh! Ooooh! |
| LAIRD | Mrs Naughtie? |
| MRS NAUGHTIE | Yes? |
| LAIRD | This is very important. Could you pick me up some of that crystallised ginger as you swing past? |
| MRS NAUGHTIE | Right ho. Ooooh! |
| HAMISH | What's happening? |
| DOUGAL | Here she comes, swinging through the air. |
| LAIRD | Dougal, you grab one leg; Hamish, you grab the other. |
| DOUGAL | Then what? |
| LAIRD | Make a wish. Ha ha ha! No, hang on tight, up we go. |
| | ***Helicopter and winch noise up*** |
| DOUGAL | Ohh – don't look down! |
| HAMISH | Don't look up! |
| DOUGAL | What? Oh, I didn't know they still wore those. |
| LAIRD | Now, the two of you climb up Mrs Naughtie, and scramble into the helicopter. |
| MRS NAUGHTIE | I hope nobody's attempting the South Face. |
| HAMISH & DOUGAL | Ooof. Oh! Unf. |
| MRS NAUGHTIE | Mind where you're putting your feet. Why are you wearing my shoes? |
| HAMISH | They go with the pantihose. |
| | ***Body rustles and clunks*** |
| DOUGAL | Hup! Well, here we both are in the helicopter. |
| HAMISH | Why did you say that? |
| DOUGAL | It seemed appropriate. |

| | |
|---|---|
| MRS NAUGHTIE | *[Off]* Ooooo-oooh! |
| HAMISH | Jings, Mrs Naughtie is still dangling on the cable. |
| LAIRD | Yes … Right, where to, gents? |
| DOUGAL | The Shortbread Department, please. |
| LAIRD | Certainly. |
| | ***Helicopter up and away*** |
| MRS NAUGHTIE | Oooooooooooh … |
| ***Band plays*** | ***Scottish link*** |
| HAMISH | Well, here we are, back home again. |
| DOUGAL | Why didn't I say that? |
| HAMISH | You had the chance. |
| DOUGAL | I can see the metropolis has gone to somebody's head. |
| HAMISH | Your Lairdship, it was very kind of you to give us a lift all the way back to the Glen. |
| LAIRD | It was the least I could do for a pair of stranded fellow Highlanders. Shame about Mrs Naughtie, though. |
| DOUGAL | Aye. I think we lost her somewhere over the Humber. |
| LAIRD | Cable snapped at 15,000 feet. Still, all's well that ends well. |
| HAMISH | I will say one thing. That Shortbread Department was a bit of a disappointment. |
| DOUGAL | Well, what do expect from a well-known department store in London's busy Oxford Street? They wouldn't know shortbread from a shagpile carpet. |
| HAMISH | Another piece of shortbread, your Lairdship? |
| LAIRD | Rather. But could you hoover it first this time? |
| HAMISH | Oh, don't be a fusspot. There you are. |
| DOUGAL | It's a lovely pattern. |
| LAIRD | Nice and chewy … |
| | ***Door bursts open*** |
| MRS NAUGHTIE | You bastards! |
| HAMISH & DOUGAL | What? |
| LAIRD | Look at the state of you, woman. All soot and seaweed. |
| MRS NAUGHTIE | Jettisoned over the Humber! Swept out to sea! If it hadn't been for that nice trawler captain who netted me off the coast of Mogadishu, I wouldn't be here at all. That's you and me finished, the lot of you. I've been to hell and back. Well may you hang your |

|                   | heads between your knees. What have you got to say for yourselves? |
|-------------------|--------------------------------------------------------------------|
| **ALL**           | Mrs Naughtie …                                                     |
| **MRS NAUGHTIE**  | Yes?                                                               |
| **ALL**           | You'll have had your tea …                                         |
| ***Band plays***  | ***Sig and oot under credits***                                    |

**THE END**

# HOGMANAY SPECIAL

Hamish and Dougal's Hogmanay Frolic

# HAMISH AND DOUGAL'S HOGMANAY FROLIC!

| | |
|---|---|
| *Band plays* | *Sig tune up and under* |
| *Announcer* | *The season's greetings from the Glen, and welcome to: 'Hamish and Dougal's Hogmanay Frolic'* |
| *Band plays* | *Sig tune up and oot* |
| | *Door opens* |
| DOUGAL | Hamish! |
| HAMISH | Dougal. You'll have had your tea. |
| DOUGAL | No. But look here, I've brought you a wee treat – the last of the turkey leftovers. |
| HAMISH | Oho! |
| DOUGAL | Oh ho ho! |
| HAMISH | Oh. Just the beak, then. |
| DOUGAL | That'll go down very well with a few chips and a sirloin steak. Now put away that oxyacetylene torch and selection of lizards. You can finish your entry for the Turner Prize some other time. |
| HAMISH | You know, I'm still bitter about last year. If only the wind had been in the right direction … |
| DOUGAL | Well, it didn't help when the breeze lifted your kilt and you shouted 'How's that for an installation?' |
| HAMISH | I'm my own worst enemy. |
| DOUGAL | No no, I think you'll find that's Big Tam at the abattoir. Now get a move on, the Laird wants to see us, up at the Big Hoose. |
| HAMISH | On New Year's Eve? Whatever for? |
| DOUGAL | He wouldn't say. But he hinted that he had a proposition to make. |
| MRS NAUGHTIE | He made one of those to me once. |
| DOUGAL | Mrs Naughtie! What are you doing round the back? |
| MRS NAUGHTIE | That's just what the Laird said. |
| HAMISH | Mrs Naughtie just popped in to run her duster over my knick-knacks. |
| DOUGAL | Well, carry on, if you don't mind me watching. |
| HAMISH | No, we must away to the Big Hoose. The Laird doesn't like to be left dangling. |
| MRS NAUGHTIE | No he does not. Oh, apart from that one time … |
| DOUGAL | Too much information, Mrs Naughtie. We'd best be on our way. |
| MRS NAUGHTIE | Well be sure to wrap up warm. The snow's three feet deep, and it's cold enough to freeze the bells off a |

|  |  |
|---|---|
|  | brass monkey with bells on it. |
| DOUGAL | Don't worry, I have thought to bring a pair of all-weather sporrans. Come on, let us strike out through the snow! |
| ***Band plays*** | ***Link*** |
|  | ***Howling wind. Sleigh bells*** |
| DOUGAL | Hamish, hurry up there. And stop playing with that brass monkey. |
|  | ***Tink tink!*** |
| HAMISH | Oh, the bells have fallen off. |
| DOUGAL | Never mind, we're here at the Big Hoose. I'll ring the bell. |
|  | ***Dong! Creak, splinter, clank clang!*** |
| HAMISH | And that's fallen off as well. |
|  | ***Door creaks open*** |
| HUMPH | Good afternoon, gentlemen. Don't just stand there shivering, go away. |
| HAMISH | And who might you be? |
| HUMPH | I might be Geri Halliwell, but in fact I am his Lairdship's butler, Lyttelton. |
| DOUGAL | Since when? |
| HUMPH | Since the day I was born, sir. |
| DOUGAL | No no, since when has his Lairdship had a factotum? |
| HUMPH | I am no factotum, sir. I am a gentleman's gentleman. |
| HAMISH | If you are, you're the only one in the village. |
| LAIRD | Lyttelton! Who's that at the door? |
| HUMPH | It's me, sir. |
| LAIRD | Well, come in, for goodness' sake. |
| HUMPH | Thank you, sir. |
|  | ***Door closes. Howling wind*** |
| DOUGAL | Oh jings! We're never going to hear about the Laird's golf competition and meet Tim Brooke-Taylor at this rate. |
| HAMISH | Dougal, do you know something I don't? |
| DOUGAL | I've said too much. Hamish, knock on the door. |
| HAMISH | Very well. |
|  | ***Knock knock knock*** |
| HAMISH | Now, what's all this about the Laird's …? |
|  | ***Door creaks open*** |
| LAIRD | Hamish! Dougal! Just wait there while I ring for the butler to let you in. |
|  | ***Ting-a-ling … clatter cling tink*** |

| | |
|---|---|
| LAIRD | Oh, it's fallen off. Sorry |
| | *Door slams shut. Howling wind* |
| DOUGAL | Oh for goodness' sake! |
| | *Long hammering on door* |
| HAMISH/DOUGAL | *[shouting to be let in]* |
| | Hoy! Ey! Oy! Ho! |
| | *Door creaks open* |
| HUMPH | Yes? |
| LAIRD | *[Shouting off]* Who is it, Lyttelton? Is it the bell-menders? |
| HUMPH | No, sir, it's those two oiks with the brass monkey again. |
| LAIRD | Has the monkey any bells on it? |
| HUMPH | Not as far as I can see, sir. |
| LAIRD | Then it's no use to me. And shut that door, there's a terrible draught. |
| HUMPH | Certainly, sir. |
| | *Door slams shut* |
| HAMISH | What are we going to do now? |
| DOUGAL | I don't know, I just don't know. But look on the bright side – we're inside the Big Hoose. |
| LAIRD | Hamish! Dougal! Delighted to see you. Just step outside and I'll get Lyttelton to let you in. |
| DOUGAL | Thank you. |
| HAMISH | Oh no! We're not falling for that one again. We'll go outside and YOU let us in. |
| LAIRD | Very well. |
| | *Door quick open and slam. Howling wind* |
| DOUGAL | Hamish … |
| HAMISH | Yes? |
| | *Punch!* |
| HAMISH | What? |
| DOUGAL | Look out. |
| | *Punch!* |
| HAMISH | What was that for? |
| MRS NAUGHTIE | To attract your attention. |
| DOUGAL | Mrs Naughtie! What are you doing here? |
| MRS NAUGHTIE | The Laird has asked me to be hostess at his reception tonight. |
| DOUGAL | Hence the scarlet basque and the fishnet stockings. |
| MRS NAUGHTIE | Yes, so let's get inside, for goodness' sake. This basque had bells on it when I left home. |

*Fiona Duncan pulls off that difficult anti-clockwise twirl of the sporran.*

| | |
|---|---|
| **HAMISH** | I'll knock at the door. |
| **MRS NAUGHTIE** | No need. I've got my own key. |
| **HAMISH** | Well, open the door. |
| **MRS NAUGHTIE** | Don't be silly. My key doesn't fit the Laird's door. I'm just going to knock with it. |
| | ***Knocking. Door opens*** |
| **HUMPH** | Ah, Mrs Naughtie. Do come in. |
| **DOUGAL** | Hamish, put your foot in the door! |
| | ***Slam*** |
| **HAMISH** | Agh! |
| **DOUGAL** | Well at least we're in. |
| **LAIRD** | Hamish! Dougal! Mrs Naughtie! So glad you're here. I'd like you to meet my special house guest. Come in, Tim! |
| **TIM** | Hello, everyone. |
| | ***Applause*** |
| **TIM** | Thank you very much. |
| **LAIRD** | That's all right. It's a little sound effect I have to make my guests feel welcome. |
| **MRS NAUGHTIE** | Wait a minute. I know you! |
| **TIM** | Well helloo! Your Lairdship, you never told me Nicole Kidman was staying here … |
| **MRS NAUGHTIE** | Ooooooh! You and your silver-tongued bullshit. You're Tim Brooke-Taylor! |
| **TIM** | Guilty as charged. Ha ha ha. |
| **MRS NAUGHTIE** | Aye, that round of applause confused me for a moment. |
| **HAMISH** | Oh Mr Tim, I've always admired your musicals. |
| **TIM** | I think you've got your Tims in a twist. Rice is the name you're looking for. |
| **HAMISH** | So you're Anneka. |
| **TIM** | No, that's a Jewish holiday. |
| **DOUGAL** | No, that was the woman with the big bottom who jumped out of helicopters. |
| **HAMISH** | And wrote *Cats*. |
| **DOUGAL** | Yes. |
| **TIM** | No. In any case, Tim Rice has nothing to do with *Cats*. |
| **DOUGAL** | Oh, is he allergic? |
| **HAMISH** | Oh, I sympathise. Mrs Naughtie's pussy has often brought me out in a rash. |
| **TIM** | Jesus Christ! |

| | |
|---|---|
| HAMISH | Superstar! Aye, that was one of yours. |
| TIM | Oh … if you say so. Now, I expect you're all busy getting ready for Hogmanay. |
| HAMISH | Och, we never celebrate Hogmanay. |
| DOUGAL | No we do not. It clashes with New Year's Eve. |
| HAMISH | We have our own celebrations in the Glen. Do you remember last year at the Sporran Polishers' dinner? |
| DOUGAL | How could I forget? We had the Loyal Toast – marmalade or honey for choice and then … |
| HAMISH | And then! |
| TIM | I'm agog. |
| DOUGAL | Oh, is that like the Masons? |
| TIM | I've said too much. Do go on, Hamish. |
| HAMISH | Well, the haggis was brought in, preceded by one of the Red Hot Chili Pipers, and someone shouted: 'Look at the moon!' |
| DOUGAL | Aye, Big Tam up to his old tricks. I wish he wouldn't do that. |
| HAMISH | Then, when he turned round and shouted: 'How's this for the Moon and Sixpence!' … |
| TIM | Mm. I suppose you had to be there … Still, it was jolly lucky he had a sixpence with him … |
| LAIRD | Ah! Here's Lyttelton with a tray of sherry. Or would you prefer a glass? |
| DOUGAL | No, that's just fine. |
| HAMISH | Fortunately we brought our own straws. *Slurps!* |
| LAIRD | Now, Mrs Naughtie, have you got the canapés? |
| MRS NAUGHTIE | The village supermarket didn't have any, so I got a can o' beans instead. |
| LAIRD | Not to worry. Lyttelton, warm the spoons. |
| HUMPH | Your Lairdship, I had an inkling that Mrs Naughtie might let us down with the canapés, so I took the liberty of eating earlier. |
| LAIRD | Oh. Well, you're all right then. As for the rest of us, there's some stale bread in the kitchen. You'll find it next to the fresh loaf. *Doorbell* |
| LAIRD | Who can that be? |
| DOUGAL | Whoever it is, they've brought their own doorbell. Hamish, away and let them in. |
| LAIRD | No no, I've got a butler for that sort of thing. Lyttelton … |

*Up goes the traditional cry: 'Keep the Viking noise down!'*

| | |
|---|---|
| HUMPH | Sir? |
| LAIRD | Tell Hamish to let them in. |
| HAMISH | Don't worry, I'm there. |
| | ***Door opens*** |
| SANDI | Hello. Filthy night. |
| HAMISH | Now there's an offer I can't refuse. |
| TIM | Sandi, is that you? |
| HAMISH | No, it's me with a frisky woman. |
| TIM | Hamish, this is Sandi Wedge, captain of the All England Ladies Golf Co-operative. |
| HAMISH | Oh, do come in. |
| SANDI | Thank you. |
| | ***Clunk!*** |
| SANDI | Oo! |
| HAMISH | Mind your head! |
| SANDI | Too late. Story of my life. It's not much fun being seven feet tall. |
| HAMISH | But you're a fine figure of a woman. |
| DOUGAL | Aye, a fine figure of two women. |
| LAIRD | Come over here and meet everybody. Mind the chandelier. |
| | ***Crash tinkle tinkle clink*** |
| SANDI | Oh, sorry. |
| LAIRD | Don't apologise, it suits you. |
| SANDI | Hello, everybody. Any of you lot play golf? |
| MRS NAUGHTIE | I play a round now and again. |
| DOUGAL | Anybody? No? Well, let it pass … |
| MRS NAUGHTIE | I'll have you know, last year I was entered in the Open. |
| SANDI | Are you a pro? |
| MRS NAUGHTIE | No, I'm a hostess. |
| SANDI | Sorry. The fishnet stockings misled me. |
| DOUGAL | In fact, Mrs Naughtie, were you not the Arbroath Ladies' Golf Champion? |
| MRS NAUGHTIE | I was indeed. Three years running, and two years just hanging around. I worked at the club, you know. |
| DOUGAL | Doing what, for goodness' sake? |
| MRS NAUGHTIE | Straining the greens. |
| HAMISH | Oh. You were the cook. |
| MRS NAUGHTIE | I was no such thing. I was junior green-strainer. |
| HAMISH | Who was the senior green-strainer? |
| MRS NAUGHTIE | The cook, who do you think? And I was a ball-washer. |
| HAMISH | Aye, I'd heard that. Or something similar. |

| | |
|---|---|
| LAIRD | But Dougal, have you never played golf? |
| DOUGAL | No, your Lairdship. I like women. |
| HAMISH | I used to play golf – I had my clubs, I had my golfballs … |
| DOUGAL | You'll have had your tee. |
| | ***Chandelier tinkling*** |
| SANDI | You played, did you? What was your handicap? |
| HAMISH | My handicap? What was my handicap? I'll tell you what my HANDICAP was! It was twenty-three. |
| DOUGAL | Aye, he was rubbish. |
| HAMISH | I could never control my swing. |
| DOUGAL | Well, it doesn't show in a kilt. |
| MRS NAUGHTIE | I've heard that you were a fair old player, Mr Hamish. They told me that in the Auchtermuchty Open you had nine and a half inches for a birdie. |
| HAMISH | Proudest day of my life. |
| ***Band plays*** | ***Link*** |
| LAIRD | Well, Lyttelton, my guests all seem to be getting on. |
| HUMPH | None of us are as young as we used to be, sir. |
| LAIRD | Indeed. Lyttelton … |
| HUMPH | Sir? |
| LAIRD | Have you laid out my accoutrements? |
| HUMPH | I have, sir. But may I draw your attention to the dandruff on your sporran? |
| LAIRD | Ah yes, there was a heavy fall of it at the hairdresser's. |
| HUMPH | I took the liberty of taking it to the dry cleaner's. As a result, I fear, it's gone rather limp. |
| LAIRD | Story of my life. And have you pressed my dicky? |
| HUMPH | It wasn't me, sir. |
| LAIRD | My dress shirt. |
| HUMPH | Ah. I gave it a kiss with the steam iron, sir. |
| LAIRD | You're a gem, Lyttelton. |
| HUMPH | I aim to please, sir. |
| LAIRD | So I see. Shall we rejoin the guests? |
| HUMPH | Certainly, sir. You'll find them at the end of this short passage of music. |
| ***Band plays*** | ***Link*** |
| | ***Door opens*** |
| LAIRD | Ah, there you all are. Sandi, can I press you to a vol-au-vent? |
| SANDI | Sounds messy, but fun. Lead on, tiger! |
| TIM | Oh, excuse me, Sandi, you seem to have a smudge on your nose. |

# HOGMANAY PUNCH

The original Scottish cocktail, this tried and tested favourite has been passed down over the years and never fails to please. Wherever Scots get together for a get-together and drinks are on the menu, sooner or later the traditional Hogmanay Punch is bound to come up. A sure-fire way to make your New Year's Eve go with a swig!

INGREDIENTS: 1 bottle of good Scotch Whisky, 1 litre Gin, ½ pint Brandy, 1 eggcupful Avocaat, 4 litres Vermouth, 1 Noilly Prat, 0.75 pints Polish (Vodka), 0.75 pints Polish (Mr Sheen), ¼ gallon Lager, 1 slice lemon (optional)

METHOD: Drink

| | |
|---|---|
| SANDI | Oh, that'll be when I forgot to duck going under the railway bridge. |
| LAIRD | I can't see it. |
| TIM | Take a look through my binoculars. |
| LAIRD | Yes, I see it now. |
| TIM | You might be lucky enough to spy a ptarmigan on her lower slopes. |
| DOUGAL | Allow me to remove that smudge with my hankie, Miss Sandi. |
| | *Tinkling chandelier* |
| SANDI | Who said that? |
| DOUGAL | I did. Hamish, give me a bunk up. |
| HAMISH | Hup! etc. |
| DOUGAL | Oooooooh …! etc. |
| *Band plays* | *Drum roll under* |
| LAIRD | Nice drummage, Lyttelton. |
| HUMPH | Thank you, sir. |
| *Band plays* | *Drum roll – cymbal crash!* |
| HAMISH | No. No good. |
| DOUGAL | No, sorry. |
| MRS NAUGHTIE | Let me have a try. |
| DOUGAL | Ah, Mrs Naughtie. Never without your trusty see-saw. |
| MRS NAUGHTIE | Lyttelton … |
| *Band plays* | *Drum roll* |
| HAMISH & DOUGAL | One, two, three … HUP!!! |
| | *Thud! Boing! Whistle! Chandelier tinkle … clatter … thud!* |
| LAIRD | Are you all right there, Mrs Naughtie? |
| MRS NAUGHTIE | Oh yes. The floor broke my fall. But do you realise she's got your chandelier on her head? |
| | *Tinkling chandelier* |
| SANDI | Never mind the chandelier, is that smudge still there? |
| TIM | Leave it to me. Your Lairdship, I couldn't help noticing your ancestral trampoline. May I? |
| LAIRD | Be my guest. Lyttelton! |
| HUMPH | Yes, sir. |
| | *Drum roll* |
| | *Boing!* |
| TIM | Oooh! |
| | *Boing!* |
| TIM & ALL | Oooh! |
| | *Boing!* |

| | |
|---|---|
| TIM & ALL | Oooooooh! |
| | *Glass crash!* |
| | *Pause* |
| | *Knocking at door* |
| LAIRD | Let him in, Lyttelton. |
| HUMPH | Very good, sir. |
| | *Door opens* |
| COLIN | Good evening. I'm Colin Sell. You booked a pianist |
| HUMPH | Yes we did. Where is he? |
| COLIN | Look here, my man, I am the pianist, and I expect to be treated in a manner befitting a musician of my calibre. |
| HUMPH | Of course, sir. If you'd be kind enough to step into this cupboard. |
| COLIN | That's more like it. |
| | *Cupboard open* |
| HUMPH | You'll find a curly sandwich and half a bottle of warm light ale. Make yourself at home. |
| | *Slam shut* |
| COLIN | *[Muffled]* Thank you. |
| HUMPH | Bloody musicians … |
| TIM | *[Coming back]* Hello, everyone. That dip in the goldfish pond did me a power of good. How's the smudge? |
| | *Tinkling chandelier* |
| SANDI | Oh bugger the smudge, let's play golf! |
| LAIRD | Well, do you know, I believe you just have time for a round before supper. |
| TIM | I say, what a spiffing idea. Hamish and Dougal can be our caddies. |
| SANDI | Splendid. Where's the golf course? |
| LAIRD | It's out the back, just past the ornamental swamp. You can't miss it, it's shaped like a piano. |
| TIM | A golf course shaped like a piano? How unusual. |
| LAIRD | Oh no, silly me, that is the piano. The golf course is shaped like a banjo. |
| SANDI | That's more like it. To the golf! |
| | *Chandelier tinkling* |
| *Band plays* | *Link* |
| | *Howling wind. Footsteps trudging through the snow* |
| DOUGAL | Oh, what have you got me into here, Hamish? Oh, the weight of these clubs. |

| | |
|---|---|
| HAMISH | What about me? I'm the one giving you a piggyback. |
| DOUGAL | Why can't they carry their own clubs? |
| HAMISH | Dougal, golf is a game going back 500 years, and nobody has ever thought of asking that question before. |
| TIM | Come on, you two, keep up. |
| DOUGAL | Who does he think he is? |
| HAMISH | You must remember. *The Goodies*? He was in that. |
| DOUGAL | Was he? |
| HAMISH | Oh aye, there was him, Bill Oddie, and … |
| DOUGAL | The other one. |
| HAMISH | No, I don't remember him. |
| DOUGAL | Me neither … though if the truth be told, I'm more of a *Monty Python* man myself. |
| HAMISH | Ha ha! Oh yes! 'Nice to see you … to see you nice!' |
| DOUGAL | Where the devil have they got to? |
| HAMISH | They're over there in the deep snow. Oh no! I can see him, but what's happened to Miss Sandi? |
| DOUGAL | She's disappeared. |
| TIM | No, it's all right, I'm sitting on her head. |
| HAMISH | Are you all right with him on your heid, Miss Sandi? |
| SANDI | Oh yes, it takes my mind off the chandelier. Now off you get, we're at the first tee. |
| | ***Tinkling chandelier*** |
| SANDI | Right then, Tim. Do you want to drive off? |
| TIM | Yes I do. I've forgotten my golf balls. |
| | ***Car drives off*** |
| SANDI | He could have borrowed mine. Well, boys, do you fancy a threesome? |
| DOUGAL | Well, that's very kind of you, but we don't usually go that far on a first date. |
| HAMISH | Speak for yourself. |
| | ***Car drives back and screeches to a halt in a flurry of snow*** |
| TIM | Silly me. My balls were in my pocket all the time. |
| ALL | Ha ha ha! |
| ***Band plays*** | ***Link*** |
| ALL | Ha ha ha … |
| HAMISH | In his pocket all the time! Oh dear … |
| SANDI | OK, Tim, tee off. |
| TIM | Bit difficult to see in this light. If it wasn't for your chandelier I couldn't see anything at all. Stand back! ***Swooosh!*** |

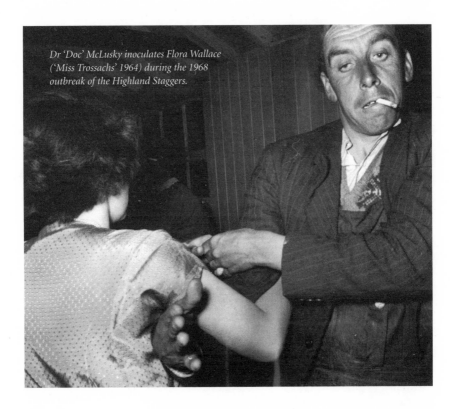

*Dr 'Doc' McLusky inoculates Flora Wallace ('Miss Trossachs' 1964) during the 1968 outbreak of the Highland Staggers.*

| | |
|---|---|
| TIM | What was that? |
| HAMISH | I don't know but here comes another one! |
| | *Swooooosh!* |
| DOUGAL | They're flying low tonight. |
| SANDI | That one nearly had my chandelier off. |
| | *Swoooosh! Swoooosh!* |
| TIM | Fore! |
| | *Swooooosh!* |
| HAMISH | Five! |
| TIM | Right ho. My turn. |
| | *Swoosh. Clack! Wheeee! Ricochet! Ricochet!* |
| | *Ricochet! Ball bounces into hole* |
| HAMISH | Look at that, he's got a hole in one. |
| DOUGAL | Looks to me like he's got a hole in both. |
| HAMISH | Avert your gaze, Miss Sandi. |
| SANDI | Who said that? |
| TIM | For goodness' sake, we're playing golf, not '*Quote Unquote*'. |
| SANDI | Stand well back, I've got a very wide swing. |
| DOUGAL | Ye-es … |

| | |
|---|---|
| SANDI | I had these clubs made to measure. |
| HAMISH | Look at the size of that thing! It must be ten feet long. |
| DOUGAL | Well hit it with a golf club. |
| | *Whack! Cat/snake hiss! Swoooooosh!* |
| DOUGAL | That won't be back in a hurry. |
| HAMISH | Whatever it was. |
| DOUGAL | Play on, Miss Sandi. |
| SANDI | I will. |
| | *Swoosh. Clack! Wheeee! Ricochet! Ricochet!* |
| | *Ricochet! Ball bounces into hole* |
| TIM | Well done. We're level pegging. |
| DOUGAL | Congratulations. A fine evening's sport. Now, let's away back to the Big Hoose … |
| TIM | No no no. We haven't finished the round. |
| DOUGAL | What? |
| SANDI | We still have seventeen more holes to play. |
| DOUGAL | Come off it! Nobody in their right mind would go through that another seventeen times. |
| TIM | Oh yes. It takes ages. |
| DOUGAL | Well, what a stupid bloody waste of time. |
| TIM | Do you know, you're absolutely right. |
| SANDI | He is, isn't he? |
| TIM | Yes. Well, you won't catch me wasting my time with this golf malarkey ever again. Come on, back to the Big Hoose. |
| HAMISH | Aye, and don't forget, Dougal, we have to prepare for tonight's big New Year's festivities. |
| DOUGAL | Then what are we waiting for? |
| *Band plays* | *Link* |
| | *Bathwater splashing. Echo* |
| LAIRD | *[Hums]* Ah, most relaxing. A little more hot water if you'd be so kind, Lyttelton. |
| HUMPH | Certainly, sir. |
| | *Water poured into bath* |
| LAIRD | I must be sure to look my best for the traditional village New Year's Eve festivities. |
| TIM | Yes. What form do these festivities take, exactly? |
| DOUGAL | It's the Grand New Year's Eve Festival. We … oh, will you pass the soap? |
| TIM | Here you are. |
| DOUGAL | Thank you. Yes, we lead the parade round the village, bearing the Flaming Yorkshire pudding. |

*Splashing and tinkling chandelier*

| | |
|---|---|
| SANDI | But why a flaming Yorkshire pudding? Why not something Scottish, like a Big Mac? |
| HAMISH | The Flaming Pudding is a reminder of Bloody Yorky. |
| TIM | Language! |
| DOUGAL | Bloody Yorky, the infamous Duke of York, the Butcher of the Glens. |
| TIM | The Grand Old Duke of York? |
| DOUGAL | That's him. |
| TIM | The one who had 10,000— |
| HAMISH | No, the other one. |
| TIM | Oh, pity. |
| DOUGAL | Old Yorky was linked with the Highland Clearances. |
| HAMISH | Special offer on porridge, two cabers for the price of one, sporrans slashed! |
| DOUGAL | Everything must go … |
| MRS NAUGHTIE | And it did. What a sale that was! |
| HAMISH | This water's getting cold. Splash in a bit of hot, Mrs Naughtie. |
| MRS NAUGHTIE | I can't even see the taps. Ah, there we are. |

*Twist!*

| | |
|---|---|
| DOUGAL | That's not doing any good. Try the tap. |
| MRS NAUGHTIE | Oh, Mr Dougal. |
| DOUGAL | No, no, no harm done. You can try again, if you like. |
| MRS NAUGHTIE | You know, it was Bloody Yorky that burned down the local factory belonging to Sir Harry's sister, Estee Lauder, in what became known as the infamous Glen Close Mascara. |
| DOUGAL | No he didn't. |
| MRS NAUGHTIE | Oh no, you're right, that was me. |
| HAMISH | Mrs Naughtie makes the pudding every year. Then she sets it alight. |
| MRS NAUGHTIE | I'm a very careless woman. |
| DOUGAL | Then Hamish and I carry the pudding up and down the High Street, in and out of the houses … |
| HAMISH | Oh ho ho. Do you remember last year, the first place we went into with the pudding? |
| DOUGAL | And you shouted: 'Welcome to the Pudding Club!' |
| HAMISH | And the Mother Superior burst into tears. |
| DOUGAL | She soon got over it though. |
| HAMISH | Aye, she was distracted by the convent burning to the ground. |

| | |
|---|---|
| LAIRD | Oh, look at the time! We'd better be on our way. Everybody out of the bath. |
| MRS NAUGHTIE | After you. |
| LAIRD | Where are the towels? |
| | *Door opens* |
| LAIRD | Ah, Lyttelton, is that you? |
| COLIN | No. Did you order a pianist? |
| LAIRD | Get out! This is a private bathroom. |
| ALL | Yes! How dare you! Get out! etc. etc … |
| TIM | And take that piano with you! |
| *Band plays* | *Link* |
| | *Exterior crowd scene. Distant bagpipes* |
| DOUGAL | Is everybody ready? |
| ALL | Och aye! |
| LAIRD | Is the pianist here? |
| HUMPH | No, sir. |
| LAIRD | Splendid! Where is he? |
| HUMPH | I sent him to have a quiet lie down in the giant wicker figure of a man on the cliff-top, sir. |
| LAIRD | I hope he doesn't get too cold up there. |
| HUMPH | No chance of that, sir. |
| HAMISH | Let the parade begin. |
| DOUGAL | Ignite the pudding! |
| MRS NAUGHTIE | Pudding ignitement is … GO!!! |
| | *Match scratch: flame whummmph!!!!* |
| DOUGAL | Oh. Well, that didn't last long. |
| HAMISH | Have you no' got a bigger pudding, Mrs Naughtie? |
| MRS NAUGHTIE | No. Oh wait, what's this in my handbag? Tissues … lipstick … novelty boomerang … oh, and a Yorkshire pudding! |
| HAMISH | That's more like it. It's the size of a Volkswagen! |
| DOUGAL | Put a match to it and away we go. |
| | *Match strike and fire crackle* |
| DOUGAL | Always a magic moment. |
| HAMISH | Aye, it's worth it just to see the look of wonder and anticipation in the eyes of the fire brigade. |
| DOUGAL | Hoist the flaming pudding, and away we go! |
| | *Band plays and crowd marching in parade behind the flaming pudding, carried by Hamish and Dougal. The band plays 'On Ilkley Moor Baht'At' in a very Scottish manner* |
| HAMISH | Jings, Dougal! Mind out! |

|  |  |
|---|---|
| | ***Bus approaching fast, horn blaring*** |
| DOUGAL | That bus is taking the corner too fast! He's heading for Moira Anderson's World of Kippers! |
| HAMISH | No, he's swerving off towards the Highland Bap and Oatcake Experience. |
| DOUGAL | Throw the flaming pudding at it. |
| HAMISH | Why? |
| DOUGAL | I'm sick of the sight of the damn thing. |
| HAMISH & DOUGAL | Hup! |
| | ***Flame roar, bus horn, skid, flumph!*** |
| HAMISH | What's happened? I can't bear to look. |
| DOUGAL | It's all right, I was going to describe it for the listeners anyway. Oh no! The bus has skidded off the road and lodged in that great snowdrift. |
| MRS NAUGHTIE | It was an accident waiting to happen. |
| HAMISH | What's that written on the side of the bus? 'BBC Hogmanay Celebrity Special'. 'This way up.' |
| DOUGAL | Jings, Hamish! Look at the faces at the windows. |
| MRS NAUGHTIE | They'll be all the top stars heading for the BBC *Hogmanay Cavalcade* in Edinburgh. There's every famous Scots celebrity in the world on that bus, on the way from their homes in England. |
| HAMISH | Crivens! I haven't seen so many famous Scottish faces since Prime Minister's Question Time. |
| DOUGAL | Sean Connery and the Crankies … |
| MRS NAUGHTIE | Trevor MacDonald, Naomi Campbell … |
| HAMISH | And there's wee Moira Stewart. And look there, the bard of the bothy himself, the great Rabbie Lionel Blue. |
| | ***Hammering at bus door*** |
| DOUGAL | They're trying to get out of the bus. Help me open the door. |
| | ***Bus door creaks open*** |
| COLIN | Did you order a pianist? |
| HAMISH | Never mind that. Do you know any first aid? |
| COLIN | You hum it, I'll play it, sunshine. |
| HUMPH | Excuse me. Is this man bothering you, sir? |
| COLIN | Yes he is, as a matter of fact. |
| HUMPH | Good. |
| JAMES | Let me out, let me out! |
| MRS NAUGHTIE | Stand aside! I know that voice! Let me through, I'm getting into the bus. |

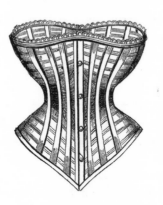
of

e,
!”

ost,
n

N!

Can
Once
ger

ere's a hectic

fe in the village!'

MARVEL AT THE SI

## The Battle

|  | ***Creaking metal as Mrs Naughtie forces open the door and clambers into the bus*** |
|---|---|
| JAMES | Is that you, Mother Naughtie? |
| MRS NAUGHTIE | You know fine it is, wee Jimmy. And somebody needs a haircut, young man! |
| JAMES | I've got a very heavy schedule. |
| MRS NAUGHTIE | I'll 'heavy schedule' you, you wee rascal. When are you going to get a proper job? Like Dale Winton? |
| JAMES | I have got a proper job, you know I have. Radio 4, every morning from six till nine. |
| MRS NAUGHTIE | When all right-minded folk are listening to Terry Wogan. Why can't you be like him? Now, there is a programme. |
| JAMES | Mother, I'm a commentator on the social and political scene. |
| MRS NAUGHTIE | Common is the word! |
| JAMES | Mother Naughtie, Mr Humphrys and I … |
| MRS NAUGHTIE | Mr Humphrys? Who does he think he's fooling with his 'I'm free!' You need to choose your friends more carefully … |
| JAMES | Mother, sorry to interrupt you, but we must move on. |
| MRS NAUGHTIE | You spend too much time with that Humphrys character. That's why you've got that silly Welsh accent. Coming up here without telling your mother. Imagine how I feel. My own flesh and blood … I dread to ask if you're keeping your kilt clean, and eating plenty of haggis … |
| JAMES | I'm going to have to cut you short there, I'm afraid. We're out of time. |
| DOUGAL | Now then, what's going on here? |
| JAMES | Help, can you get us out of the bus? |
| DOUGAL | Don't you worry, Taffy. We'll have you out in a twinkling. |
| JAMES | Make it quick. That Janet Street Porter's driving us all mad. And she's not even Scottish. |
| HAMISH | Mr Naughtie, can I trouble you for an autograph? |
| JAMES | Certainly. What name? |
| HAMISH | Yours please. |
| JAMES | Oh! |
| HAMISH | Mr Naughtie! What's the matter? |
| JAMES | I must be in shock. I could swear I just saw a seven-foot woman with a chandelier on her head. |

| | |
|---|---|
| SANDI | Hello. |
| JAMES | Oh. |
| | *Thud* |
| SANDI | Why has that man fainted? |
| LAIRD | Stand back, everyone. |
| DOUGAL | It's the Laird! |
| LAIRD | Let me through, I'm a toff. |
| HAMISH | The Laird always takes charge in situations like this, and sells tickets. |
| LAIRD | Now here's the position. One coach-load of so-called celebrities; fact. Stuck in snow drift; fact. One flaming Yorkshire pudding completely ruined; fact. Goodnight. |
| ALL | But but but … |
| LAIRD | Well, what do you expect? |
| TIM | Hello, everyone. |
| | *Applause* |
| TIM | Thank you for that heartfelt sound effect. Now I have an idea. It's nearly midnight, these celebrities won't get to the BBC in Edinburgh now, so why don't we have a star-studded Hogmanay frolic right here in the Glen!? |
| HAMISH | You just mind your own business, pal. |
| DOUGAL | No, he's got a point. Our New Year's Eve's parade is ruined, so we might as well go along with their Hogmanay nonsense. |
| LAIRD | That's the ticket! Everybody back to the Big Hoose for the Hogmanay frolic! |
| *All* | *[Without much enthusiasm] hooray!* |
| *Band plays* | *Link* |
| LAIRD | Well here we all are in the Big Hoose. |
| TIM | Brilliant observation! |
| HAMISH | Aye, he doesn't miss much. |
| DOUGAL | Come on, everybody – gather round the piano. |
| COLIN | At last! |
| HAMISH | Aye, that's it. Now, all together: one, two, three … |
| ALL | HEAVE!!! |
| | *Glass window crash!* |
| ALL | HOORAY! Out it goes! |
| DOUGAL | Ladies and gentlemen: I have an announcement to make. |
| HAMISH | Go on then. |

| | |
|---|---|
| DOUGAL | That was it. |
| LAIRD | Ladies and gentlemen, I have a better announcement to make. Midnight is approaching. So let everyone step up to the steaming bowl and help themselves to a glass of mulled porridge. |
| ALL | HOORAY! |
| JAMES | Your Lairdship, I'm very worried. We were all booked by the BBC to do a broadcast at the stroke of midnight, but we're not at the studio and they'll get cross. Our careers are in the balance here – all the best newsreading jobs have already been given to the Children in Need Dancers. |
| LAIRD | Not to worry. I have a small broadcasting studio here in the Big Hoose. It's just through this door. |
| | ***Door creaks open*** |
| COLIN | Did you order a pianist? |
| LAIRD | Yes, you'll find the piano outside. Hup! |
| COLIN | Woooooh! |
| | ***Glass window crash!*** |
| JAMES | It's true, you have got a studio here. |
| LAIRD | Of course. There we are – tape machine, record deck, microphone. |
| JAMES | Oh good heavens, there's even an old script: 'Germany calling, Germany calling …' |
| LAIRD | Ah yes. Happy days … |
| HAMISH | There's no' much time to go, your Lairdship. What are we going to broadcast? |
| LAIRD | I shall naturally sing a song. It's what my public expects. Perhaps you'd all like to join me? |
| DOUGAL | We'd prefer to stop you, but … |
| LAIRD | Not an option. |
| ALL | ***Murmurs of grudging assent*** |
| LAIRD | Now what's that song all you Scotch people always sing at New Year? |
| DOUGAL | Yes of course, I know the one you mean. It's 'Auld … McDonald Had a Farm' … no … |
| HAMISH | No … what is it again … 'Auld Smokey, On Top Of …?' |
| DOUGAL | 'Auld Fashioned Way, Dance in the' … Er … |
| TIM | 'Auld Lang Syne'! |
| HAMISH & DOUGAL | What? |
| TIM | 'Auld Lang Syne'. That's what you sing at Hogmanay. |
| DOUGAL | Well you might, but we've never heard of it. |

*Gordon Gaye (left) about to pip Dingle McCouthy to win the All-Comers'*
*Standing Still on One Leg contest. (3 hours 52 minutes!)*

| | |
|---|---|
| HAMISH | Come on let's do 'Caledonian Rhapsody' … |
| JAMES | Scaramouche, Scaramouche, can you do the Highland Fling? |
| MRS NAUGHTIE | Shut your noise, laddie. |
| JAMES | Sorry, Mum. |
| TIM | No. It has to be 'Auld Lang Syne'; you must know the words: |
| | 'And there's a haund my trusty fiere, |
| | And gie's a haund o thine, |
| | And we'll tak a right guid-willie waught, |
| | For auld lang syne.' |
| DOUGAL | Mrs Naughtie, cover your ears! |
| MRS NAUGHTIE | What is he talking about? |
| DOUGAL | No idea. What language is that? |
| JAMES | It's not Welsh. |
| HAMISH | And you'd know, Taffy. |
| LAIRD | It's an old Scots tradition! Like first-footing. |
| HAMISH | First-whatting? |
| DOUGAL | He's lost me now. |
| LAIRD | At New Year a tall dark stranger brings you gifts. |
| | ***Knock at door*** |
| LAIRD | That'll be First Foot now. |
| | ***Door opens*** |
| LAIRD | Hello. What gifts do you bring? A piece of coal? A slice of black bun? A wee dram? A generous cheque? |
| COLIN | I've got a piano. |
| LAIRD | Then bring it in and strike up 'Auld Lang Syne'. And everybody else join in! |
| ***Band plays*** | ***Auld Lang Syne*** |
| ALL SING | Should auld acquaintance be forgot, |
| | And never brought to mind? |
| | Should auld acquaintance be forgot, |
| | And auld lang syne? |
| | |
| | CHORUS: |
| | For auld lang syne, my dear, |
| | For auld lang syne, |
| | We'll tak a cup of kindness yet, |
| | For auld lang syne! |
| | |
| | And there's a hand my trusty fiere, |
| | And gie's a hand o thine, |

And we'll tak a right guid-willie waught,
For auld lang syne!

CHORUS:
For auld lang syne, my dear,
For auld lang syne,
We'll tak a cup of kindness yet,
For auld lang syne!

| | |
|---|---|
| **HAMISH** | Quiet, everyone – listen for the church bell chiming midnight … |
| **LAIRD** | We'll broadcast it to the nation, any minute now. Any time … hang on … wait for it … |
| **DOUGAL** | Jings! |
| Hamish | Was that the bell? |
| **DOUGAL** | No, it was me. Jings, Hamish! We've forgotten this cold weather. The church bell will have frozen and fallen off like all the others. |
| **HAMISH** | Jings! |
| **LAIRD** | Was that the bell? |
| **HAMISH** | No, it was me. There will be no bells on a night like this. We'll have to find an alternative for the midnight chimes. |
| **LAIRD** | The entire nation is tuned in to our broadcast, waiting for the New Year bongs. |
| **HUMPH** | I have an idea, if I may be permitted to elucidate? |
| **LAIRD** | Of course, and as soon as you've finished, you must tell us your idea. |
| **HUMPH** | There is a way we could broadcast 'alternative' bongs to the nation, sir. Miss Sandi! |
| | ***Tinkling chandelier*** |
| **SANDI** | Yes, how can I help? |
| **HUMPH** | I believe you still have your golf clubs? Good. Do you think you could hit the Forth Bridge from here? |
| **LAIRD** | Good thinking, Lyttelton! |
| **SANDI** | The Forth Bridge? It's a bit of a long shot … |
| **DOUGAL** | Aye, but it would make a hell of a bong. |
| **HAMISH** | You'd have to do it twelve times in a row … |
| **SANDI** | Well … it's miles and miles away … |
| **TIM** | You can do it, Sandi. |
| **LAIRD** | It'll take a while for the balls to get there … |
| **DOUGAL** | Then you'd better start right away! |

| | |
|---|---|
| SANDI | Very well. |
| HUMPH | I know this is implausible, sir, but it is our only chance. |
| SANDI | Stand back. Here I go! |
| | *Swoosh-clack many times and golf balls whistle away into the far distance … continues under* |
| TIM | Nice try, but I'm afraid they don't look quite on target … |
| SANDI | Those are just my sighting shots, to help me get the range. |
| TIM | I wonder what they'll hit. |
| HAMISH | I wonder … I wonder … |
| DOUGAL | Well I think we're about to find out! |
| | *'Westminster chimes consisting of sample object hit by the golf balls: a bus, a wooden shed, a plate glass window, a cow; a ricochet, a water splash, a passer-by [scream], a giant dustbin. [Or other sounds, depending on best appropriate effects]* |
| TIM | Getting closer … |
| SANDI | Now for the Forth Bridge … |
| | *Swoosh-clack – twelve times and golf balls whistle away … Continues under* |
| LAIRD | Bang on target! |
| | *Golf balls hit the forth bridge twelve bongs continue under* |
| | *[Perhaps, after each hit, we hear the golfball trickle down the metalwork of the bridge]* |
| ALL | HOORAY! Happy New Year! |
| | |
| *Band plays* | *Auld lang syne* |
| | |
| ALL SING | Should auld acquaintance be forgot, |
| | And never brought to mind? |
| | Should auld acquaintance be forgot, |
| | And auld lang syne? |
| | |
| | CHORUS: |
| | For auld lang syne, my dear, |
| | For auld lang syne, |
| | We'll tak a cup of kindness yet, |
| | For auld lang syne! |

*Undertaker's receptionist Maggie Doon welcomes the 1,000th visitor to the Chapel of Rest.*

And there's a hand my trusty fiere,
And gie's a hand o thine,
And we'll tak a right guid-willie waught,
For auld lang syne!

CHORUS:
For auld lang syne, my dear,
For auld lang syne,
We'll tak a cup of kindness yet,
For auld lang syne!

**Band plays**          **Sig tune credits and oot**

**THE END**

# FOLK OF THE GLEN

## MRS MCALISTER

Visitors to the post office and general shop will be assured of a warm welcome from our village postmistress Mrs McAlister. Pop in for a second-class stamp and you'll be greeted with a warm smile, a cheery word, a cup of tea and a home-baked bannock, a peck on the cheek and a pat on the bum. And if that's not worth every penny of 24p, I don't know what is. (Larger envelopes and packages or a full body massage will cost a little more.)

Mrs McAlister has been a stalwart of the Village Drama Society for many years and scored another notable triumph last Christmas when she took the role of Rocky Balboa in her own stage adaptation of the film, *Rocky 3*.

## THE REVEREND HUSH

His charitable works are legendary, as no one has ever seen concrete evidence of them. Mind you, it is well known that when Old Meg came calling at the back door he did buy her entire stock of lucky heather. Shortly afterwards Old Meg was sadly run over by a bus as she left the vicarage.

The popular vicar comes from a large family, his mother possibly being the largest. It is from her that he has inherited his big bone structure, which he proudly displays at the bottom of his allotment, polished and gleaming in the sun.

Over the years that I have known him, the Reverend Hush has constantly amazed me by the ingenuity of his many schemes for raising money and subsequently evading capture. Television was quick to adopt his idea of rummaging around in people's attics to find forgotten treasures which could be sold at auction to raise a tidy sum, although the TV executives added the refinement of telling the householders first.

*Opposite: A bold pose from five-year-old Alan Dooley, seen here in his dog costume.*

# THIRD SERIES

*Two weary stags hitch a lift on a couple of passing ponies.*

# GAMBLING FEVER!

| | |
|---|---|
| *Band plays* | *Sig tune up and under* |
| *Announcer* | *You'll Have Had Your Tea. The doings of Hamish and Dougal. Today, 'Gambling Fever!'* |
| *Band plays* | *Sig tune up and oot* |
| | *Knock on door. Door opens* |
| DOUGAL | Hamish! You'll have had your tea … |
| HAMISH | Well … |
| DOUGAL | Come away in. |
| HAMISH | Thank you. Jings, Dougal, it's a wee bit dark in here. |
| DOUGAL | What? |
| HAMISH | I think I'll stand over here by the window. |
| DOUGAL | Very well. It's not like you to hog my shaft of sunlight. |
| HAMISH | It's still a bit gloomy. Can you see me quite clearly? |
| DOUGAL | As clearly as I want to, yes. |
| HAMISH | Not clearly enough, it seems. Do you still have that big theatrical spotlight left over from the Ham-Dram's production of *Ben Hur*? |

*'Cocktail Hour!' The Hon 'Tooter' Gillespie awaits the arrival of his guests.*

| | |
|---|---|
| DOUGAL | The one we used for the chariot race? |
| HAMISH | To pick out the Emperor's box, yes. |
| DOUGAL | Yes of course. Why do you ask? |
| HAMISH | I was wondering if you'd care to switch it on? |
| DOUGAL | Oh anything for a quiet life. Here you are. |
| | *Spotlight switched on* |
| HAMISH | Oh! Oh I'm dazzled. Don't point it in my eyes. Point it … a little higher up. |
| DOUGAL | Oh very well, but I really don't … WHAT? WHAT? |
| HAMISH | What? |
| DOUGAL | What in the world is that on your heid? |
| HAMISH | What? |
| DOUGAL | That! |
| HAMISH | Oh this? I wasn't going to mention it, but now you've drawn attention to it, I suppose you'll want to drag the information out of me. |
| DOUGAL | Well, what is it? |
| HAMISH | Well, if you must know, it's a tweed sporran cosy. |
| DOUGAL | But why is it on your head? |
| HAMISH | Well, it would be a wee bit ostentatious to wear it on my sporran. |
| DOUGAL | Fair point. But wherever did you get it? |
| HAMISH | Since you ask, I won it. |
| DOUGAL | You won it? |
| HAMISH | It was first prize in this week's Glen McLottery. It was a roll-over. And my ticket came up. |
| DOUGAL | What did it cost you? |
| HAMISH | Just one pound. Every week for the last ten years. |
| DOUGAL | Some people get all the luck. |
| HAMISH | Exactly. And that's why I'm away to the races. Perhaps you would care to accompany me? |
| DOUGAL | All right, as long as you don't wear that sporran cosy on your heid. |
| HAMISH | Take off my lucky cosy? Are you mad? Come on – to the racecourse! Luck be a Laddy tonight, don't wear your sporran too tight …! |
| *Band plays* | *Link. William Tell?* |
| | *Crowd noise, racecourse atmos* |
| HAMISH | Come on, Crazy Tam! Crazy Tam! Go, Crazy Tam! Crazy Tam, come on! |
| DOUGAL | Aye, come on, Crazy Tam, there's people in the queue behind you. Place your bet and piss off! |

| | |
|---|---|
| HAMISH | Ah here we are. Good afternoon Honest Dodger MacDodgy. I would like to place a bet of one hundred thousand pounds on Nijinsky in the 2.30. |
| | Unfortunately I don't have a hundred thousand pounds, and Nijinsky's dead, so I'll have 50 pee each way on Dandy Dinmont. |
| | *Cash register* |
| LAIRD | *[Over the tannoy]* *[Pop squeak]* Good afternoon ladies and gentlemen. Is this bugger on? *[Blows into mike]* Good afternoon ladies and gentlemen. Welcome to the Bravely-Borne Handicap. The runners and riders are making their way to the Starting Gate. Leading the way is the evens favourite, Evens Favourite, and the 100-to-1 shot, Dandy Dinmont. Followed by the horse I have entered myself, Double Entendre. But now I can see the Steward's signalling … yes, the bar's about to close, so let's get this race up and running. |
| HAMISH | Oh, Dougal. I'm sitting on the edge of my seat with excitement. |
| DOUGAL | Well sit further back, you'll find it less stimulating. |
| HAMISH | Look, there's 50 pee riding on that Dandy Dinmont. |
| DOUGAL | Pity they couldn't afford a jockey. Ha ha ha! |
| HAMISH | This is no time for jokes. It's a tragedy they couldn't afford a jockey. |
| DOUGAL | They're under starter's orders … |
| LAIRD | *[Tannoy]* On your marks … get set … |
| | *Gunshot!* |
| | *Horses galloping off* |
| | *Gunshot!* |
| | *More gunshots!* |
| DOUGAL | What's going on? |
| HAMISH | It's Mrs Naughtie. |
| DOUGAL | Mrs Naughtie, our housekeeper-stroke-cleaning lady? What's she doing, blazing away with a Kalashnikov AK47? |
| HAMISH | There's only one way to find out. Mrs Naughtie? |
| MRS NAUGHTIE | Yes? |
| HAMISH | What are you doing, blazing away with a Kalashnikov AK47? |
| MRS NAUGHTIE | I am registering my protest in the only way I know how. |

|  |  |
|---|---|
| | ***Gunshot, ricochet*** |
| HAMISH | Jings! She's taken the top off my lucky Cosy! |
| MRS NAUGHTIE | Horse-racing is a cruel and barbaric sport, and I am here to put an end to it! |
| DOUGAL | What, by shooting all the horses? |
| MRS NAUGHTIE | Oh I haven't, have I? It's the Laird I was aiming for. No hard feelings, your Lairdship. |
| LAIRD | *[Tannoy]* Not for some time now, Mrs Naughtie. Meanwhile back at the race, all the horses seem to have run away, apart from my own, Double Entendre, who is on the final stretch, the only runner left in … just a minute, what's this? Dandy Dinmont coming up fast on the rails. |
| | ***Train whistle: toot toot!*** |
| HAMISH | Come on Dandy! |
| DOUGAL | Look at that wee dog go! |
| HAMISH | And Dandy Dinmont wins by a wet nose! Hoorah! |
| LAIRD | So Hamish, you win this time. *[Aside]* But I shall get my revenge. I shall take advantage of his gambling fever, and use it against him. I shall bleed him dry! Ha ha ha ha ha! |
| ***Band plays*** | ***Link*** |
| MRS NAUGHTIE | Mr Dougal, I've been silent long enough. |
| DOUGAL | That's a matter of opinion, Mrs Naughtie. |
| MRS NAUGHTIE | There's something I just have to get off my chest. |
| DOUGAL | What is it? |
| MRS NAUGHTIE | It's Marmite. Och it gets everywhere. |
| DOUGAL | Doesn't it just. After you with the Marmite flannel. |
| MRS NAUGHTIE | There. That's better. |
| DOUGAL | Aye, waste not want not. |
| MRS NAUGHTIE | Mr Dougal, it's Mr Hamish. He's bothering me. |
| DOUGAL | Aye, he's bothering me too. |
| MRS NAUGHTIE | What – every night? |
| DOUGAL | No no, not every night … |
| MRS NAUGHTIE | He has a new lover now – and Madam Gambling is a demanding mistress. |
| DOUGAL | But he keeps winning. What can we do, Mrs Naughtie? |
| MRS NAUGHTIE | I've tried everything. To stop him going to the Betting Shop, I hid all his kilts. |
| DOUGAL | Good thinking. |
| MRS NAUGHTIE | But he still went. Marching away down the High |

|                  | Street as pleased as Punch. Oh, I still go hot and cold whenever I rerun that video. |
|------------------|---|
| DOUGAL           | Speak of the devil – here he comes now, in his stretch limousine. |
|                  | *Horn toots. Long car effect passing the door* |
| DOUGAL           | The back end will be along in a minute. |
|                  | *Car door open and slam* |
| HAMISH           | *[Off]* Thank you Galloway. Pick me up in an hour, I'm away to try my luck at the tombola. |
|                  | *Horn toots. Long car effect driving off* |
|                  | *Door opens* |
| HAMISH           | Hello. |
| MRS NAUGHTIE     | Eeeeek! |
| HAMISH           | Well, it's you that hid the kilts. |
| DOUGAL           | Hamish! What are you doing, coming here in a fancy limousine, smoking expensive cigars and flashing your wad? Did nobody ever tell you that's vulgar? |
| HAMISH           | You're just jealous. |
| DOUGAL           | Put it away, we've all seen it. |
| HAMISH           | Oh very well. |
| DOUGAL           | It's all right, Mrs Naughtie. It's safe to get out of the bath now. |
| MRS NAUGHTIE     | At last! |
| MRS NAUGHTIE.    | *Getting out of bath* |
| HAMISH           | Is that Marmite, Mrs Naughtie? |
| MRS NAUGHTIE     | Oh! Flannel, Mr Dougal. Turn your backs, gentlemen, please. |
| *Band plays*     | *Link into Scottish dance music. Ends* |
|                  | *Genteel applause* |
| LAIRD            | Thank you, Ewan and Kirsty. That was as fine an exhibition of potholing as you're likely to see this evening. |
| MRS NAUGHTIE     | I must say, this is an improvement on last year's church social. |
| DOUGAL           | Oh, I enjoyed that. |
| MRS NAUGHTIE     | Hm! A little sumo wrestling goes a long way with me, I'm afraid. Those women looked ridiculous. |
| *Band plays*     | *Fanfare* |
| LAIRD            | And that tells me it's bingo time! |
| HAMISH           | Hooray! I've got a bingo card here with my name on it. |
| LAIRD            | Off we go. Eyes out for a full English. |

*Farmer Bob Cruddenloch bounces up to the games aboard his prize ram, Space-Hopper.*

|  | *Bingo balls rattle round in drum* |
| LAIRD | Ahem. On its own … number fourteen. |
| MRS NAUGHTIE | This is the devil's work! Gambling has no place at a church social. Where's that vicar? |
| VICAR | Here I am. |
|  | *Gunshot* |
| LAIRD | Calm down, Mrs Naughtie. Good shot by the way. We shan't be seeing him again this side of Michaelmas. |
| MRS NAUGHTIE | I want no part of this. I'm off, and you're lucky I'm leaving you with your balls intact |
|  | *Door slam* |
| HAMISH | Right, your Lairdship, on with the bingo! |
| LAIRD | clickety-click – seventy-four. |
| HAMISH | Yes! |
| LAIRD | Doctor's orders – key of the door. |
| HAMISH | Yes!!! I'm cooking tonight! |
| DOUGAL | But you cooked last night. |
| LAIRD | Two fat ladies … |
| HAMISH | Yesss!!!!! |
| LAIRD | No, you two fat ladies over there. Could you sit down please, I can't see the room. |
|  | *Thud thud* |
| LAIRD | Thank you. Where was I? Oh yes, all the fours – eighty-eight. |
| HAMISH | House! |
| LAIRD | Could somebody pass me a set of well-gritted teeth? Thank you, Tam. Congratulations, Hamish. |
| HAMISH | Have I won the big prize? |
| LAIRD | Yes. Free life membership of my new casino. |
| HAMISH | Yes! |
| LAIRD | You'll be very welcome. *[Aside]* Said the spider to the fly! Ha ha ha ha! |
| *Band plays* | *Link* |
| Laird | Welcome to Mac Vegas! |
| ALL | *Cheer!* |
|  | *Excited crowd atmos* |
| HAMISH | Jings, Dougal, this is punter's paradise! |
| DOUGAL | Och, it's just the Big Hoose with a makeover. He's just pushed back the furniture and slung a bit of tinsel on the old stag's antlers. |
| HAMISH | Look over there! A one-armed bandit! |
| DOUGAL | Where? |

| | |
|---|---|
| HAMISH | There, playing the fruit machine. |
| DOUGAL | That's no bandit – that's One-arm Tam. What a loser! |
| HAMISH | Oh no – the man's a winner! Remember One-arm Tam won a big bet that night at the sawmill. |
| DOUGAL | I thought they sewed it back on. |
| HAMISH | They did, just before he won that other big bet at the All-comers Alligator Wrestling. |
| DOUGAL | Aye, I suppose some people are just born lucky, like Stumpy McPhee. |
| HAMISH | Oh look, the fruit machine is free and I've got a bulging sporran! |
| DOUGAL | Well, you know what they say: a fool and his money butter no parsnips. |
| HAMISH | Right, bawbee in the slot, and a good yank on this – just for luck – and here we go! |
| | *Lever pulled. Whirring. Clunk. Clunk. Clunk* |
| HAMISH | Look at that! Three melons! |
| | *Thump. Thump. Thump* |
| HAMISH | I'll put those in my string bag. It's deep-fried melon and chips tonight. |
| LAIRD | Congratulations, Hamish. I see you're still on your winning streak. Here, have a buttered parsnip. On the house. |
| HAMISH | Thank you. |
| LAIRD | And Dougal, can I interest you in a game? |
| DOUGAL | Such as what? |
| LAIRD | Why don't you try shooting craps? |
| DOUGAL | Oh very well. Pull! |
| | *Twang. Gunshot!* |
| LAIRD | You missed. |
| DOUGAL | Thank goodness for that. |
| LAIRD | Now if you'll excuse me, I really must go over there and ignore you. |
| MRS NAUGHTIE | Place your bets! Place your bets! |
| DOUGAL | Mrs Naughtie! What are you doing here? |
| MRS NAUGHTIE | Shh!! Not a word. I'm here undercover. |
| DOUGAL | Well, not that much cover, in that costume. Too much cleavage! |
| HAMISH | You should see her from the front. |
| MRS NAUGHTIE | I've changed my tactics. Oh, they were chafing me. *[Confidentially]* But now, Mr Dougal, I am out to destroy this temple of depravity from within. |

*Entrants eagerly await the result of the 'Ladies Hat in the shape of a UFO' contest.*

| | |
|---|---|
| **DOUGAL** | Good luck to you, Mrs Naughtie. I'm right behind you. |
| **MRS NAUGHTIE** | Oooh! Cold hands, warm sporran. |
| **DOUGAL** | Not a word to Hamish. |
| **MRS NAUGHTIE** | Have you all placed your bets? *Rien ne va plus*! |
| **HAMISH** | Fingers crossed! |
| | ***Roulette wheel spin, ball thrown in, spinning goes on and on and on …*** |
| **DOUGAL** | Jings, Mrs Naughtie, you're a wonder on that unicycle! |
| **HAMISH** | 50p says she falls off. |
| **DOUGAL** | You're on! |
| **MRS NAUGHTIE** | No I'm not. Oooooooooh … |
| | ***Crash!*** |
| **DOUGAL** | Damn you, Hamish, here's your money. |
| **HAMISH** | Oh, I'm on a roll. |
| **MRS NAUGHTIE** | So am I. I landed awkwardly on the buffet. |
| **DOUGAL** | Take this vol-au-vent and cover your modesty, woman. |
| **HAMISH** | Right, on with the gaming. What's it to be? Chemin de fer? *Vingt-et-un*? Guess the weight of the vicar? |

| | |
|---|---|
| DOUGAL | Hold on, we don't want to miss the famous Mac Vegas cabaret. Mrs Naughtie will be doing her tribute to Meatloaf. |
| HAMISH | Oh, yes. I believe it's just like the real thing. |
| DOUGAL | It is, I had it for tea yesterday. |
| LAIRD | May I have a roll on the drums! |
| *Band plays* | ***One-armed drum roll*** |
| LAIRD | Thank you, Tam. And we look forward to your accordion solo later. But now it's cabaret time. Sadly Mrs Naughtie has told me she will not be able to oblige tonight, so I'm not going to let her do the show. Instead I shall be entertaining you with my tribute to Scotland's own – Tom Jones! |
| ALL | Hoorah! |
| LAIRD | Take it away, Tam. |
| *Band plays* | ***Tams accordion intro*** |
| LAIRD SINGS | ***'Its not unusual'*** |
| ALL | ***React between the lines*** |
| | ***Applause at the end*** |
| LAIRD | Thank you, thank you. Hamish, Dougal, help me off with this underwear. |
| HAMISH | The ladies still go wild and no mistake. That's Mrs McVitie's surgical stocking, if my memory serves. |
| DOUGAL | Aye, your Lairdship, you're festooned with more whalebone than Moby Dick. |
| LAIRD | Yes, they still throw their flimsies at me – but it'll take more than that to shut me up. |
| HAMISH | Well, the gambling fever is still upon me, and I'm going for the big one. |
| LAIRD | And when you get back, Hamish, how about placing a really … enormous bet? |
| HAMISH | Bring it on! |
| DOUGAL | Have some sense, man … |
| HAMISH | I see a big coup in the offing. |
| | ***Big moo!*** |
| LAIRD | Get that big coo out of my casino. There's serious gambling to be done. |
| HAMISH | I'm ready for anything. Do your worst. |
| LAIRD | Good. I have here a perfectly ordinary pack of cards. |
| | ***Cards riffle*** |
| MRS NAUGHTIE | Manners! |
| LAIRD | Now, Hamish – name a card, any card at all. |

| | |
|---|---|
| HAMISH | Seven of clubs. |
| LAIRD | No. Bad luck, that's two thousand pounds you owe me. |
| HAMISH | Best of three. |
| LAIRD | Very well. Think of a card, any card at all. |
| HAMISH | Three of diamonds. |
| LAIRD | No, I was thinking of the king of hearts. Bad luck. That's four thousand pounds. *[Aside]* Like candy from a baby. |
| HAMISH | All right – double or quits. |
| DOUGAL | No, Hamish, hold it right there. Oh, that's better. Now step aside, let me play the game in your place. |
| HAMISH | No, I can win this, I feel it in my water. |
| DOUGAL | Sit on him, Mrs Naughtie. |
| MRS NAUGHTIE | With pleasure! |
| LAIRD | Hmm, what's going on here? |
| DOUGAL | It's just you and me, your Lairdship. Game on! |
| LAIRD | Then so be it. Think of a card, any card at all … |
| DOUGAL | No, your Lairdship. You think of a card! |
| LAIRD | What? But …but … |
| DOUGAL | You don't like it when the boots are down and the chip's on the other foot. Come on, think of a card … |
| LAIRD | The … the … the ten of … diamonds. |
| DOUGAL | DAMN! |
| HAMISH | Oh Dougal! |
| DOUGAL | I'm sorry, old friend. I thought I'd cracked his system. |
| LAIRD | That'll be eight thousand … well, let's round it up to ten thousand pounds. |
| HAMISH | Oh Dougal, we're ruined. I've certainly learned my lesson. |
| MRS NAUGHTIE | I bet you haven't. |
| DOUGAL | I bet he has. |
| LAIRD | What do you bet? |
| HAMISH | Ten thousand pounds! |
| ALL | *Laugh* |
| *Band plays* | *Music up and oot* |

*THE END*

# CLOOTIE DUMPLING

Universally acknowledged to be the only way to serve clooties.

INGREDIENTS: 1 doz clooties, 1 box dumpling mix

METHOD: Plunge the clooties into boiling water and leave until they stop moving. Drain off the water then quickly combine the clooties with the dumpling mix. Cook and serve.

SUGGESTION: A bottle of 1954 Chateau Léoville Poyferré vin de Bordeaux will take away the taste.

*Big Tam at work and play.*

# THE TALE OF BIG TAM
## A CELEBRATED LOCAL RESIDENT

Let me tell you the tale of Big Tam McLeod
Who you can always notice in a crowd.
He stands approximately six foot eight
And furthermore I wish to state,
He tips the scales at eighteen stone,
One of a kind, of him there is no clone.
People still recount the tale
Of how, despite an in-growing toenail,
He delivered letters throughout the area
With also, it is rumoured, a touch of malaria.
He is our postman, but much more than that,
He plays in our cricket team as opening bat,
Though I must confess, if the truth be told,
Not for some years, as the ground was sold
Six years ago to a commercial buyer
And now it is part of the Tesco empire.
But talking of Tam, people long have admired
How, when married three times, he stoutly sired
Seven sons and a daughter, Morag by name,
Who he seldom sees, which is a great shame.
They all went abroad, for they never forgave
An incident that occurred while Tam was digging a grave.
The facts are not clear but the result was dire
(It concerned a trampoline and the Women's Institute choir),
But no matter, for his name still resounds;
One year in the Lottery he won ten pounds
And once was voted Local Trainspotter of the Year.
So well done, Tam! It is quite clear
You truly should be extremely proud –
'Tis a fact – there is only one Tam McLeod!

Kirsty McGonagall (no relation)

# THE SUBSIDENCE ADVENTURE

| | |
|---|---|
| *Band plays* | *Sig tune up and under* |
| *Announcer* | *You'll Have Had Your Tea. The doings of Hamish and Dougal. Today, 'The Subsidence Adventure'* |
| *Band plays* | *Sig tune up and oot* |
| | *Door opens* |
| HAMISH | Dougal! You'll have had your tea … |
| DOUGAL | Ho ho, there's more to life than tea! |
| HAMISH | Why the big smile on your face? |
| DOUGAL | I finally did it: I stuck it up in the post office window. |
| HAMISH | Did anybody see it? |
| DOUGAL | I want everybody to see it. I got Mrs McVitie to do the lettering on it. |
| HAMISH | What does the lettering say? |
| DOUGAL | It says: 'You name it, we're up for it'. |
| HAMISH | We? |
| DOUGAL | That's what it says on the postcard. |
| HAMISH | The postcard? Oh, when you said you stuck it up in the window, I thought you meant— |
| DOUGAL | Oh no, Hamish. You'd never catch me doing that. |

# You Name It, We're Up For It

**BUILDERS TO THE GENTRY NO JOB TOO BIG, NO FEE TOO SMALL.**

**TWO HODS ARE BETTER THAN ONE.**

**NEVER KNOWINGLY UNDER-PINNED.**

Don't Bother With Google, Here's HAMISH AND DOUGAL!

| | |
|---|---|
| HAMISH | Well, they caught you last time. |
| DOUGAL | Aye, but the magistrate let me off. |
| HAMISH | On the grounds of insufficient evidence. |
| DOUGAL | Yes, yes. Now this postcard; if it doesn't drum up business for our new enterprise, I don't know what will. I have a copy of it here. |
| HAMISH | Oh yes. 'Builders to the Gentry.' |
| DOUGAL | 'No Job Too Big, No Fee Too Small.' |
| HAMISH | 'Two hods are better than one.' |
| DOUGAL | 'Never knowingly under-pinned.' |
| HAMISH | 'Don't bother with Google, |
| BOTH | Here's Hamish and Dougal!' |
| HAMISH | That'll have them beating a path to the door. |
| | ***Knocking on door*** |
| DOUGAL | Here's the first one now! |
| | ***Door opens*** |
| DOUGAL | Mrs Naughtie! |
| MRS NAUGHTIE | I was just beating a path to your door when I remembered: the Laird asked me to see you. He noticed the postcard in the post office window. |
| HAMISH | Re-sult! |
| MRS NAUGHTIE | And he would like to book a French lesson at half past three. |
| DOUGAL | That was not our postcard, Mrs Naughtie. |
| HAMISH | Speak for yourself. |
| DOUGAL | What? |
| HAMISH | Eh bien, Madame Naughtie, trois heures et demi c'est parfait pour moi et Milord. Et son habituelle discipline sauvage? |
| MRS NAUGHTIE | D'accord. Merci bien. |
| HAMISH | À bientôt, madame. |
| DOUGAL | Hamish! |
| HAMISH | What? |
| DOUGAL | You never cease to amaze me. I'm discovering there's a whole new side to you that is an undiscovered continent to me! |
| HAMISH | Well, I had the fishnets and leather boots, I thought I might as well put them to good use. |
| DOUGAL | How's it going? |
| HAMISH | Not as well as I hoped. That's why I'm getting into this building game with you. |

| | |
|---|---|
| DOUGAL | Not in those boots, pal! |
| MRS NAUGHTIE | Oh, builders! That's it! That's what the Laird wanted. He saw the other postcard, and he said get those two builders up to the Big Hoose right away. So you'll have to reschedule his French lesson. |
| HAMISH | Sacre bleu! |
| DOUGAL | Och, come on, you haggis-eating suspender-monkey; to the Big Hoose! |
| **Band plays** | **Link** |
| DOUGAL | Right, here we are at the Big Hoose. |
| HAMISH | You say that every time we come here. |
| DOUGAL | What do you expect me to say? |
| HAMISH | Touché, mon brave. |
| MRS NAUGHTIE | I'll ring the doorbell. |
| HAMISH | Why do you have to say that? |
| MRS NAUGHTIE | So everybody knows I'm here. |
| | **Ding dong! Door opens** |
| LAIRD | Ah there you are, Mrs Naughtie |
| MRS NAUGHTIE | *[To Hamish]* See? *[To Laird]* It's Hamish and Dougal, I've brought them up the way you wanted. |
| LAIRD | And they're a credit to you, Mrs Naughtie. Dougal. And Hamish … *[Confidential]* ahem – I'm afraid I've been very very naughty boy … |
| HAMISH | Pas devant les enfants! |
| LAIRD | Comment? |
| HAMISH | Leave it out, your Lairdship? |
| LAIRD | Oh! I didn't realise I had. I deserve a jolly good spanking. |
| HAMISH | I can still fit you in at half past three … |
| DOUGAL | If you've quite finished! |
| LAIRD | To be continued. Now, Dougal, I believe you two are starting out in the building business. |
| DOUGAL | 'Erections while you wait.' |
| LAIRD | Good. I've got a few problems that need sorting here at the Big Hoose. |
| HAMISH | Which as you know is where we are … |
| LAIRD | Fact is, I've got dry rot, rising damp, falling arches and a touch of subsidence. |
| HAMISH | But you keep smiling. |
| LAIRD | Quite a bit of work, so I wondered if you could give me a quote? |

| | |
|---|---|
| DOUGAL | Certainly. 'Half a league, half a league, half a league onward, Into the Valley of Death rode the six hundred ...' |
| LAIRD | Oh, that's a bit more than I was hoping for ... |
| HAMISH | We could knock a bit off for you. |
| DOUGAL | How about 'rode the four hundred'? |
| LAIRD | Make it quarter of a league and we've got a deal. |
| DOUGAL | Done! |
| | ***Tea tray rattle*** |
| MRS NAUGHTIE | Here we are, mugs of tea all round. Who's the twenty-four sugars? |
| HAMISH | That's mine. I'm cutting down. |
| MRS NAUGHTIE | Your Lairdship, I know you're partial to Earl Grey and a chocolate Hobnob. |
| LAIRD | Yes, but I haven't seen him for years. |
| HAMISH | Now he was a naughty boy. |
| MRS NAUGHTIE | And Mr Dougal, you're the Camomile and Peppermint Pansy. |
| DOUGAL | That's me. Down the hatch! |
| ALL | ***Slurrppp!!!*** |
| DOUGAL | Right. Let's get to work. |
| HAMISH | Hi hooooo ...! |
| Dougal | Quiet Hamish! Now your Lairdship, where would you like us to start? |
| LAIRD | My most urgent problem is the eaves. |
| MRS NAUGHTIE | Oh, you poor thing. Put your head between your knees while I get a bucket. |
| LAIRD | If I could put my head between my knees I'd never leave the house. |
| DOUGAL | Right, Hamish, you go and see to the foundations and sort out this subsidence. |
| HAMISH | Very well. What will you be doing? |
| DOUGAL | I shall be in the bathroom, rubbing down and making good. Let's get to work. |
| ***Band plays*** | ***Link*** |
| LAIRD | What can be taking them so long, Mrs Naughtie? |
| MRS NAUGHTIE | Well, that's builders for you. |
| LAIRD | It's been six months now, and they're still standing there. |
| MRS NAUGHTIE | They haven't moved a muscle. |
| DOUGAL | Good news, your Lairdship! |

*Maisie and Mollie Montrose represent the village in the 'Crochet a Marquee' competition.*
*(They came 26th! Better luck next year, ladies!)*

| | |
|---|---|
| **Laird** | What is it? |
| **Dougal** | We can start on Tuesday. |
| **Hamish** | Slave-driver! |
| ***Band plays*** | ***Link*** |
| **Mrs Naughtie** | Well, another six months, and it's amazing what they've done. |
| **Laird** | Yes. Bugger all. |
| **Hamish** | Mrs Naughtie, this tea is stone cold. |
| **Dougal** | Oh, by the way, your Lairdship, I've prepared this revised estimate. |
| **Laird** | But you've doubled the price! |
| **Dougal** | Well, the job's taken a lot longer than expected. |
| **Laird** | Then there's no time to waste. Get to work! |
| **Hamish** | Oh give us a break! |
| ***Band plays*** | ***Link*** |
| **Dougal** | Though I say it myself, that was a good day's work. |
| **Laird** | Let's hope the first of many. |
| **Dougal** | I'll away to see how Hamish has got on with those foundations. |
| **Laird** | Carry on. If you want me, I'll be in the larder. |
| | ***Lada drives off*** |
| **Dougal** | *[Calls]* Hamish? |
| **Hamish** | What is it? |
| **Dougal** | The Laird did his Lada joke again. Now how do these foundations look? |
| **Hamish** | See for yourself, I've laid them all out on the lawn. |
| **Dougal** | You dug them out? |
| **Hamish** | I did. And I'm pleased to report the foundations are all in excellent condition. |
| **Dougal** | But, but … the Big Hoose now has no foundations, therefore there is every likelihood that it could … |
| | ***Lada screeches to a halt*** |
| **Laird** | Everything all right? |
| **Dougal** | Yes. |
| | ***Alarming creaks and groans from the Big Hoose*** |
| **Dougal** | Don't be alarmed by those noises coming from the Big Hoose, your Lairdship. |
| **Laird** | I'm not alarmed. I can see the foundations laid out on the lawn, and they look in perfect condition. |
| **Dougal** | But, but … |
| **Laird** | Now come along into the Big Hoose and I'll sort out your wages. |

| | |
|---|---|
| DOUGAL | But but … |
| LAIRD | Come on, Dougal, come on, Hamish! |
| HAMISH | Quel dommage! |
| | *Footsteps off to the Big Hoose* |
| *Band plays* | *Link* |
| | *Chains locks etc – clang!* |
| LAIRD | Well, that's my wallet open. What's the damage? |
| DOUGAL | None at all. |
| LAIRD | I mean what do I owe you? |
| DOUGAL | For the damage? |
| LAIRD | Damage? What damage? |
| | *More alarming creaks and groans* |
| HAMISH | Let's get out of here! |
| LAIRD | Oh don't worry Hamish. We often hear noises – this is an old hoose. I got it from a second-hand hoose dealer. |
| DOUGAL | Where's Mrs Naughtie? |
| LAIRD | Upstairs, taking a bath. |
| | *Creak crack clank (getting louder) clank-clank-clank-clank …* |
| LAIRD | Ah here she comes now. |
| | *Bath crashes through the door* |
| MRS NAUGHTIE | Oh! I haven't ridden a bath downstairs since Rag Week at Housekeepers' College. |
| HAMISH | Don't be embarrassed, Mrs Naughtie, you're quite decent; it is a bubble bath. |
| MRS NAUGHTIE | It wasn't when I got into it. Oh, I don't know where to put my face! |
| HAMISH | That's the least of your worries. Nice tattoo, by the way. |
| MRS NAUGHTIE | Thank you. It's a pattern I got from Woman's Weekly. |
| | *More groans and cracks from the hoose, and then a continuous rumbling …* |
| ALL | Oooooh! |
| DOUGAL | I swear I felt the ground move just then. |
| LAIRD | So did I, Dougal. We must do this more often. |
| HAMISH | Your Lairdship, I hope you don't mind me butting in, but did you see a tree go past the window just then? |
| LAIRD | My answer to that is: yes, I do mind you butting in. |
| DOUGAL | The hoose is on the move! |
| HAMISH | So it wasn't a moving tree? Thank goodness for that. |
| DOUGAL | The hoose is accelerating doon the hill … |

| | |
|---|---|
| MRS NAUGHTIE | And we all know what lies at the bottom of the hill! |
| LAIRD | Yes. Do you know if this hoose stops at the post office? |
| DOUGAL | If it doesn't, we'll all end up in the loch! |
| LAIRD | Don't be ridiculous … |
| | *Mighty splash as the Big Hoose lands in the loch* |
| MRS NAUGHTIE | I needn't have got out of that bath. |
| HAMISH | I don't believe it: the hoose is floating. |
| LAIRD | I was just thinking: 'what a stroke of luck that we're not weighed down by heavy foundations'. |
| | *Splashing and bubbling* |
| DOUGAL | Careful, everybody! Nobody move … |
| HAMISH | Look, it's leaning at an alarming angle! |
| MRS NAUGHTIE | It's a few years since you last said that. |
| | *Crash and splash as the hoose turns turtle* |
| DOUGAL | Well, here we are upside down … |
| HAMISH | And it's all gone dark! |
| DOUGAL | Hamish, your kilt's over your head. |
| MRS NAUGHTIE | That reminds me, I must defrost those turkey giblets for the weekend. |
| LAIRD | Right everybody, listen to me … |
| | *[Pause]* |
| | This is a little song I first heard at my mother's knee. She had a tin leg that picked up Radio Caroline. |
| | *[Starts to sing]* 'Strangers in the night …' |
| DOUGAL | Sh! Be quiet! |
| LAIRD | Did you hear something? |
| DOUGAL | Yes, you singing. Be quiet. |
| HAMISH | What are we going to do? Here we are, trapped upside down in the Big Hoose in the loch. |
| DOUGAL | He said by way of a recap. |
| MRS NAUGHTIE | Wait a minute! This reminds me of a film I once saw. |
| LAIRD | Yes, me too. In fact we saw it together. |
| MRS NAUGHTIE | Oh, that was you, was it? If I'd known at the time, I'd have kept my hand on my popcorn. |
| DOUGAL | What was the film? |
| MRS NAUGHTIE | *The Poseidon Adventure.* |
| HAMISH | What happened in that? |
| MRS NAUGHTIE | Oh, I left before the end – too far-fetched. |
| LAIRD | Right, let's examine the situation. Here we are in the library, and we need to get up to the door, fifteen feet |

above our heads. Now, you know those ladders they
have in libraries, so you can reach the books on the
top shelves?

| | |
|---|---|
| HAMISH | Yes? |
| LAIRD | Well, I've always wanted one of those. I've never been able to see the top-shelf books until now. Good Lord! Is that a rather damp *Lady Chatterley*? |
| MRS NAUGHTIE | No, it's me, your Lairdship. |
| LAIRD | So it is. Could you pass me that filthy magazine? |
| DOUGAL | Come on! Concentrate! If we all stood on each other's shoulders, the top one could reach the door. |
| HAMISH | I'm game! |

***Shotgun blasts***

| | |
|---|---|
| LAIRD | Sorry! Force of habit. |
| DOUGAL | It's all right, nobody's hurt. Apart from Hamish. Now here's what we do. Your Lairdship, get up on my shoulders. |
| LAIRD | Right ho. Hup! |
| DOUGAL | Mrs Naughtie, up on his Lairdship's shoulders. |
| MRS NAUGHTIE | I'm there. Hup! Hup! Oooooh! |
| LAIRD | Don't look down, Mrs Naughtie. |
| DOUGAL | And Hamish, up on Mrs Naughtie's shoulders. |
| HAMISH | Here I go! Hup! Hup! Hup! |
| MRS NAUGHTIE | Ooooh! |
| LAIRD | Don't look up, Mrs Naughtie! |
| DOUGAL | Right. We have now formed a human ladder. When I give the word, we all scramble up each other to the doorway fifteen feet above us. OK? |
| ALL | *[Doubtful]* Ye ...es ... |
| DOUGAL | Fine, here we go. One, two, three ... |
| ALL | FOUR! |
| DOUGAL | And here we all are. That wasn't too difficult, was it? |
| LAIRD | No, though a little implausible. |
| HAMISH | But how are we going to get oot? |
| LAIRD | Well, if I remember that film right, they attracted attention by tapping on the pipes. |
| DOUGAL | Aye, good idea. But I don't see any pipes. |
| MRS NAUGHTIE | Oh, I know where to find the pipes! |
| DOUGAL | Then what are you waiting for, woman? |
| MRS NAUGHTIE | Off I go. |

***Running feet away***

says our Social Editor
Morag Ravation.
Hen Nights are
especially popular
and the eggs certainly
come in handy!

Mrs

VISIT OUR

# MUSEUM
# OF THE GLEN!

To a background of Andy Stewart's greatest hits,
you can see glass cases full of historic relics
Including a dirk once owned by Moira Anderson.
(dirk: a ceremonial dagger thrust down
the stocking, known as a *SKHEAN DHU*
which is Gaelic for oh my legs bleeding!)

(B

Enjoy a
Grand Tour of

THE BIG

| | |
|---|---|
| *Band plays* | *Link* |
| | *Running feet back again* |
| MRS NAUGHTIE | Here we are, enough pipes to go round. |
| LAIRD | Splendid. |
| MRS NAUGHTIE | And I've brought you a good supply of shag tobacco to go with them. |
| LAIRD | Light up, everybody! |
| HAMISH | Are those not the wrong kind of pipes? |
| MRS NAUGHTIE | I thought you might say that, so I've brought these as well. |
| | *Bagpipes starting up* |
| DOUGAL | Those are the wrong kind of pipes too – under any circumstances. |
| HAMISH | I think what we need are water pipes, Mrs Naughtie. So that we can tap out our messages. |
| MRS NAUGHTIE | Oh, you mean … like these? |
| | *Pile of pipes dropped on the ground* |
| LAIRD | Good work, Mrs N. Right, everyone, start tapping. |
| ALL | *Start tapping pipes* |
| DOUGAL | Just a minute! Mrs Naughtie, where did you get these pipes from? |
| MRS NAUGHTIE | From the post office. |
| LAIRD | But how …? |
| MRS NAUGHTIE | I swam ashore, popped into the post office, got the pipes – I'd previously noticed they had them on special offer this week – and then Boatman Tam the boatman rowed me back here in his dinghy. |
| DOUGAL | Mrs Naughtie, where is Boatman Tam the boatman now? |
| MRS NAUGHTIE | In his boat, tied up outside the bathroom window. |
| HAMISH | Who tied up Boatman Tam? |
| MRS NAUGHTIE | Oh, that was me. Saving him for later. |
| DOUGAL | Then we're saved! To the boat! |
| LAIRD | Yes! Mrs Naughtie, you untie Boatman Tam; Dougal, you help with the oars; Hamish, you take the rudder; and me, I'll take your money for the tickets. |
| ALL | *Hoorah!* |
| *Band plays* | *Link* |
| DOUGAL | Well, Hamish, it's good to be home again. |
| HAMISH | You don't have to tell me. So why do you? |
| DOUGAL | Just so we all know where we are. Home again and |

stony broke. If you ask me, it was bit mean of the Laird to refuse to pay us a penny.

HAMISH    Aye, especially as he's making a fortune running cruises to the Hebrides aboard the Big Hoose.

DOUGAL    And I'll tell you this: I've had enough of this building game.

HAMISH    Me too. Leave it to the experts.

DOUGAL    From now on we should stick to what we know.

HAMISH    Yes. I once stuck to something I didn't know, and it wasn't a pleasant experience.

DOUGAL    Ah, Mrs Naughtie, thank you for bringing in the tea and putting the tray on the table.

HAMISH    There you go again, explaining everything!

MRS NAUGHTIE    Now, I'm pouring you both a nice cup of tea.

HAMISH    She's doing it too, now!

*Pouring tea*

DOUGAL    She's pouring you a cup, Hamish.

HAMISH    I can see that!

MRS NAUGHTIE    Walnut whip?

HAMISH    Now you're talking!

*Whip crack!*

DOUGAL    What the devil was that?

LAIRD    I've been a very, very naughty boy …

HAMISH    Taissez-vous, cochon!

*Whip crack!*

*Band plays*    *Music up and oot*

**THE END**

# INVERURIE JONES
## AND THE THIMBLE OF DOOM

| | |
|---|---|
| *Band plays* | *Sig tune up and under* |
| *Announcer* | *You'll Have Had Your Tea. The doings of Hamish and Dougal. Today, 'Inverurie Jones and the Thimble of Doom'* |
| *Band plays* | *Sig tune up and oot* |
| | *Thunderclap. Pouring rain* |
| | *Hammering at door* |
| HAMISH | Let me in, let me in! |
| DOUGAL | *[Off]* Who's there? |
| HAMISH | Brad bloody Pitt! Who do you think it is? |
| DOUGAL | *[Off]* We're not at home to Mrs Strop. |
| HAMISH | Open this door! |
| DOUGAL | *[Off]* No. It's pouring down with rain out there. |
| HAMISH | Oh is it? I hadn't noticed. |
| DOUGAL | *[Off]* Is that Mrs Sarcastic with you, Mrs Strop? |
| HAMISH | Let me in! |
| | *Door opens* |
| HAMISH | At last! |

*'Inverurie' Jones and fellow archaeologist-adventurers try out some new long sticks.*

| | |
|---|---|
| DOUGAL | Oh, it's you. You'll have had your tea … |
| HAMISH | I'm in no mood for tea. I'm drenched! Look at the state of this sporran. |
| DOUGAL | So that's what it is. |
| HAMISH | See how it's shrunk? |
| DOUGAL | And there's me thinking you were being molested by a wee guinea pig. |
| HAMISH | Don't be ridiculous! |
| | *Eeek eeek!* |
| HAMISH | What? My God, there is a wee guinea pig, peeping out of my sporran. |
| DOUGAL | He'll have been sheltering from the rain. Now, get out of that wet kilt and hang it over my statue of Malcolm Rifkind. No, not that one, the full-size one. |
| HAMISH | Oh, that's better. |
| DOUGAL | That's a matter of opinion. Is that an oilskin thong? |
| HAMISH | Aye, I thought it might rain. |
| DOUGAL | Come away over here by the fire, while I get the whisky bottle, and hide it. |
| HAMISH | Oh, this is sheer bliss! Steaming away on the hearth rug. |
| | *Door opens* |
| MRS NAUGHTIE | Here we are, I've brought your tea tray and … |
| | *Ooooooh!* |
| | *Dropped tray crash, clatter* |
| MRS NAUGHTIE | OOOOOOOOH! |
| | *Glass crash. Clatter. Bang* |
| MRS NAUGHTIE | OOOOOOOOH! |
| | *Crash. Smash. Tinkle tinkle. Clang. Crash* |
| DOUGAL | Careful, Mrs Naughtie. It seems you're as surprised as I was to see Brad Pitt here. |
| HAMISH | No, it's me – Hamish. |
| MRS NAUGHTIE | So that's where my oilskin thong got to. |
| HAMISH | My suede jockeys were in the wash. I just grabbed the first thing that came to hand. |
| MRS NAUGHTIE | So it was you! |
| HAMISH | Oh all right, here you are, have it back. |
| | *Snap twang!* |
| MRS NAUGHTIE | NOOO! Just a minute! Where's Mr Dougal gone? |
| HAMISH | Oh. He must have popped out. |
| MRS NAUGHTIE | Oh no, not the both of you. |

| | |
|---|---|
| **HAMISH** | Haven't you got something you ought to be doing, Mrs N? |
| **MRS NAUGHTIE** | Thanks for reminding me. I ought to be giving you your marching orders. |
| **HAMISH** | But I can't go out looking like this. |
| **DOUGAL** | Here we are. I've found my old spare pair of flared troos, my chunky Arran sweater, and a tartan bonnet. Now, Hamish, what are you going to wear? |
| **HAMISH** | I was hoping you'd lend me something. |
| **DOUGAL** | As if I wouldn't. I've got this for you. |
| **HAMISH** | Is it in this bin bag? |
| **DOUGAL** | It is this bin bag. |
| **HAMISH** | Oh, I didn't know they did them in my size. Kind of you to cut holes for my arms and legs – but what's this one for? |
| **DOUGAL** | Your head. |
| | ***Bin bag rustle as Hamish puts it on*** |
| **HAMISH** | Oh, very comfy. What do you think, Mrs Naughtie; does my bum look big in this? |
| **MRS NAUGHTIE** | It might if it covered it. |
| **DOUGAL** | Come on, Hamish, let's hit the town! |
| ***Band plays*** | ***Link*** |
| | ***Thunder. Pouring rain*** |
| **HAMISH** | I'm fed up. There's never anything to do here on a wet afternoon. |
| **DOUGAL** | You had a very pleasant half-hour in the ironmonger's, browsing through their bin bag selection. |
| **HAMISH** | Yes, but they've got their summer range in already. |
| **DOUGAL** | We could pop back to the synagogue. Catch the second house. |
| **HAMISH** | We could go for a picnic. |
| **DOUGAL** | Oh, I think one was enough. |
| **HAMISH** | When does the pub open? |
| **DOUGAL** | Tuesday. |
| **HAMISH** | You mean they've got an extension? |
| **DOUGAL** | Aye, but it doesn't help us today. We'll just have to stay here huddled in the doorway of the Museum of the Glen. |
| **HAMISH** | Wait a minute! |
| **DOUGAL** | Well, make it quick, I don't want to waste good huddling time. |
| **HAMISH** | Why don't we do what other people do, to while away a wet afternoon? |

| | |
|---|---|
| DOUGAL | We tried that. But you were sick and my hat blew off. |
| HAMISH | I'm not talking about sailing. |
| DOUGAL | Neither was I. |
| HAMISH | It's right behind us, staring us in the face. The museum! |
| DOUGAL | Of course, let's go in. |

*Door creaks open*
*Echo*

| | |
|---|---|
| HAMISH | Do you have to pay to get in here? |
| DOUGAL | No, but I've heard it's so boring you have to pay to get out. |

*Echoing footsteps wander along*

| | |
|---|---|
| DOUGAL | This is a very disappointing display. |
| HAMISH | Well, it's the best I can do with a binbag. |
| DOUGAL | Mind you, that's an interesting collection of empty shelves along that wall. |
| HAMISH | Yes. And there's some more empty shelves over here. |
| DOUGAL | Indeed. Quite different, but just as interesting. |
| HAMISH | And have you ever seen so many empty glass cases? |
| DOUGAL | I have not. And no two of them the same. |
| HAMISH | Are you thinking what I'm thinking? |
| DOUGAL | Oh, I hope not. |
| HAMISH | Shouldn't there be something on those shelves, and in those cases? |
| DOUGAL | Such as what? |
| HAMISH | Well, Wine Gums and Snickers and Twix. |
| DOUGAL | Snickers and Twix? Snickers and Twix!!? |
| HAMISH | Don't get your Snickers in a Twix! |
| DOUGAL | This is not a sweetie shop! This is a museum. In a museum, the shelves and cases are full of exhibits. |
| HAMISH | But they're empty. |
| DOUGAL | Exactly! |
| HAMISH | Ah! |
| DOUGAL | You know what this means? |
| HAMISH | Yes. No sweeties for us. |
| DOUGAL | No, you great lummock. This means the Museum of the Glen has been looted! |

*Clap of thunder*

| | |
|---|---|
| LAIRD | Hello, you two. |
| DOUGAL | Your Lairdship. |
| LAIRD | Dougal. And … oh, it's not every day you see Brad Pitt in a binbag. |

# DEEP FRIED BUTTER
# IN BATTER

For those lazy hazy crazy days of summer, a healthy alternative to salad.

INGREDIENTS: 2lbs of lean butter, 3 pints of deep-frying lard (or diesel for the ecologically aware!) Batter mix: butter, lard, flour, ½ pint of cooking ale, organic salt, 1 battery egg, 1 mains egg, suet and dripping (garnish).

METHOD: Cut the butter into strips and leave to dry. Make the batter mix, beating well until the eggs are powdered. Shape the butter strips into goujons. Roll in the batter mix until well coated. It's a real tonic for dry skin, right enough! Now roll the goujons of butter in the remaining batter mix and coat with oil. Decorate with dabs of suet and dripping. Make sure the fat is good and hot in the fryer – a reliable smoke alarm will alert you when it is *au point*. Fry the battered butter until crisp and golden broon. Sprinkle with sugar and enjoy!

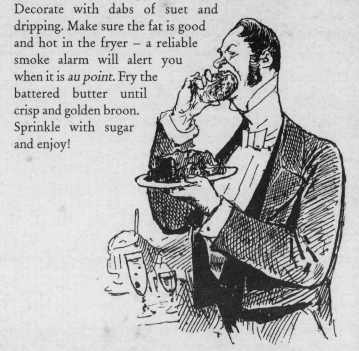

| | |
|---|---|
| DOUGAL | Your Lairdliness, something awful has occurred. |
| LAIRD | Oh no! Not on the same day the Museum of the Glen has been looted. What could be worse than that? |
| DOUGAL | Oh. You've rather taken the wind out of my sails … |
| HAMISH | Your Lairdship …? |
| LAIRD | What is it, Brad? |
| HAMISH | Has … everything been taken? |
| LAIRD | I'm afraid it has, Brad. |
| DOUGAL | Oh no! Does that include the museum's most famous exhibit? |
| LAIRD | Yes: the Thimble of Doom! |
| *Band plays* | *Dramatic chord* |
| DOUGAL | The Thimble of doom? |
| | *Clap of thunder* |
| LAIRD | Yes, the Thimble of Doom! |
| *Band plays* | *Dramatic chord* |
| HAMISH | Not the Thimble of Doom! |
| | *Duck quack* |
| HAMISH | Dougal, there's one thing that puzzles me. |
| DOUGAL | Yes? |
| HAMISH | What the hell is the Thimble of Doom? |
| DOUGAL | It's a mysterious ancient thimble. It was first discovered in the Great Pyramid of Cheops. |
| HAMISH | The display in Tam the Butcher's window? |
| LAIRD | Yes, how it came to be there is a mystery. But there are those who say the Thimble bestows upon whoever wears it unholy powers. |
| DOUGAL | And now it's been stolen! |
| HAMISH | Who could have done this terrible thing? |
| | *Glass crash. Thud!* |
| DOUGAL | Look what's been hurled through the window. It's Mrs Naughtie with a message attached. |
| MRS NAUGHTIE | Forgive the intrusion, but a gentleman gave me this message for you, and then threw me through the window. |
| LAIRD | Mrs Naughtie, what an experience. Sit down here and tuck in to this Twix. You've met Brad Pitt and his duck? |
| | *Quack!* |
| MRS NAUGHTIE | Oh yes, I never forget a binbag. |
| HAMISH | I am not Brad Pitt! |

| | |
|---|---|
| MRS NAUGHTIE | Then what are you doing with his duck? |
| HAMISH | Doh! |
| DOUGAL | Look what this message says. 'I have the legendary Thimble of Doom. I intend to use its ancient mystical powers to crush Scotland under the heel of my own brutal dictatorship. Hoping this finds you as it leaves me, all the best, yours, Inverurie Jones'. |
| *Band plays* | ***Dramatic chord*** |
| | ***Clap of thunder*** |
| | ***Duck quack*** |
| LAIRD | I might have known it! The unscrupulous treasure hunter Inverurie Jones has stolen the legendary Thimble of Doom and made off with it. |
| DOUGAL | We must track him down. |
| HAMISH | Let's look him up in Yellow Pages, under Unscrupulous Treasure Hunters. |
| DOUGAL | Don't be a fool, man. There's hundreds of them. |
| MRS NAUGHTIE | He can't have got far. Oh! I have a biplane, with its engine idling, parked right outside in the High Street. |
| DOUGAL | What are you doing with a biplane out there? |
| MRS NAUGHTIE | Monday is my day for crop-dusting. |
| LAIRD | I didn't know you went in for crop-dusting. |
| MRS NAUGHTIE | Oh your Lairdship, hadn't you noticed how bright and shiny your plums are? |
| LAIRD | Yes, they've attracted many an admiring glance, but I didn't realise it was all down to you. |
| DOUGAL | Come on, everybody! Into the plane and after the thief! |
| *Band plays* | ***Link*** |
| | ***Crop-duster bi-plane flying erratically*** |
| HAMISH | Oh Dougal, I don't like this. I haven't been flying since the Highland Games when I forgot to let go of the caber. |
| DOUGAL | Well, at least you landed in the porridge dump. Now calm down, old friend, Mrs Naughtie's coming round with the trolley. |
| MRS NAUGHTIE | Duty-free shortbread? Presentation haggis? Packet of three? Three peanuts, that is … |
| DOUGAL | A large glass of whisky for Hamish. |
| MRS NAUGHTIE | Sounds like a fair swap. |
| DOUGAL | Cheers. |

| | |
|---|---|
| LAIRD | Stewardess! |
| MRS NAUGHTIE | Yes, sir? |
| LAIRD | Could you be a dear and ask the pilot who's flying this thing? |
| MRS NAUGHTIE | Oh, I knew there was something! Excuse me! Pilot coming through! |
| HAMISH | It's all right, Mrs Naughtie, I've got the controls. |
| MRS NAUGHTIE | Mr Hamish! I didn't know you could fly a plane. |
| HAMISH | Oh, I knew there was something! |
| | *Plane diving. Crash into rainforest* |
| *Band plays* | *Link* |
| | *Rainforest atmos* |
| DOUGAL | Well, here we all are in the rainforest. |
| HAMISH | I didn't know there were any rainforests in Scotland. |
| DOUGAL | I think they've only just had one put in. |
| LAIRD | This is exactly the sort of place where Inverurie Jones would be hiding. Right, everybody spread out. |
| ALL | *Oh ah groans of pleasure etc.* 'That's better!' etc … |
| LAIRD | No, what I had in mind was an intensive search of the entire rainforest. You three go over there, and I'll search right here. |
| DOUGAL | Very well, your Lairdship. Consider this rainforest well and truly searched. |
| HAMISH | See you later. |
| MRS NAUGHTIE | Missing you already. |
| | *Tramping away through the undergrowth* |
| LAIRD | Goodbye and good hunting! *[Aside]* Poor fools! Little do they know that I am Inverurie Jones! Yes, I've been leading a double life as popular Laird of the Big Hoose, and unscrupulous treasure hunter. Those three meddling fools will never leave the rainforest alive, and the power of the Thimble of Doom will be mine, all mine! Ah ha ha ha hahaha! |
| *Band plays* | *Sinister link* |
| LAIRD | Oh I do like my new ring-tone. Hello? |
| VOICE | *Garble* |
| LAIRD | I'm in the rainforest at the moment, so I think that opportunities for double glazing are rather limited. Lovely to talk, ciao! |
| *Band plays* | *Different sinister link* |
| | *Tramping through undergrowth* |

| | |
|---|---|
| HAMISH | Oh Dougal, we've got to stop for a bit. I need to take the weight off my binbag. |
| MRS NAUGHTIE | And I have to powder my nose in the smallest room in the rainforest. And while I'm there I may as well have a pee. |
| DOUGAL | Well, be quick about it. In the meantime I'll rub my legs together and start a fire. |
| HAMISH | Can you start a fire by rubbing your legs together? |
| DOUGAL | No, I've got a box of matches for that. |
| *Band plays* | *Jungle drums under* |
| MRS NAUGHTIE | Listen! The drums! The rhythm of the drums! |
| HAMISH | Let's get moving! |
| DOUGAL | This is no time for dancing. |
| MRS NAUGHTIE | Spoilsport. I used to be known as the Queen of the Jitterbuggers. Of course that was before I took up dancing. |
| DOUGAL | Haud yer wheesht! Listen! |
| *Band plays* | *Drums joined by pipe band playing 'Scotland the Brave'* |
| MRS NAUGHTIE | What's that? |
| DOUGAL | Just as I feared, it's the massed pipes and drums of the McCoists – the Lost Clan of the rainforest. |
| HAMISH | The Clan McCoist? Is it true that they're New Age cannibals? |
| DOUGAL | That's right, they only eat vegetarians. |
| MRS NAUGHTIE | They're getting closer. |
| DOUGAL | We'd better run for it. The band might be taking a collection. |
| HAMISH | No. I'm going to stay here and stick it out. |
| *Band plays* | *Pipe music speeds up and rapid fade* |
| DOUGAL | Well, that's scared them off. |
| MRS NAUGHTIE | Maybe, but they've left their knitting behind. |
| DOUGAL | Their knitting? |
| MRS NAUGHTIE | Oh yes, they're a superstitious folk. They knit gigantic cardigans for the spirits of the forest. |
| DOUGAL | Ah, that would explain those enormous knitting needles lining the path. |
| HAMISH | And also that giant ball of wool at the top of the hill. |
| DOUGAL | Jings, that's a big ball of wool. |
| HAMISH | Let's just hope nothing happens to dislodge it. |
| | *Volcano erupts* |

*Alistair Coulthard shows off his prize-winning length of rope to Nigel the Highland bull.*

*Charlie Murray at the controls of his electronic bullock.*

Book into the

# Thistle McHilton
## HOLIDAY INN AND B&B.

*'Here you'll want tae stop and bide,*
*All you could ever want deep-fried!'*

You're sure of a warm welcome from your genial host,
Thistle McHilton, his lovely partner Holiday Inn
and their two sons Bert and Ben..

VISIT OUR

# MUSEUM OF THE GLEN!

To A Background Of Andy Stewarts Greatest Hits You Can
See Glass Cases Full Of Historic Relics Including A Dirk Once

| | |
|---|---|
| DOUGAL | Well, I can think of better times for a volcano to erupt. |
| | ***Rolling rumble*** |
| MRS NAUGHTIE | The enormous ball of wool has been dislodged and it's rolling down the hill towards us! |
| DOUGAL | Run for your lives! |
| | ***Running feet*** |
| HAMISH | It's gaining on us! |
| MRS NAUGHTIE | Quick, let's hide in this cave. |
| DOUGAL | No! It's full of snakes! |
| HAMISH | Quick, let's hide in this cave. |
| MRS NAUGHTIE | No! It's full of spiders! |
| DOUGAL | Quick, let's hide in this Starbucks. |
| HAMISH | No! It's full of wankers! |
| DOUGAL | Never mind. Two skinny frappachinos and a latte, please. |
| LAIRD | Do you mind? There is a queue. |
| HAMISH, DOUGAL & MRS NAUGHTIE | Your Lairdship! |
| LAIRD | Good Lord! I thought you'd all died in the wool. |
| DOUGAL | No, we escaped. |
| LAIRD | What did you find in your search of the rainforest? |
| HAMISH | A lot of wet trees. |
| DOUGAL | We were lucky to get out alive. In fact, now I think of it, you left us all in the rainforest to perish! |
| LAIRD | So what? You can't stop me now, because I have the Thimble of Doom. |
| HAMISH | Where did you find it? |
| LAIRD | I simply followed the polar bear to the wrecked airliner on the beach, and there it was. |
| HAMISH | Why didn't we think of that? |
| LAIRD | See, I slip the Thimble on and … |
| HAMISH | Where's he gone? I can't see him! |
| LAIRD | I'm still over here. |
| HAMISH | Oh, so you are. |
| DOUGAL | So now you plan to use the power of the Thimble to take over Scotland? |
| LAIRD | No, unfortunately it won't do that. But it does mean I can now darn socks without fear of a needle-related injury. Hoorah! |
| MRS NAUGHTIE | You fiend! |
| DOUGAL | But I can't believe you've done all this to us; you, our kindly Laird. |

| | |
|---|---|
| **LAIRD** | You poor fools! I am Inverurie Jones! |
| **DOUGAL** | Inverurie Jones, you must pay for your crimes. |
| **LAIRD** | Oh, there's a perfectly innocent explanation. Here, I've written it all down on this Kleenex. |
| **DOUGAL** | This is a tissue of lies! |
| **HAMISH** | More to the point, what have you done with the real Laird? |
| **LAIRD** | Hello, everyone. |
| **DOUGAL** | Your Lairdship! |
| **LAIRD** | Dougal, Mrs Naughtie … I say, Brad Pitt's let himself go … and … good Lord, my spitting image. |
| **DOUGAL** | You must have a doppelgänger. |
| **LAIRD** | No, just a cappuccino for me. Now look here, I've been away on my gap year. Anything happen while I was gone? |
| **HAMISH** | Well, it all began one rainy afternoon at the museum … |
| **LAIRD** | You don't need to tell me any more. I can work out the rest for myself. So, you must be the notorious Inverurie Jones. |
| **LAIRD** | I beg to differ. How do we know you're not Inverurie Jones? |
| **HAMISH** | How can we tell which is which? This is a nightmare! |
| **LAIRD** | Wake up, Hamish! Wake up, Dougal! For it was all a dream … |
| **HAMISH** | No it wasn't. |
| **LAIRD** | Damn! Still, it was worth a try. |
| **DOUGAL** | There's only one way to tell them apart. |
| **HAMISH** | Yes, the real Laird has a mole in the shape of a birthmark. |
| **LAIRD** | That's true. And here it is. *Zzzippp!* |
| **MRS NAUGHTIE** | Aye, that's the one. |
| **LAIRD** | Pass it around so they can all see. |
| **DOUGAL** | Well, I'm convinced. |
| **LAIRD** | No, that birthmark is a forgery. This is the real one. *Zzzippp!* |
| **ALL** | *Gasp!* |
| **HAMISH** | They're identical. What do we do now? |
| **MRS NAUGHTIE** | There is one surefire way to tell the real Laird from the imposter. Ask him to sing. |
| **DOUGAL** | Steady on, Mrs Naughtie, there's only so much flesh and blood can stand. |

| | |
|---|---|
| HAMISH | But she's right, nobody sings like the Laird. |
| LAIRD | Very well, I'm game. After you, Inverurie. |
| LAIRD | No, after you, Inverurie! |
| LAIRD | No, I insist. |
| LAIRD | So do I. |
| LAIRD | Very well. Although even I have lost track of who I am now. Here we go. Ahem. |
| *Grams* | ***Pavarotti sings 'Nessun Dorma' or some such*** <br> ***Gunshot*** |
| LAIRD | Well, that's sorted that out. |
| DOUGAL | It's good to have you back with us, your Lairdship. |
| LAIRD | It's good to be back. Ha ha ha ha ha! |
| *Band plays* | ***Sinister link*** |
| LAIRD | Hello? No, they think I'm the real one. Goodbye. |
| *Band plays* | ***Sig tune*** |

**THE END**

# THERE'S SOMETHING
# ABOUT MRS NAUGHTIE ...!

| | |
|---|---|
| *Band plays* | *Sig tune up and under* |
| Announcer | *You'll Have Had Your Tea. The doings of Hamish and Dougal. Today, 'There's something about Mrs Naughtie ...!'* |
| *Band plays* | *Sig tune up and oot* |
| | *Door opens* |
| HAMISH | Dougal! |
| DOUGAL | Hamish. You'll have had your tea ... |
| HAMISH | Well ... |
| DOUGAL | And by the way, don't you normally knock at the door before coming in? |
| HAMISH | Well, we are old friends ... |
| DOUGAL | Oh, you may as well stay, now that you're in. |
| | *Loo flush* |
| HAMISH | Oh no, don't let me interrupt you. I can see you're busy, listening to your album of vintage toilet flushes. |

*Mrs Naughtie's winning entry for the Scarf and Shortbread arrangement (over 60s).*

| | |
|---|---|
| DOUGAL | What else would I be doing in the lavatory? |
| HAMISH | Well, you might be catching up on some paperwork ... |
| DOUGAL | Well I'm not. |
| | ***Zzzzzip!*** |
| HAMISH | Why do you have a zipper on your kilt? |
| DOUGAL | It's not on my kilt. |
| HAMISH | ... OK ... |
| | ***Knocking on door*** |
| HAMISH | Oh, I see you've got a new album of the *Golden Years* of Door Knocking. |
| | ***More knocking*** |
| MRS NAUGHTIE | Hello? Let me in! |
| DOUGAL | That's a real door. Hold on a minute, Mrs Naughtie. Hamish and I are just in the lavatory together. |
| MRS NAUGHTIE | Oh. Shall I come back later? |
| HAMISH | No. Stay away. |
| MRS NAUGHTIE | What?! |
| HAMISH | It's not what you think. |
| MRS NAUGHTIE | You mean it's not a perfectly innocent misunderstanding? |
| DOUGAL | Oh, get out of the way, woman. We're coming out. |
| MRS NAUGHTIE | It's a bit late for that, if you ask me! |
| | ***Door opens*** |
| DOUGAL | There, you see? Not a hair out of place. Oops! |
| | ***Zzzzzip!*** |
| MRS NAUGHTIE | Oh gentlemen, I'm in such a state. |
| HAMISH | Pour the lady a dram, Dougal. |
| DOUGAL | Aye, she certainly looks in need of a stiff one. |
| MRS NAUGHTIE | I've just had this in the post. It's my uncle Nab. |
| HAMISH | What, in that wee envelope? |
| MRS NAUGHTIE | No, he's dead. |
| HAMISH | I'm not surprised. He couldn't breathe in there. |
| MRS NAUGHTIE | This is a letter from his solicitor. He passed away last week. |
| DOUGAL | Oh no, not two of them. |
| MRS NAUGHTIE | Apparently Uncle Nab left me his fortune in his will. It's come as a terrible shock. |
| DOUGAL | Oh Mrs Naughtie, sit down here and marry me. |
| MRS NAUGHTIE | I'm not the sort of girl who marries the first man that asks her. |

| | |
|---|---|
| DOUGAL | Quite right too. |
| HAMISH | How about the second man? |
| MRS NAUGHTIE | I'd never marry a man who was just after my money. |
| HAMISH | The thought had never crossed my mind until you mentioned it. Marry me. |
| MRS NAUGHTIE | I'm not that easy. I want to be wooed. |
| DOUGAL | You can be as wude as you like with me, baby. |
| HAMISH | Dougal! |
| MRS NAUGHTIE | Gentlemen, in the light of my good fortune, I'm sure you'll understand that I am handing in my notice. |
| DOUGAL | You're leaving us? But who's going to press my underpants? |
| MRS NAUGHTIE | You can press your own underpants. And don't tell me you don't know how. |
| HAMISH | Mrs Naughtie, I respect your wishes. |
| DOUGAL | What?! |
| HAMISH | In fact, to celebrate your aforementioned good fortune, and for no other reason, why don't you come away with me, to the Malcolm Rifkind Tea Rooms. |
| MRS NAUGHTIE | Oo-oooh …! |
| HAMISH | There we can share a pot of Mazzawattee, then hitch up our kilts and dance cheek to cheek. |
| MRS NAUGHTIE | I can almost see it now! |
| HAMISH | Sorry! |
| | *Zzzzzip!* |
| MRS NAUGHTIE | But I must think deeply about your offer. Now, will you excuse me while I pop upstairs and escape through the bathroom window. |
| | *Footsteps run upstairs. Crash of glass* |
| DOUGAL | Hamish! You Jezebel! |
| HAMISH | What? |
| DOUGAL | I meant Judas. I always get those two mixed up. |
| HAMISH | Oh, I remember Jessie Bell. Thirty pieces of silver well spent, as I recall … |
| DOUGAL | Hamish! How dare you try to snatch Mrs Naughtie from under my nose? |
| HAMISH | All's fair in love and war. |
| DOUGAL | To the victor the spoils! |

| | |
|---|---|
| HAMISH | Who dares wins! |
| DOUGAL | … Nice to see you, to see you nice! |
| HAMISH | Just you wait, Dougal, I'll sweep that lassie off her feet. |
| DOUGAL | She won't thank you for that. |
| HAMISH | We shall see. She won't be able to resist my advances. Now, where's my mobile? |
| | ***Zzzzip!!!!!*** |
| HAMISH | Still warm. |
| | ***Old-fashioned phone dialling*** |
| DOUGAL | I see you've got a big old one there. |
| HAMISH | Sh! Hello, Malcolm Rifkind Tea Rooms? Hello, Tam, I'd like to book a table this afternoon please. Oh, and two chairs while you're at it … |
| TAM | *[Distort surprised noises]* |
| HAMISH | Yes, two. |
| ***Band plays*** | ***Link into tea-room piano dance music*** |
| | ***Establish tea-room atmos*** |
| HAMISH | Can I tempt you to a Hobnob? |
| MRS NAUGHTIE | Behave yourself! This is a respectable establishment, with tablecloths and those lovely potted palms. |
| HAMISH | Yes, they were delicious. |
| MRS NAUGHTIE | Oh, I love the ambience. |
| | ***Distant ambulance siren goes by*** |
| HAMISH | Aye, on its way to the Cottage Hospital, no doubt. |
| MRS NAUGHTIE | Yet another cottage-related injury. |
| HAMISH | That's our tune! Time for … dancing! |
| | ***Dancing feet*** |
| MRS NAUGHTIE | Oh, you dance divinely. |
| HAMISH | Thank you. Would you care to join me? |
| MRS NAUGHTIE | Well, I can't dance and play the piano. |
| HAMISH | What? I can't hear you for that bloody piano! |
| | ***Piano music ends*** |
| WAITRESS (GG) | Good afternoon. Everything to your satisfaction? |
| HAMISH | I'm working on it. |
| WAITRESS | Oh, you rascal! |
| HAMISH | Wait a minute, you're new. I haven't seen you in these parts … |
| WAITRESS | Do you mind? I'm a real waitress. Now, are you the one that ordered the crumpet? |
| HAMISH | No, but now you're here, I could nibble a little tart. |

| | |
|---|---|
| **WAITRESS** | Oh, you naughty boy. What about your girlfriend on the piano? |
| **HAMISH** | Oh, she's not my girlfriend, that's merely a business arrangement. |
| **MRS NAUGHTIE** | What's this, Hamish? Chatting up the waitress? |
| **HAMISH** | Well no, but it's a thought. |
| **MRS NAUGHTIE** | Is it indeed? |
| **HAMISH** | No no. Oh Mrs Naughtie, or may I call you … Fiona? |
| **MRS NAUGHTIE** | Very well, but I'd prefer you to use my name. |
| **HAMISH** | Then Beyonce it is. |
| **WAITRESS** | Will there be anything else? |
| **HAMISH** | I sincerely hope so. Now, could I have the bill please? |
| **WAITRESS** | Certainly. And will you require the rest of the duck costume too? |
| **HAMISH** | What? |
| **DOUGAL** | *[For the waitress is he]* The duck costume you wore at the Bill Oddie Theme Night at the public baths. |
| **HAMISH** | Wait a minute! You're not a real waitress, are you! Take off that false beard. |
| | ***Rrrrip!*** |
| **HAMISH** | Dougal! This waitress looks just like Dougal! |
| **DOUGAL** | It is me, you great tumshie! |
| **MRS NAUGHTIE** | Oh Mr Dougal. What are you up to? |
| **DOUGAL** | Never mind what I'm up to. Ask your fancy man here what he's playing at. |
| **MRS NAUGHTIE** | Well, it looks like Scrabble … |
| **HAMISH** | How many 'T's in 'titillate'? |
| **DOUGAL** | Four. But perhaps you can explain to Mrs Naughtie why you were chatting up a beautiful and highly talented young waitress, and expecting Mrs N herself to pick up the tab? |
| **HAMISH** | Your point being? |
| **DOUGAL** | Look at you, you snake in the grass. |
| **HAMISH** | I must get this zip fixed. |
| **DOUGAL** | I know what you're after. |
| **HAMISH** | Don't let this zip mislead you. |
| **MRS NAUGHTIE** | What kind of man would take me out, not for myself as a woman, but because of my great wealth, having recently inherited a vast fortune? |
| | ***Whoooosshhh!*** |
| **LAIRD** | Good afternoon, everybody. |

Proud possessor of
Three Michelin Tyres!

Enjoy a
Grand Tour of

# THE BIG
# HOOSE

## With Big Tam
## our Local Guide

(Not during pub opening hours)

'There's a hectic
social life in the village!'

says our Social Editor
Morag Ravation.
Hen Nights are

| | |
|---|---|
| **MRS NAUGHTIE** | Your Lairdship! |
| **HAMISH** | What a surprise. |
| **LAIRD** | Is that Mrs Naughtie, Hamish? I've never seen you looking so gorgeous. |
| **HAMISH** | Thank you. It's just a new feather … |
| **LAIRD** | Now, you tantalising young minx, how about a fresh pot of tea? |
| **MRS NAUGHTIE** | I don't mind if I do. |
| **LAIRD** | I was talking to the waitress. *[Confidentially]* Listen, my dear, once I've got the old girl's money, how about me and you going for a high old time in Rio de Janeiro? |
| **HAMISH** | Your Lairdship, that's Dougal! |
| **DOUGAL** | You mind your own business. *[Waitress]* One pot of tea coming up! *[Goes off singing]* I feel pretty … |
| **LAIRD** | Now my dear Mrs Naughtie, or may I call you my little nest-egg? Let me take you away from all this. |
| **MRS NAUGHTIE** | On yer bike, you muckle waste of space! |
| **LAIRD** | How dare you! A vast fortune doesn't make you my equal, you know. It just makes you unbelievably attractive. |
| **MRS NAUGHTIE** | Go away and leave me alone, the lot of you. I need time to think. |
| ***Band plays*** | ***Link*** |
| **MRS NAUGHTIE** | *[Tearful]* Oh misery me! This vast fortune is more trouble than it's worth. It's true what they say: Saddam had no weapons of mass destruction. But what use is that to me? Oh cruel fate! Where will it all end? |
| **DOUGAL** | Is that you, Mrs Naughtie? |
| **MRS NAUGHTIE** | Yes? |
| **DOUGAL** | Keep it down, will you? |
| **MRS NAUGHTIE** | I'm sorry. I didn't see you there, on top of my wardrobe. |
| **DOUGAL** | You never do, Mrs N. |
| **MRS NAUGHTIE** | Oh Mr Dougal, it's so good to see you. You're the only one I can trust. I don't know where to turn – I'm at the end of my tether. |
| **DOUGAL** | I told you to keep it down. |
| **MRS NAUGHTIE** | ***Wails!*** |
| **DOUGAL** | Mrs Naughtie, or may I call you Judas? Jezebel! |

|                    | Never mind. You're a woman who needs cosseting. |
|--------------------|---|
| MRS NAUGHTIE       | I'm already wearing one. |
| DOUGAL             | Then let yourself go, Mrs Naughtie. |
|                    | ***Twwangggg!*** |
| MRS NAUGHTIE       | Jings, that's better. Mr Dougal, you're the one who saved me from those unscrupulous gold-diggers. When I saw you dressed up as that waitress, I said to myself 'That's my kind of man.' |
| DOUGAL             | And you're my kind of woman, Mrs Naughtie. Let's throw caution to the winds, and hit the town. |
| MRS NAUGHTIE       | What are we waiting for? |
| DOUGAL             | Just waiting for me to get out of this waitress costume. |
| ***Band plays***   | ***Link*** |
|                    | ***Pub atmos*** |
| DOUGAL             | Ready for another, Mrs N? |
| MRS NAUGHTIE       | Do you mind if I have a drink first? |
| DOUGAL             | Same again? |
| MRS NAUGHTIE       | No, I'm serious, I'd like a drink. |
| DOUGAL             | Of course. Now this bar is famous for its twelve-year-old malt whisky. |
| MRS NAUGHTIE       | Do they have any malt whisky for grown-ups? |
| DOUGAL             | Ha ha ha … no. Well, we'd better be on our way. The lady's paying. Taxi! The lady's paying … |
| ***Band plays***   | ***Link*** |
|                    | ***Café atmos*** |
| MRS NAUGHTIE       | Oh, that looks delicious. |
| DOUGAL             | Yes, the food here's always reliable. |
| MRS NAUGHTIE       | Mmmm! |
| DOUGAL             | You sound as if you're enjoying that. |
| MRS NAUGHTIE       | Oh yes. I really am. |
| DOUGAL             | You're not faking it? |
| Mrs Naughtie       | No. Mmmm! Mmmmmmm! Ah! Ooooh! Oooooooh. |
|                    | ***[Full 'Harry Met Sally' treatment leading to a climax!]*** |
| YOUTH              | Do you want fries with that? |
| DOUGAL             | Why not? The lady's paying. |
| MRS NAUGHTIE       | Hang about! I've paid for everything tonight. The drinks, the food, the moonlight buggy ride, the flowers and chocolates, your dry-cleaning and a small motorcycle. |
| DOUGAL             | Even though I really wanted a big motorcycle. |

# LANARKSHIRE HOTPOT

A local dish found all over the world, this Scottish treat satisfies the hungry and stuffs a mattress for the weary.

INGREDIENTS: 3 medium-sized muttons, 2 tbsps clapshot (I find Hungarian tbsps are best!), 1 lb potted hough, 1 sprig of stovies, 3-4 slices of Atholl brose, 6 ripe cranachans, ¾ gms tablet

METHOD: First heat your pot. Brown the muttons on all three sides and place on a draining net. Peel the cranachans and crush with the stovies and allow to settle while you liquidise the rest of the seasoning.

Marinade one or other of the chickens (it doesn't matter which) in a pint of flambé, stirring in the asparagus lumps a little at a time.

Suddenly warm the leeks. Cook under a low oven for 2 hours or leave overnight if you're not bothered. Serve your Hotpot with a generous sprinkling of fluid ounces.

| | |
|---|---|
| MRS NAUGHTIE | You're as bad as the rest. Taking advantage of me, just because of my enormous fortune. |
| | ***Whoooosshhh!*** |
| LAIRD | Good evening, everybody. |
| MRS NAUGHTIE | Your Lairdship! |
| LAIRD | Is this man bothering you? |
| MRS NAUGHTIE | What I need is a knight in shining armour. |
| DOUGAL | Oh, I've got some shining armour and you're welcome to spend the night in it. |
| MRS NAUGHTIE | This fortune of mine is such a burden, I don't know how to cope. Your Lairdship, you know what it's like to be obscenely rich. |
| LAIRD | I was once, dear lady, but I have recently fallen upon hard times. Hence my interest in you. |
| MRS NAUGHTIE | *[Aside]* Jings! The Laird, interested in me? |
| LAIRD | Here, you tantalising bundle of fun, let me run my fingers lightly through your purse. |
| MRS NAUGHTIE | Oooh! |
| LAIRD | Do you have your cheque book handy? |
| MRS NAUGHTIE | I do. |
| LAIRD | Then let me take you away from all this ... |
| | ***Ships siren*** |
| MRS NAUGHTIE | Manners! |
| LAIRD | Pardon me, I was overcome with excitement. Come, let us away on an exotic cruise to faraway places ... |
| | ***Ships siren*** |
| LAIRD | I see you're as excited as I am. Let us be gone! |
| ***Band plays*** | ***Link. Calypso*** |
| | ***Sea, seagulls, ship under way, siren*** |
| LAIRD | I always think the West Indies look their best at this time. |
| MRS NAUGHTIE | It's so romantic, out here on deck in the middle of the night. |
| LAIRD | I want you to look at the moon. |
| MRS NAUGHTIE | Oh! What a sight! Is that the Sea of Tranquility? |
| LAIRD | No, just a birthmark. |
| MRS NAUGHTIE | Och, pull down your silk dressing gown. You'll catch cold. |
| LAIRD | Mrs Naughtie, would you be so kind as to light my cigarette? |
| MRS NAUGHTIE | By all means. |

| | |
|---|---|
| | *Footsteps hurry along. Match strike* |
| LAIRD | *[Distant]* Thank you, Mrs Naughtie. |
| MRS NAUGHTIE | Oh I do like a man with a long cigarette holder. |
| DOUGAL | Good evening, Mrs Naughtie. |
| MRS NAUGHTIE | Mr Dougal. |
| HAMISH | And Mr Hamish. |
| DOUGAL | Do we find you all alone? |
| MRS NAUGHTIE | No, I'm with the Laird. |
| HAMISH | Where is he? |
| LAIRD | *[Distant]* I'm over here! |
| | *Footsteps as the threesome go to join the Laird* |
| DOUGAL | Good evening your Lairdship. |
| LAIRD | Hm! I see you've managed to drag yourself up on deck. |
| DOUGAL | Och, it's just an old waitress costume … |
| LAIRD | In that case, it's cocktails all round! |
| ALL | Ha ha ha ha ha ha ha …! |
| *Band plays* | *Link* |
| DOUGAL | Well it's good to be home, but what a cruise that was. |
| HAMISH | Twice round the world, including a stop off at DFS Carpet Warehouse. |
| DOUGAL | Not forgetting the hot air balloon trip across the M6. |
| HAMISH | From one side right to the other. |
| DOUGAL | It must all have cost Mrs Naughtie a fortune, but as far as I'm concerned, it was worth every penny. |
| | *Knock at door* |
| DOUGAL | Come in. |
| | *Door opens* |
| HAMISH | Mrs Naughtie! Whatever's wrong? |
| MRS NAUGHTIE | I've just had the final bill for the cruise, and it's cleaned me out. Every last penny gone. |
| DOUGAL | Oh, Mrs Naughtie! That's… no surprise. |
| MRS NAUGHTIE | Therefore, gentlemen, I am asking if you can please give me back my old job as your cleaner-stroke-housekeeper? |
| HAMISH | Then it would just be like old times! |
| MRS NAUGHTIE | Oh, yes! |
| DOUGAL | I'm sorry, the post has already been filled. Goodbye. |
| | *Door closes firmly* |
| HAMISH | Well, it was nice to see Mrs Naughtie again. |

| | |
|---|---|
| DOUGAL | Oh yes. Time for tea? |
| HAMISH | Certainly. |
| | ***Bell tinkles. Door opens*** |
| LAIRD | You rang, sir? |
| DOUGAL | Tea for two, Laird. |
| HAMISH | And be quick about it. |
| DOUGAL | Oh, and Laird … |
| LAIRD | Yes, sir? |
| DOUGAL | My old waitress costume really suits you. |
| LAIRD | Thank you, sir. I was wondering about getting a rise … |
| HAMISH | And did you? |
| LAIRD | Sadly, no, sir. Will there be anything else? |
| HAMISH | Oh, I hope not. |
| ***Band plays*** | ***Music up and oot*** |

**THE END**

# FOLK OF THE GLEN

## Myself: The Laird

My papa, the McCoist of McCoist of that ilk, sadly passed away shortly before my conception. How he would have wished to be there for that momentous occasion. Nevertheless I was born to the title of Laird of the Glen. Mama and I lived at the Big Hoose where my early schooling was carried out by a succession of governesses, each one more fearsome than the one before. My favourite was Nanny Goering, who arrived by parachute in the late 1940s, a jolly roly-poly kind of woman with a wicked sense of fun.

I was sent away to Eton College as a four-year-old boy, but they sent me back as they already had one. I went to Glen Academy school where I was always top of the class, excelled at sports, and was loved and admired by staff and pupils alike until I was expelled for lying. It wasn't long before show business beckoned, and I joined the troupe of Alice Moffat's 'Tumbling Tots' where I soon became the star turn in my little duckling costume until my second wife put her foot down.

My third wife was a model, and I built her from a kit. However, I was soon hankering after the companionship of a real woman, so I set off in search of a wife, and soon found one whose husband wasn't that bothered. Two years of bliss ensued and then we got married. I had a distinguished career in the army, serving in three world wars and successfully starting a fourth. After my discharge (which was successfully cleared up with a series of injections) I returned to the Big Hoose and the Glen that I love. In time, Glen left and I was alone once again. There was nothing for it but to throw myself wholeheartedly into the loch. Since then I have devoted myself to good works in the neighbourhood, visiting the sick and the needy and finding similar simple entertainments.

*An unusual wedding.*

# LOOK WHO'S STALKING

| | |
|---|---|
| *Band plays* | *Sig tune up and under* |
| *Announcer* | *You'll Have Had Your Tea. The doings of Hamish and Dougal. Today, 'Look Who's Stalking'* |
| *Band plays* | *Sig tune up and oot* |
| | ***Knocking at door. Three times*** |
| DOUGAL | There, that's the shelf put up. |
| | ***Knock at door*** |
| DOUGAL | Jings, this is a noisy screwdriver. |
| | ***Knock at door*** |
| HAMISH | *[Off]* Hello! |
| DOUGAL | A talking screwdriver? This is devil's work. |
| | ***Door opens*** |
| HAMISH | Dougal, are you deaf? Or have you been at the paint stripper again? |
| DOUGAL | Certainly not. I only keep the twelve-year-old stuff for special occasions. |
| HAMISH | Now, isn't there something you're forgetting to ask me? |
| DOUGAL | Oh yes. Do you have a screwdriver that is not possessed by demons? |
| HAMISH | I'm afraid not. Where would I get a thing like that? |

*All in the day's work for a gillie! Hamish and Dougal push a boulder uphill to provide somewhere for the Laird to hide behind while he changes into a kilt.*

| | |
|---|---|
| DOUGAL | Well, that's all I had to ask you. |
| HAMISH | Really? Do the words kettle, pot, bags, milk, sugar and teacup bring anything to mind? |
| DOUGAL | Oh of course! Hamish, you'll have had your tea … |
| HAMISH | No, I've no time for that. Look here, have you seen what's in this morning's paper? |
| | *Paper rustle* |
| DOUGAL | Goodness me! I didn't even know you had a cat. |
| HAMISH | Oh, not that paper, this paper. |
| | *Paper rustle* |
| DOUGAL | Hmmm. Oh look at that! 'Local woman bursts into flames.' |
| HAMISH | No no, you're looking under 'Court and Social'. |
| DOUGAL | Oh! 'Dog eats garage'! |
| HAMISH | And it's not in the Sports Section either. Front page, man! |
| DOUGAL | Oh, that's dreadful! 'Price 50p'! |
| HAMISH | The headline! |
| DOUGAL | 'Local paper price hike'? |
| HAMISH | The one underneath! |
| DOUGAL | 'My stalker nightmare – by Beyonce Naughtie. Well-known housekeeper terrorised by Laird lookalike.' |
| HAMISH | Aye, that'll be Laird Lookalike of Auchtermuchty. |
| DOUGAL | Away, you great numpty! Laird Lookalike died in 1998. |
| HAMISH | You don't think they mean this stalker looked like our own dear Laird? |
| DOUGAL | In answer to that query, just take a look at this photograph. |
| HAMISH | That looks nothing like the Laird. |
| DOUGAL | That's Mrs Naughtie. I admit her face is very blurred. |
| HAMISH | Oh, I remember, that was taken just after the wine tasting. |
| DOUGAL | Aye, but peeping out of the bushes behind her is a familiar face … |
| HAMISH | Jings! I was never at that wine tasting. |
| DOUGAL | Quite. So that must be the Laird Lookalike wearing a Hamish-shaped mask! |
| HAMISH | And look! He's wearing the Laird's bonnet. I'd know that feather anywhere. |
| DOUGAL | With good reason … |

| | |
|---|---|
| HAMISH | Aye. Oh … you never forget a goose like that. |
| | *'The Birdy Song' ring-tone* |
| DOUGAL | Oh, that'll be my mobile. Avert your gaze while I pull it out. Mmyello? Oh!!! |
| HAMISH | What is it? |
| DOUGAL | It's his Lairdship! |
| HAMISH | Ask him if I can have the mask back. |
| DOUGAL | Sh! |
| HAMISH | What does he want? |
| DOUGAL | I've no idea. |
| HAMISH | Why don't you ask him? |
| DOUGAL | Oh yes. Ahem. What do you want, your Lairdship? Yes. Yes. Yes? Yes. Ye-ess. Yes! Yes! Yes. Yes. |
| HAMISH | What did he say? |
| DOUGAL | He just wants to know if it's me. |
| HAMISH | Ask him if he's seen his picture in the paper. |
| DOUGAL | Are you mad? Not you, your Lairdship, we all know that. We were just noticing there was absolutely nothing about you in this morning's edition of the *Glen Bugle*. Oh, you saw that on the front page, did you? I agree, it's a disgrace. 50p! Very good, sir, we'll see you shortly. Goodbye. |
| HAMISH | So, what did he want? |
| DOUGAL | I've no idea, he just said 'get your arses up to the Big Hoose without delay.' |
| HAMISH | Oh, not another of those parties … |
| *Band plays* | *Link* |
| LAIRD | … and the doctor said, 'I suggest you paint it blue and join the police!' |
| HAMISH & DOUGAL | *Laugh* |
| LAIRD | But that's enough about me. Hamish, I see you've got an empty glass. Let me get you another one. |
| | *Glass chink* |
| HAMISH | Oh, thank you. Another empty glass. |
| LAIRD | And there's more where that came from. Now, you're probably wondering why I sent for you. |
| DOUGAL | Well, we did think you might have explained over dinner last night. Or breakfast this morning … |
| LAIRD | The thing is, tomorrow sees the start of the stalking season. |
| HAMISH | Really …? |
| LAIRD | Oh yes. And it's no secret that I am a passionate stalker. |

| | |
|---|---|
| **DOUGAL** | Well … none of us are human. |
| **LAIRD** | I can't wait to get at it again. |
| **HAMISH** | He's frightening me … |
| **LAIRD** | In fact I've got a party of dedicated stalkers coming up from London. |
| **HAMISH** | The man's a monster! |
| **DOUGAL** | Mrs Naughtie won't be safe in her own bloomers. |
| **HAMISH** | We must warn her at once. |
| **DOUGAL** | You keep him talking, I'll … escape. |
| **LAIRD** | Oh Dougal, before you escape; a couple of days ago I was on my rounds when I heard voices plotting to poach my salmon. I leapt over the fence and caught my gillies in the gorse bush. |
| **HAMISH** | Jings! |
| **LAIRD** | Jings indeed, Hamish. So I got rid of them. |
| **DOUGAL** | Double jings. |
| **LAIRD** | I was sorry to lose them. People often admired my gillies, in fact I used to show them off on the Glorious Twelfth. |
| **HAMISH** | You'll miss them. |
| **LAIRD** | Not as much as I'll miss my two gamekeepers. And this is where you come in. I need someone to help me and my guests with the stalking. |
| **DOUGAL** | Stalking is against every principle that we hold most dear, but if there's money involved, you can count on us. |
| **LAIRD** | One, two. So I can. Let's shake on it. |
| **HAMISH** | Jings! That's a funny handshake. |
| **LAIRD** | Damn! I keep forgetting you're not mystical members of the Royal and Ancient Order of … I've said too much. Forget my funny handshake. |
| **HAMISH** | If only it were that easy. And I'd better readjust my sporran. |
| **LAIRD** | Very good, you two. Report for duty first thing. I want to see you there at quarter past sparrow-fart. |
| ***Band plays*** | ***Link*** |
| | ***Boing! Twang! Boing! Twang!*** |
| **MRS NAUGHTIE** | Wooo! Wheeeee! Whoopeeee! Wooo! |
| **DOUGAL** | A word with you, Mrs Naughtie, when you've finished your early morning bungee jump. |
| **MRS NAUGHTIE** | Help me down. |
| **HAMISH** | Where are those secateurs? |

*Clip. Twang. Whistle. Thud*

| | |
|---|---|
| MRS NAUGHTIE | Thank you. |
| DOUGAL | Well, that's brought the colour to your cheeks. |
| HAMISH | And your face has gone red as well. |
| MRS NAUGHTIE | It's the only thing that gets my juices going in the morning. |
| DOUGAL | Have you tried prunes? |
| MRS NAUGHTIE | Prunes and bungee jumping? I don't think so. |
| DOUGAL | Mrs Naughtie, we have a matter of some delicacy to discuss with you. |
| MRS NAUGHTIE | Oh, and which delicacy would that be? I haven't forgotten that business with your cocktail sausages. |

*Paper rustle*

| | |
|---|---|
| HAMISH | Mrs Naughtie, have you seen this? |
| MRS NAUGHTIE | Oh, you've got a cat. |
| HAMISH | Oh not again. Mrs N, cast an eye over my *Bugle*. |

*Punch*

| | |
|---|---|
| HAMISH | Ow! |
| DOUGAL | Look at the story here – 'My stalker nightmare – by Beyonce Naughtie. Well-known housekeeper terrorised by Laird Lookalike.' |
| MRS NAUGHTIE | It's all true. It all began one morning as I was putting the washing out. It had caught fire when I carelessly knocked out my pipe. Suddenly I saw a face peeping out of the gazebo. We have an outdoor one, you know. |
| DOUGAL | You must have been mortified. |
| MRS NAUGHTIE | No, I was stone cold sober. |
| HAMISH | What did you do? |
| MRS NAUGHTIE | I ran into the house and got my grandfather's old service revolver. By the time I got outside again ... |
| HAMISH | He was gone? |
| MRS NAUGHTIE | No, he was sitting in a deckchair with some sandwiches. We got chatting about this and that, and then he went away. |
| DOUGAL | But who was he? Did you recognise him? |
| MRS NAUGHTIE | Did I not mention that throughout our encounter, his face was hidden behind a copy of *Stalkers' World*. |
| DOUGAL | So you never saw him again. |
| MRS NAUGHTIE | I never saw him the first time. When he was gone I ran into the house, had a couple of stiff ones and got mortified off my face! |

'How will I manage to smoke this salmon?'
wonders Pipeman of the Year Bill McAllan.

| | |
|---|---|
| HAMISH | You poor wee soul. If we'd known what you were going through we'd have come and watched. |
| MRS NAUGHTIE | Well, it was soon after that the flowers and messages began. |
| HAMISH | What, every day? |
| MRS NAUGHTIE | Or as often as I could afford to. But he never replied. |
| DOUGAL | How did you know where to send them? |
| MRS NAUGHTIE | Och, everybody knows the Laird lives at the Big Hoose. |
| DOUGAL | Are you telling us your stalker was the Laird? |
| MRS NAUGHTIE | Yes. |
| HAMISH | But how do you know? |
| MRS NAUGHTIE | It was the phone calls. At first it was the heavy breathing, but once I'd got that under control, I was able to hear what he said. |
| DOUGAL | What did he say? |
| MRS NAUGHTIE | I recorded the last call he made. Listen! |
| | **Tape machine start. Hiss under** |
| LAIRD | **[Distort]** Hello, Mrs Naughtie, this is the Laird speaking. Whoops, as you were. Hello, Mrs Naughtie, this is ... Dougal speaking. Not the Laird. |
| DOUGAL | The swine! He's passing himself off. |
| MRS NAUGHTIE | That's what I thought. Disgusting. |
| LAIRD | **[Distort]** Yes, this is Dougal all right. And not the Laird as you might have thought. Now, Mrs Naughtie, what do you think of my Laird impression? |
| HAMISH | You're very good at this, Dougal. |
| DOUGAL | That's not me! Listen! |
| LAIRD | **[Distort]** I say, Mrs Naughtie, as a matter of interest ... what knickers are you wearing today? |
| MRS NAUGHTIE | **[Distort]** Oh, my favourites. The cerise flannel ones with reinforced double gusset and daffodils all over them right down to the knee. |
| LAIRD | **[Distort]** ... is there anyone else there I can speak to? |
| MRS NAUGHTIE | **[Distort]** Who is this? |
| LAIRD | **[Distort]** It's me. Not the Laird. |
| | **Click. Dial tone** |
| HAMISH | Well, we're no further on. |
| DOUGAL | Aye, the mystery deepens. |
| | **Phone rings** |
| DOUGAL | Leave this to me. |

*Phone pick up*

| | |
|---|---|
| DOUGAL | Myello? |
| LAIRD | *[Distort]* Hello. Dougal here. |
| DOUGAL | Oh really? Well, it's Dougal here as well. |
| LAIRD | Ah, well, glad to know neither of us is the Laird. Sorry, wrong number goodbye. |

*Click. Dial tone*

| | |
|---|---|
| HAMISH | Who was that? |
| DOUGAL | Only me. I'd dialled the wrong number. |
| HAMISH | We'll never find out who's been making Mrs Naughtie's life hell. |
| MRS NAUGHTIE | And you haven't seen what was pushed under my front door this morning. Look at this. |
| HAMISH | Oh my God! |
| DOUGAL | You don't see many of those north of the border. |
| HAMISH | And still warm. |
| MRS NAUGHTIE | Oh, I just want it to be over. |
| DOUGAL | I'm afraid it's only just begun, Mrs Naughtie. His Lairdship has invited a party of experienced stalkers up from London. |
| MRS NAUGHTIE | Experienced stalkers? Oh, look at me! I'd better change into my little backless kilt. |
| HAMISH | Away you go then. And this time be sure to get it the right way round. |

| | |
|---|---|
| *Band plays* | *Link* |
| | *Party hubbub, champagne corks popping etc* |
| LAIRD | Quiet, everybody. Now as you know, you're all here for a weekend stalking in the Glen. I think you know the routine. I've located a very attractive stag, and you've all got your binoculars, bunches of flowers and mobile phones, and a little something to slip under the door. Unfortunately I won't be able to join you. Following an unfortunate stalking incident last year, I've been served with a restraining order, which forbids me from going within 500 yards of any attractive stag. So I'll be staying here to keep Mrs Naughtie company, as I leave you in the capable hands of Hamish and Dougal, my trusty gillies. |
| DOUGAL | Just a minute! |
| LAIRD | Oh, is it on? I do love that Nicholas Parsons. You can't imagine anyone else doing it the way he does. |
| HAMISH | Your Lairdship, we have a bone to pick with you. |

*Lord Raglan, up for the shooting, takes advantage of one of the many outdoor toilets dotted about the moor. He is attended by Big Tam, the plumber.*

| | |
|---|---|
| LAIRD | I've just had lunch. Off you all go. |
| DOUGAL | Oh, very well. Follow me. |
| | ***Cheers, hunting horn, gunshots etc fading*** |
| LAIRD | So, Mrs Naughtie, alone at last. |
| MRS NAUGHTIE | You certainly are! |
| | ***Footsteps running off*** |
| LAIRD | Come back! Women! I'll never understand them. Now, before my fellow members of the Royal and Ancient Order arrive, I shall just have time to polish my regalia. |
| ***Band plays*** | ***Link*** |
| | ***Moor atmos, wind*** |
| ROB (G) | Buffy Capstick! |
| CAP (B) | Good Lord, Disgusting Robinson. When was the last time? |
| ROB | Behind the bicycle sheds on Founders Day. |
| CAP | So it was. Did you ever find those handcuffs? |
| ROB | Did I ever! |
| CAP | Well, while we're waiting for that stag to show up, would you care for a bite? |
| ROB | You smooth-talking rascal. |
| CAP | Now let's see what we've got in here. |
| | ***Paper rustling*** |
| CAP | *[Cont.]* Well, I've got tuna baps and oatmeal dumplings. |
| ROB | But you keep smiling. Can I offer you a dram? |
| CAP | Most kind. Oh, is that a new flask? |
| ROB | Yes. I had a hip flask replacement last summer. But isn't that a doily peeping out of your waistcoat? |
| CAP | Yes, I had a lace-maker fitted last month. |
| ROB | You lucky dog. |
| CAP | Where have those two gillies got to? |
| ROB | Here they come now. |
| CAP | I can't wait to hear what they've got to say for themselves. |
| DOUGAL | Ah, there you are, gentlemen. I see you're enjoying each other's baps and dumplings. |
| ROB | That's no concern of yours. |
| CAP | It's a private matter. |
| ROB | Now have you spotted this stag yet? |
| HAMISH | We have indeed. He's just up there on the horizon. |
| ROB | I can't see him. |

| | |
|---|---|
| HAMISH | No, that horizon. |
| ROB | Oh yes. Fine looking beast … |
| DOUGAL | Fine looking beast … |
| CAP | Fine looking beast … |
| HAMISH | Fine looking beast … |
| ALL | Fine looking beast. |
| DOUGAL | Well, I'm glad all four of us are agreed on that. |
| ROB | Oh yes. Fine looking beast … |
| DOUGAL | Fine looking beast … |
| CAP | Fine looking beast … |
| HAMISH | Fine looking beast … |
| ALL | Fine looking beast. |
| | ***Rifles cocked*** |
| HAMISH | What on earth are you doing? |
| ROB | We're cocking our rifles. |
| HAMISH | But I thought stalking was all flowers and phone calls. |
| ROB | No, that's just the foreplay. |
| | ***Bang! Bang! Ricochet*** |
| LAIRD | *[Off]* Steady on, you nearly hit me! |
| HAMISH | That stag spoke! |
| DOUGAL | With the voice of the Laird. |
| HAMISH | It's coming towards us. |
| | ***Bang! Bang! Ricochet*** |
| LAIRD | Stop that! It's me. |
| DOUGAL | We can see it's you. But why are you speaking in the Laird's voice, stag? |
| LAIRD | I am the Laird. |
| H&D&R&C | So he is. |
| LAIRD | Hello, you four. Has anyone seen Mrs Naughtie? |
| CAP | Course we have. She was the centrefold in last month's *Housekeeping Babes*. |
| ROB | And I believe I just saw her taking a bath in a mountain stream. |
| LAIRD | Splendid! Well, that's my afternoon taken care of. |
| | ***Hooves clip clop off*** |
| | ***Bang! Bang! Ricochet!*** |
| LAIRD | *[Off]* Will you stop that? |
| ROB & CAP | Sorry! |
| ***Band plays*** | ***Link*** |
| HAMISH | Dougal? |
| DOUGAL | Yes, Hamish? |

| | |
|---|---|
| HAMISH | That was one of the most bizarre afternoons I can ever remember. |
| DOUGAL | Aye. What on earth could have been behind the Laird's strange behaviour? |
| | ***Knock at door – door opens*** |
| LAIRD | Hamish! Dougal! You must have been wondering what on earth could have been behind my strange behaviour. |
| HAMISH | No no, we hardly noticed. |
| DOUGAL | Completely passed us by. |
| LAIRD | Nevertheless, I think I owe you an explanation. You see, I have long been a member of the Royal and Ancient Order of Stags. |
| HAMISH | Ah, now it all falls into place. |
| LAIRD | Oh good. Well, now you're comfy, I'll continue. The thing is, I was recently installed as Grand High Worshipful Pointy Antler. |
| DOUGAL | Aha! So that's why you were out on the moor dressed as a wild stag. |
| LAIRD | No no, that's just a little role-play thing I've got going with Mrs Naughtie. |
| | ***Door opens*** |
| MRS NAUGHTIE | I thought I recognised that voice! My Big Stag! |
| LAIRD | Ho ho, my wee Nymph of the Glen! |
| HAMISH | Dougal, I feel a complete gooseberry. |
| DOUGAL | I'm sorry, I must have left it on the chair. |
| HAMISH | So what are we going to do now? |
| LAIRD | Well, I don't know about you, but I'm so happy I could sing! |
| HAMISH | Dougal! Do something! |
| | ***Gunshots. Ricochets*** |
| LAIRD | No! Yaroo, you rotters! |
| | ***Clip clop hooves clatter about*** |
| ALL | Ha ha ha ha ha! |
| | ***More gunshots. Ricochets*** |
| ***Band plays*** | ***Music up and oot*** |

***THE END***

# PORRIDGE VOTES!

| | |
|---|---|
| *Band plays* | *Sig tune up and under* |
| Announcer | *You'll Have Had Your Tea. The doings of Hamish and Dougal. Today, 'Porridge Votes!'* |
| *Band plays* | *Sig tune up and oot* |
| | *Street atmos, van driving along* |
| LAIRD | *[Loudhailer]* Good morning, everybody. This is your Laird shouting at you. As you know we are in the run-up to the local by-election, and I'm sure you all know exactly how you are going to vote for me. Just write my name next to the cross on your ballot paper. You also know what we stand for, in the Countryside Christian Phalangist Jackboot on the Necks of the Poor Soft-hearted Reform Liberal Party. And remember, thanks to the Electoral Register, I know where you live. |
| | *Click* |
| | *Knock on door* |
| DOUGAL | *[Off]* Come in. |
| | *Door opens* |
| HAMISH | Dougal! |
| DOUGAL | Hamish. You'll have had your tea … |
| HAMISH | I've had it up to here! Did you hear his Lairdship just then, canvassing for the election? |
| DOUGAL | I could hardly miss it! |
| HAMISH | The Countryside Christian Phalangist Jackboot on the Necks of the Poor Soft-hearted Reform Liberal Party indeed! |
| DOUGAL | Can you explain that in words of one syllable? |
| HAMISH | Aye, the first one. |
| LAIRD | *[Loudhailer]* Could you pass that plate of fairy cakes please? |
| HAMISH | Oh, your Lairdship, I didn't see you sitting there. |
| LAIRD | *[Loudhailer]* Yes, I'm out canvassing. |
| HAMISH | I thought that was you driving past in the van. |
| LAIRD | *[Loudhailer]* Oh no, that's why I've got the loudhailer. I can do my canvassing in comfort. Two lumps please. |
| DOUGAL | I tell you this, Hamish, I shall be glad when this by-election is over and done with. |
| HAMISH | Me too. Have you decided which way you're voting? |

*Scary Mary, the mad wee pest o' the Glen.*

| | |
|---|---|
| DOUGAL | That's a private matter. It's a secret ballot, Hamish. Even the Prime Minister's bodyguards leave him to it when he's inside that Booth. The truth is I'm undecided at the moment, I could swing in any direction. I might go for the Independent: Big Tam Berlusconi. He's giving away ice creams and offering free sprinkles. |
| HAMISH | Thanks for the warning. |
| DOUGAL | Aye. Big Tam's promised a chicken in every pot … |
| HAMISH | And a haggis in every chicken … |
| DOUGAL | And a horse's head on every pillow. |
| HAMISH | Good old Big Daft Tam. I didn't realise he'd been released into the community. |
| DOUGAL | He's the best of a bad bunch. A parcel of rogues, the lot of them. |
| HAMISH | They should be taken out and shot. |
| DOUGAL | That's too good for them. I'd shoot them first, and then take them out. |
| HAMISH | Aye, for a spot of dinner and dancing … |
| DOUGAL | And then I'd shoot them again. |
| HAMISH | Damn them all! |
| LAIRD | *[Loudhailer]* So, can I count on your votes on Thursday? |
| HAMISH | Oh your Lairdship, I'd forgotten you were there. |
| LAIRD | *[Loudhailer]* Well I can't stay here all day; those widows and orphans aren't going to threaten themselves. Goodbye. |
| DOUGAL | Goodbye, your Lairdship. |
| LAIRD | *[Loudhailer]* I'll let myself out. |
| DOUGAL | Not in here you won't! |
| | ***Door open and shut*** |
| HAMISH | I thought he'd never go. |
| LAIRD | *[Loudhailer – off]* I heard that! |
| DOUGAL | Oh! I've half a mind to stand against the Laird and run for the seat myself. |
| HAMISH | Well you'll have my vote as long as you don't put your back out. |
| DOUGAL | But no, Hamish. The cut and thrust of political life is not for the likes of you and me. |
| HAMISH | No. |
| | ***Door opens*** |

| | |
|---|---|
| MRS NAUGHTIE | *[Loudhailer]* If you've finished with the tea things, I'll clear away. |
| DOUGAL | What's this, Mrs Naughtie? Don't tell me you're hitting the campaign trail as well! |
| MRS NAUGHTIE | *[Loudhailer]* I certainly am. I lodged my deposit first thing after breakfast. |
| HAMISH | Oh, do sit down, my dear. |
| MRS NAUGHTIE | *[Loudhailer]* I've no time for that. As soon as I've done these dishes, I'll be spending the afternoon on the stump. |
| HAMISH | Aye, those fishcakes have a mind of their own. |
| DOUGAL | What party do you represent, Mrs Naughtie? |
| MRS NAUGHTIE | *[Loudhailer]* Our local ladies have been martyrs to static electricity lately. That's why we have formed Women Against Nylon Knitwear. |
| HAMISH | So that's W. A. N … have you thought this through Mrs Naughtie. |
| MRS NAUGHTIE | *[Loudhailer]* Yes, we were going to call ourselves Scissor Sisters, but we felt that was rather rude. Vote for Naughtie, ladies! Get the sparks off your chest! Vote for me! |
| | ***Door shuts*** |
| DOUGAL | Oh, this is terrible. Now there's two of them! |
| LAIRD & MRS NAUGHTIE | *[Loudhailer]* We both heard that! |
| HAMISH | We can't have either of them winning the seat. |
| DOUGAL | Neither one of them is fit to lick the bootlaces of our dear ex-MP, wee Jock Asbo. |
| HAMISH | He was a character. |
| DOUGAL | Aye. He was great on television. |
| HAMISH | *Crimewatch UK.* |
| DOUGAL | More than once. What's he doing now? |
| HAMISH | Three years. |
| DOUGAL | A travesty of justice. It wasn't his fault his insurance company burned down. |
| HAMISH | Dougal, it's up to you to fill his shoes. |
| DOUGAL | Oh, I don't know. I did it once and he wasn't too pleased. |
| HAMISH | No! You must answer the call! |
| DOUGAL | Yes. And when I've finished, I'll put myself forward. |
| HAMISH | And I'll be your right hand. |

*Pastrycook Davy Mutch ices the village for a bet.*

| | |
|---|---|
| DOUGAL | I can see it now. |
| LAIRD | *[Loudhailer]* We all can! |
| HAMISH | Comes the moment, comes the man. |
| | ***Knock at door*** |
| DOUGAL | Who is it? |
| MAN | It's the man. |
| DOUGAL | Go away. |
| HAMISH | Parliament, here you come! |
| DOUGAL | Aye. And now I must away and polish up my manifesto. |
| HAMISH | I'll draw the curtains. |
| ***Band plays*** | ***Link*** |
| | ***Street atmos*** |
| MRS NAUGHTIE | Good afternoon, Mr Hamish. |
| HAMISH | Good afternoon, my good woman. I didn't recognise you without your loudhailer. |
| MRS NAUGHTIE | No. It hasn't been the same since I used it to strain the sprouts. But I hope I can count on your support. |
| HAMISH | You keep your hands to yourself. |
| MRS NAUGHTIE | Oh Mr Hamish, I'm still the same woman I was when I put you over my knee in the nursery. |
| HAMISH | That was last week, this is now. And Mr Dougal is my man in the upcoming battle of the ballots. |
| MRS NAUGHTIE | And this is his campaign headquarters, is it? |
| HAMISH | Yes, since they cancelled the bus, we thought we'd use the shelter. |
| MRS NAUGHTIE | Are you getting many supporters? |
| HAMISH | Well, it gets a bit quiet, and then three come along at once. |
| MRS NAUGHTIE | Well, may the best man win. |
| LAIRD | *[Loudhailer]* And here I am. Hello, you two … |
| HAMISH | Oh God, here he comes … |
| LAIRD | *[Loudhailer]* What are you up to behind the bus shelter? Having a snog? |
| HAMISH | No, this is the headquarters of Dougal's Scot-kip Party. |
| LAIRD | *[Loudhailer] [Amplified aside]* Poor deluded fool, he's got no chance against my vote-rigging skills. Oooh, that reminds me, I've got a 50,000 majority to pop in the post. Oh power, the great aphrodisiac! Come along, Mrs Naughtie, let's find some mud and have a wrestle. |

| | |
|---|---|
| MRS NAUGHTIE | What? |
| LAIRD | [*Loudhailer*] You'll find it's all part of the rough and tumble of politics. |
| MRS NAUGHTIE | Oooh! Against my better judgement, I must decline your kind offer. |
| | ***Feet running away*** |
| LAIRD | [*Loudhailer*] Come back! Don't be a stranger to bliss! I've knocked up hundreds of women voters. |
| | ***More feet running away*** |
| HAMISH | Kids! Now let's see if Dougal's in. |
| | ***Knock at door*** |
| DOUGAL | [*Off*] I can't hear that, there's no door on this bus shelter. |
| KIRSTY | Good afternoon. Who shall I say it is? |
| HAMISH | I've no idea, I've never seen you before. |
| DOUGAL | Ah, Hamish, say hello to my new personal secretary, Kirsty McWirsty. |
| KIRSTY | How do you do, and there's nothing going on. |
| HAMISH | I should hope not. People are going to put two and two together … |
| KIRSTY | We're not into foursomes either. |
| HAMISH | How about an eightsome? |
| KIRSTY | And we're not at home to Mrs Funny Business. |
| HAMISH | I should hope not. I wouldn't want to see Dougal splashed all over the front page and hung out to dry by the tabloids. |
| DOUGAL | I have nothing to hide. Here's my leaflet. |
| HAMISH | Let me see: <br> 'Clean as a whistle <br> Sharp as a thistle <br> Goodbye to sleaze <br> Vote for me please. <br> Vote for Dongal.' |
| DOUGAL | I'll kill that printer! |
| KIRSTY | If you want me I shall be out the back in the mud patch. |
| | ***Sploosh!*** |
| HAMISH | Where did you find her? |
| DOUGAL | I'd gone to the park to read my copy of *The Lady*, and I was leafing through the bushes when I spied her sunbathing. |

| | |
|---|---|
| HAMISH | Topless? |
| DOUGAL | No no, I was wearing a hat. |
| HAMISH | I hope nothing happened. |
| DOUGAL | Well put it this way, we were soon back to basics. |
| HAMISH | Just be careful. Any hint of carryings-on, and you're finished before you've even started. |
| DOUGAL | Funnily enough, that's what she said. Right, it's time I did some doorstepping. Come on. |
| **Band plays** | **Link** |
| DOUGAL | Well, here we are in the village high street. |
| HAMISH | I know that. |
| DOUGAL | Let the door stepping commence. |
| | ***Knock knock. Feet running. Ding dong. Feet running. Door knocker. Feet running. Doorbell. Feet running. Westminster chime doorbell. Feet running. Knock knock. Feet running*** |
| DOUGAL | Oh, that was good fun. |
| HAMISH | Dougal, aren't you supposed to wait for them to open the door? |
| DOUGAL | Then they'd know who it was! |
| HAMISH | That's the point. They want to get the measure of you. |
| DOUGAL | Oh … all right then. |
| | ***Door knock. Door opens. Scream! Door slam*** |
| HAMISH | OK. When I said 'get the measure of you', I didn't mean … oh, never mind. |
| DOUGAL | Now let's see, there's only one house left. |
| HAMISH | No number but … oh look, 'Berchtesgarten. |
| | ***Riffling through register*** |
| DOUGAL | Oh yes, Mr and Mrs McBigot. |
| HAMISH | Oh yes, *Daily Mail* on the doorstep, and a pint of semi-skimmed bile. |
| DOUGAL | And a sign, look: 'No Circulars, No Hawkers, No Beggars, and No Progress of Any Kind' |
| HAMISH | They sound like a couple of floaters to me. |
| DOUGAL | Well, here goes. |
| | ***'Land of Hope and Glory' door chime*** |
| | ***Door opens*** |
| MR McB | Who are you? Are you religious fanatics? |
| DOUGAL | Certainly not! |
| MR McB | Well we are. Piss off! |
| | ***Door slam*** |

| | |
|---|---|
| HAMISH | Put them down as a yes. |
| DOUGAL | So far so good. |
| HAMISH | We've just got to be sure we get your message across. I could be your chiropractor! |
| DOUGAL | What? |
| HAMISH | Your spine doctor. |
| DOUGAL | That's spin doctor, you great tumshie! |
| HAMISH | Who cares? Come on. It's all over bar the shouting. |
| LAIRD | *[Loudhailer]* Vote for me, everybody, or I'll release the hounds. |
| MRS NAUGHTIE | *[Loudhailer]* Vote for me, ladies, this is my Pledge, and this is my J Cloth. And now, some handy hints around the home … |
| HAMISH | I hope we don't get to see her Flash. |
| DOUGAL | Right, time for my keynote speech. Pass me that tuning fork. |
| | *Ping!* |
| DOUGAL | Me me me me. Vote for me me me me. Fellow voters, I stand before you … |
| LAIRD | *[Loudhailer]* Sit down, you're pissed. |
| DOUGAL | I stand before you as one of you. |
| MRS NAUGHTIE | *[Loudhailer]* I always had you down as one of them. |
| DOUGAL | Nevertheless, we are all sick and tired of Punch and Judy politics … |
| LAIRD | *[Loudhailer]* That's the way to do it! Ha ha ha! |
| DOUGAL | But wait till you see what I've got to offer you. |
| MRS NAUGHTIE | *[Loudhailer]* Been there, seen that, not impressed. Oh I am enjoying myself. |
| LAIRD | *[Loudhailer]* Why, what are you doing? |
| LAIRD & MRS NAUGHTIE | *[Laugh]* |
| DOUGAL | These are serious matters, and, if you join my party … |
| HAMISH | If it's anything like your Christmas Party, count me out. |
| DOUGAL | My party … |
| HAMISH | I've had more fun at the dentist's. |
| DOUGAL | My party … |
| HAMISH | When you promised us a buffet with things on sticks, I didn't know you meant your parents. |
| LAIRD & MRS NAUGHTIE | *[Laugh]* Oh that's a good one! Oh that's funny. etc |

| | |
|---|---|
| HAMISH | Your mother is so ugly her reflection looks the other way. |
| LAIRD & MRS NAUGHTIE | *Laugh* |
| HAMISH | Your mother is so fat, when she walks down the street, the mice jump into the chemist's shop! |
| LAIRD & MRS NAUGHTIE | *More laughter* |
| DOUGAL | Hamish, you haven't quite got the hang of this electioneering, have you? |
| HAMISH | Oh, I've got plenty more up my sleeve! |
| DOUGAL | Hamish, you're supposed to be on my side. |
| HAMISH | Oh, don't tell me I've got it wrong again. Oh deary me. |
| DOUGAL | Now don't take on. You just go and lie down in a darkened room, and I'll be along in a minute to beat the living daylights out of you. |
| HAMISH | It'll be just like old times. |
| DOUGAL | Yes. And in conclusion, ladies and gentlemen, don't be deceived by the Laird's right-wing neo-fascist rants about VAT on children's clothing. And don't be seduced by wishy-washy woolly Mrs Naughtie's promise of free shortbread. The polls open first thing tomorrow. Be there, and vote for me. |
| HAMISH | He's right you know. 'Just let me spin it, and Dougal will win it!' |
| DOUGAL | That's not a very good slogan, Hamish. |
| HAMISH | Well, what do you expect from a chiropractor? |
| *Band plays* | *Link* |
| DOUGAL | Well, here we are at the polling station. |
| HAMISH | You're doing it again. |
| DOUGAL | Now to cast our votes. Are the photographers here? |
| ROB | Aye, Rob from the *Bugle*. Can you get a move on? It's half-day closing and I need to get to the chemist's. |
| DOUGAL | Ah yes, to get the film developed? |
| ROB | No, to pick up my special ointment. |
| DOUGAL | Right, Hamish, into the polling booth. |
| | *Curtain swish. Heavy disco music* |
| DOUGAL | What's that? |
| HAMISH | That's the pole. But who is that? |
| DOUGAL | That's Kirsty McWirsty! |
| HAMISH | She's giving that pole a fair old polish. |

| | |
|---|---|
| DOUGAL | I don't like the look of this. |
| HAMISH | You speak for yourself. |
| DOUGAL | If you ask me, we've been set up! |
| ROB | Right, everybody – a nice startled look for the camera. Everyone smile and say 'Jings!' |
| ALL | Jings! |
| ROB | Hold it right there. |
| DOUGAL | Not you, Kirsty! |
| ROB | Too late! |
| | *Camera flash and camera motor drive to wind on the film and not to be confused with the sound of a car driving off* |
| *Band plays* | *Link* |
| DOUGAL | Oh Hamish, thanks to the other side's dirty tricks, I am Donald Ducked. |
| HAMISH | No no, the people know what you're really like. |
| DOUGAL | That's the problem. |
| HAMISH | Come along, Dougal, look the world in the face, and come out fighting. |
| | *Punch* |
| DOUGAL | Aye, that feels better. Come on, Hamish, they'll be announcing the election result any minute. |
| *Band plays* | *Link* |
| | *Crowd atmos* |
| RETURNING OFFICER | As returning officer for the constituency of Inverapenny, I declare the votes cast are as follows: Tara Palmer Tompkinson … |
| COMENTATOR | 24 Hour Party. |
| RET | 69. Jeffrey Archer … |
| COMM | Day Release Working Party. |
| RET | 5,633 … he says. The Crankies … |
| COMM | Fandabedozie Party. |
| RET | 2 votes. Sir Sean Connery … |
| COMM | Scottish Nationals in the Bahamas Party. |
| RET | Shix hundred and sheventy-shix. George Galloway … |
| COMM | Suspect Party. |
| RET | 476 votes for Moustache of the Year. His Lairdship the McCoist of McCoist of that ilk … |
| COMM | Countryside Christian Phalangist Jackboot on the Necks of the Poor Soft-hearted Reform Liberal Party. |

| | |
|---|---|
| RET | Minus 12 votes. |
| LAIRD | Bugger! Here, what happened to the 50,000 postal votes I sent in? |
| RET | You should have put stamps on them. |
| LAIRD | Damn you! Just because I'm a laird you think I'm made of stamps! |
| RET | Ms Beoncie Naughtie … |
| COMM | W A N … Knitwear Party. |
| RET | 15,501 votes. |
| MRS NAUGHTIE | Yippee! |
| RET | Dougal McDougal … |
| COMM | 24 Hour Opening Alliance. |
| HAMISH | This is it! |
| RET | 15,502 votes. |
| HAMISH | Yes! |
| DOUGAL | I'd like to thank the returning officer, and the police for turning a blind eye … |
| RET | I haven't finished yet. |
| ALL | What? |
| RET | Ms Kirsty McWirsty … |
| COMM | Spin on This Party. |
| RET | 328,978. And I hereby declare that Kirsty McWirsty is the duly elected member for this constituency, and don't forget your promise, Kirsty! |
| *Band plays* | *'For She's a Jolly Good Fellow.'* |
| | *Glasses clinking* |
| LAIRD | Quiet now, everybody. I'd like to thank you all for coming along to the wedding at such short notice. On behalf of my dear wife Kirsty and myself, I'd especially like to thank Mrs Naughtie for being such a splendid matron of honour, and of course Hamish and Dougal for stepping in at the last minute as the bridesmaids. |
| KIRSTY | You tell 'em, tiger! |
| LAIRD | I'm telling them, dear. We make a formidable husband and wife team, like the Hamiltons with sex, and tomorrow who knows, it could be Number Ten. In fact it will be, as you're my wife Number Nine. |
| HAMISH | Shall we away home and drown our sorrows? |
| DOUGAL | No, let's stay here and drown the Laird. |

| | |
|---|---|
| LAIRD | Come on, you two, this is no time for bitterness … Not on this, our special day. Oh I'm so happy … I could sing! |
| *Band plays & Laird* | *'Things Can Only Get Better'* |
| HAMISH & DOUGAL & MRS NAUGHTIE | No! Stop him! etc etc! |
| | *Splash!* |
| LAIRD | *Gurgles his way through the song … then gives up the struggle* |
| | *Splash!!* |
| HAMISH & DOUGAL & MRS NAUGHTIE | Hooray! |
| *Band plays* | *Sig tune up and oot* |

**THE END**

# THE GREAT GLEN DISASTER

'Twas in the year of Our Lord eighteen hundred and
eighty nine,
Which will be remembered for a very long time,
There was gloom on many faces
With news of scattered showers and snow in high places.
Young Alistair McKuik who was out for a stroll
Unexpectedly tripped over a sausage roll.
As he fell with a cry, he seized hold of the fence,
Which crashed to the ground with a clatter immense.
The noise startled some sheep, whose panic was large
And they leaped into the canal and on to a barge.
The bargee, a man Allan Dooley by name,
Lost control of his craft, which was a great shame.
It crashed into the lock gates with a mighty sound,
Causing considerable flooding for yards around.
Two collies were drowned, I'm sorry to say,
And their funeral was held on the following Wednesday.
The grief of the owners was tragic to see,
The next week one threw a brick at the local MP.
The other became a nun, the poor wee soul
And all because of a sausage roll.
To this day, folk still speak of the great disaster,
Which makes them weep and their hearts beat faster
And fills them full of the most painful woe
And often spoils the mood of the weekly bingo.

MORRIS MCGONAGALL (NO RELATION)

*Village vet Wullie Bonnet, at his road-kill clinic,*
*hears the news that over 30 fish have been drowned in the flood*

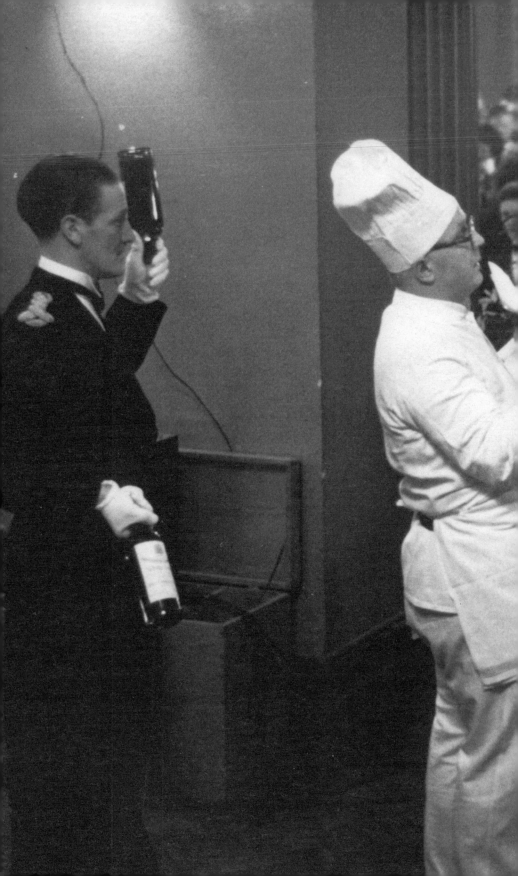

# BURNS NIGHT SPECIAL

Burns Night!

# BURNS NIGHT!

| | |
|---|---|
| *Band plays* | *Sig tune up and under* |
| *Announcer* | *You'll Have Had Your Tea. The doings of Hamish and Dougal. Today, 'Burns Night!'* |
| *Band plays* | *Sig tune up and oot* |
| | *Knock knock* |
| **DOUGAL** | Oh, who can this be? |
| **HAMISH** | *[Off]* It's me! |
| **DOUGAL** | I was talking to myself! |
| **HAMISH** | *[Off]* So was I! |
| **DOUGAL** | What do you want? |
| **HAMISH** | *[Off]* Who are you talking to now? |
| **DOUGAL** | You you great numpty! What do you want? |
| **HAMISH** | *[Off]* Oh, I'm fed up with shouting through this letterbox. |
| **DOUGAL** | Why have your brought a letterbox? |
| **HAMISH** | In case the post comes while I'm out. |
| **DOUGAL** | But if it does, the postie will just push your letters through the door. |
| **HAMISH** | He can't. |

*Moira Baxter entertains on her mutton harmonica.*

| | |
|---|---|
| DOUGAL | Why not? |
| HAMISH | I've got the letterbox here with me! You great thickie. |
| DOUGAL | Oh, come in, for goodness' sake. |
| | *Door opens and shuts* |
| HAMISH | At last. |
| DOUGAL | Ah Hamish, there you are. You'll have had your tea … |
| HAMISH | Yes, I had a cup while I was waiting. Euch, no sugar! When will I ever learn? |
| DOUGAL | Now just put down that stupid letterbox. |
| HAMISH | Aye. Wait a minute, there's a letter here for you. |
| | *Spang!* |
| HAMISH | Must have gone to the wrong address. |
| DOUGAL | Oh jings! Callum the Postie needs his eye testing. |
| HAMISH | How's that going to help when he can't read nor write? |
| DOUGAL | Now, let's turn our attention to this letter. |
| HAMISH | Aye, who's it from? |
| | *Letter ripped open. Rip. Ripriprip. Riiiip. Rip rip rip!* |
| DOUGAL | Now we'll never know. |
| HAMISH | Wait a minute: give me the pieces. We can stick it. |
| DOUGAL | My sentiments precisely. |
| HAMISH | No no no, stick it together with this handy roll of sticky-backed plastic. |
| | *Sellotape zips, rustle of paper* |
| HAMISH | There. It's from the Laird. |
| DOUGAL | Oh. |
| | *Letter ripped open. Rip. Ripriprip. Riiiip. Rip rip rip!* |
| HAMISH | Why have you torn it up again? |
| DOUGAL | It'll just be another of his hare-brained projects he wants to lumber us with. |
| LAIRD | Hello? Is anybody in? |
| HAMISH | Jings! It's the Laird, shouting through my letterbox. |
| LAIRD | Hamish! Is that you? |
| HAMISH | Yes, but I'm not at home. |
| LAIRD | Damn! Where are you? |
| HAMISH | I'm round at Dougal's. |
| LAIRD | Top-hole! I'll be over in five minutes. Ciao! |
| *Band plays* | *Link* |
| HAMISH | I always loved that tune. |
| DOUGAL | How that got to be the Christmas Number One I'll never know. Now put away your iPod, the Laird's going to be here in five minutes! |

259

*Door opens*

| | |
|---|---|
| MRS NAUGHTIE | Oh my aching feet. I'm a martyr to bunions! |
| DOUGAL | Tomato and onions? Put them in the fridge. |
| HAMISH | Mrs Naughtie! What are you doing here? This is Tuesday. You normally have it off. |
| MRS NAUGHTIE | True, but don't tell me you've forgotten the date. |
| DOUGAL | The date? Which one of us were you expecting to …? |
| MRS NAUGHTIE | No no no! This is Twelfth Night. I've come to take down your fripperies. |
| HAMISH | But we're not wearing any. |
| MRS NAUGHTIE | So I see. And may I suggest you put some clothes on before his Lairdship arrives. |
| DOUGAL | We're just this minute out of the jacuzzi. |
| MRS NAUGHTIE | I didn't know you'd got a jacuzzi. |
| DOUGAL | Well, it wasn't until Hamish got into it. |
| HAMISH | Oh, be fair, it was my sporran full of Refreshers that did it. |
| DOUGAL | Aye. More than once. |
| MRS NAUGHTIE | Now come along! Let's get rid of these decorations. |
| DOUGAL | But I always wear them on special occasions. |
| MRS NAUGHTIE | And very smart you look, wreathed in paper chains with a fairy on your hat. |
| HAMISH | And his baubles swinging in the breeze. |
| MRS NAUGHTIE | But it's bad luck to wear them. |
| DOUGAL | After Twelfth Night? |
| MRS NAUGHTIE | No, in public. And Mr Hamish, you can let down the inflatable Santa. |
| HAMISH | Right you are. |

*Lengthy fart sequence*

| | |
|---|---|
| HAMISH | Right. Now where's that inflatable Santa? |

*Door opens*

| | |
|---|---|
| LAIRD | Hello, everyone! Do you mind if I open a window? |
| DOUGAL | Carry on. |

*Glass smash*

| | |
|---|---|
| LAIRD | Ah, that's better. Now, Dougal, I sent you a letter. I hope you haven't torn it up. |
| DOUGAL | Your Lairdship, I cannot tell a lie. What letter? |
| LAIRD | The letter that arrived this morning. |
| DOUGAL | Oh, that letter? It was delivered to Hamish by mistake. |
| HAMISH | So I brought it straight to Dougal. |
| DOUGAL | And I got the letter in the end … |
| HAMISH | And then you tore it up. |

| | |
|---|---|
| DOUGAL | Yes. No, I read it with great interest. |
| LAIRD | Good. So what's your answer. |
| DOUGAL | Well, the answer is … yes … that is it would have been yes if not for the proviso that, had you sent it yesterday, then definitely yes or even no, depending of course on the exact terms I would say yes … or not, if when the … when the answer you are eh … the answer is … possibly … conditions are such that … such and such … then I say to you … as I expect you want to hear … To hear our answer which is … quite simply … this answer … is … is … is … |
| | *Long farting sequence* |
| LAIRD | Hamish! |
| HAMISH | I'm just letting down Santa. |
| DOUGAL | Hamish, you're letting everybody down. |
| LAIRD | Look here, as you'll remember from my letter, I am planning a big party for everyone in the Glen. We are going to celebrate Burns Night. |
| HAMISH | But November the 5th is months away. |
| LAIRD | We commemorate the birth of our Scottish National Poet Rabbie Burns on January 25th. Will you two organise the traditional Burns Night Supper? Yes or no? Yes? Splendid. Over to you. Goodbye. |
| | *Whoosh!* |
| *Band plays* | *Link* |
| | *Echoey atmos. Footsteps* |
| DOUGAL | Well, here we are in the public library. |
| HAMISH | I know that. |
| DOUGAL | No, it's the title of that book there. 'Well, here we are in the Public Library.' By E. Nesbitt. |
| HAMISH | Which book? |
| DOUGAL | That one on the shelf … |
| HAMISH | Here in the public library? |
| DOUGAL | Yes. |
| HAMISH | Dougal, why are we here in the public library? |
| DOUGAL | We are here … in the public library, to find out what the hell is Burns Night. |
| HAMISH | Oh look, here's a book: *What the Hell is Burns Night.* |
| DOUGAL | Who's it by? And this better be funny! |
| HAMISH | It's called *What the Hell is Burns Night* by His Royal Highness the Duke of Edinburgh. |
| DOUGAL | You made that up. |

| HAMISH | No, he really exists. |
| DOUGAL | Duke of Edinburgh, eh? He should know what he's talking about, being a Scotsman. |
| HAMISH | I thought he was German … |
| DOUGAL | He's no more German than Zorba the Greek. Give me that book. We'll find all we need in here. |
| HAMISH | Let's hope so, because I've never heard of Burns Night. |
| DOUGAL | Of course you haven't. You're a Scotsman. Burns Night is an old English tradition invented by foreigners. |
| HAMISH | Where is it celebrated? |
| DOUGAL | Everywhere but Scotland. Come on, we'd better get this book home and start boning up. |
| HAMISH | Don't worry, I've already started! |
| *Band plays* | *Link* |
| MRS NAUGHTIE | All right, you two, that's enough boning up. You ought to be poring over this book. |
| HAMISH | That's just what we've been doing! |
| DOUGAL | That's right, and now we know exactly how to organise the perfect Burns Night celebration. Mrs Naughtie, you will be in charge of Burns Night catering. |
| MRS NAUGHTIE | Very well, I shall serve a delicious seafood platter with sauce Marie Rose and mixed leaf salad … |
| HAMISH | Oh no, the book says it has to be the traditional meal. Haggis. |
| MRS NAUGHTIE | And what might that be, may I ask? |
| DOUGAL | It's a traditional dish the English believe we eat. |
| MRS NAUGHTIE | Oh, like a deep-fried Mars bar? |
| HAMISH | No thanks, I've just had three. |
| | *Fart* |
| HAMISH | Santa! |
| DOUGAL | Apparently the vegetables to accompany the haggis are traditionally tatties and neeps. |
| MRS NAUGHTIE | Oh, you've lost me there. |
| DOUGAL | See, here's a picture of a haggis, tatties and neeps. |
| MRS NAUGHTIE | Ooooooh! Are you sure this isn't a medical dictionary? |
| DOUGAL | No, look, it says this shows the traditional haggis, made from oatmeal and onion … |
| MRS NAUGHTIE | Oh, a vegetarian dish. |
| DOUGAL | Not quite. You add a pound of suet plus the liver, heart and lungs of a sheep all minced up and stuffed |

|                |                                                                                          |
| -------------- | ---------------------------------------------------------------------------------------- |
|                | into a dead sheep's stomach.                                                              |
| MRS NAUGHTIE   | Oh! I can't see Nigella getting her laughing gear round that lot!                        |
| HAMISH         | All washed down with a fine malt whisky.                                                  |
| MRS NAUGHTIE   | It would have to be!                                                                      |
| DOUGAL         | Speaking of which, we'd better pay a visit to the Drive-Thru Distillery to place our very large order for the party. |
| HAMISH         | Then what are we waiting for?                                                             |
| DOUGAL         | This bus.                                                                                 |
|                | *Bus draws up, doors open, doors shut, bus drives off*                                    |
| HAMISH         | Dougal …                                                                                  |
| DOUGAL         | Yes …?                                                                                     |
| HAMISH         | Why didn't we get on that bus?                                                            |
| DOUGAL         | Did you not realise? That was the phantom bus that haunts the village.                    |
| HAMISH         | How do you know?                                                                           |
| DOUGAL         | Did you not notice how it glided through that wall of my sitting room and then out through the other. |
| HAMISH         | Ooooo! A phantom bus.                                                                      |

| | |
|---|---|
| DOUGAL | Aye. |
| | *Crash! Clatter of rubble, bus draws up, doors open* |
| DOUGAL | This … is the real one. |
| HAMISH | Two singles to the distillery please. |
| | *Ding ding! Bus drives off. Crashes through other wall* |
| *Band plays* | *Link* |
| DOUGAL | Well, here we are at the Drive-Thru Distillery. |
| HAMISH | Why do you keep doing that? |
| DOUGAL | It's a trick I learned from the wireless. |
| LAIRD | *[Distort]* Good morning. Welcome to the Drive-Thru Distillery. |
| HAMISH | You see, you needn't have bothered. |
| DOUGAL | How was I to know he was going to do exposition? |
| LAIRD | *[D]* Can I help you? |
| HAMISH | Good morning. |
| DOUGAL | Good morning, Hamish. Now leave this to me. Where's that list of mine? Oh yes, in my sporran. Somewhere in … here … Ah … eh … |
| | *Sporran fumbling* |
| HAMISH | Dougal … |
| DOUGAL | Not now, Hamish, I've nearly got my hand on it. |
| HAMISH | Dougal, that's my sporran you're fumbling in. |
| DOUGAL | Oh, I'm sorry. |
| HAMISH | No, please carry on. |
| DOUGAL | Very well. But I don't know how I come to be wearing your sporran. |
| HAMISH | Well, we did dress rather hurriedly after the jacuzzi … |
| LAIRD | *[D]* Look here, are you going to place an order or not? |
| DOUGAL | Aye, here's the list. We'd like … a lot of whisky please. |
| HAMISH | Do you have anything on special offer? |
| LAIRD | *[D]* This is your lucky day! With every twenty-five cases of GlenCampbell twelve-year-old malt, you get a free commemorative millennium beer mat. |
| HAMISH | Jings! That's an offer you can't refuse. |
| DOUGAL | Now hold on, Hamish. We've already got a beer mat. |
| LAIRD | *[D]* Or with fifty cases of Glen Campbell you get a free ceremonial teatowel with a picture of Mao Tse Tung on it. |
| DOUGAL | Och, we're up to here with those. |
| LAIRD | *[D]* Or, with 100 cases, you get a free electronic sporran alarm. |

| | |
|---|---|
| HAMISH | Better late than never. |
| DOUGAL | It's a deal! Now let me just have a rummage for my chequebook … |
| HAMISH | Here it is! |
| DOUGAL | Spoilsport. Now, who shall I make this cheque out to? |
| LAIRD | Oh leave it blank, I'll fill in the name when I'm writing the amount. |
| DOUGAL | That's very kind of you. |
| | ***Sign and rip out cheque*** |
| LAIRD | *[D]* Well, you'd better be on your way; I notice the bus driver's getting a little impatient. |
| | ***Rude bus horn: parp parp!*** |
| HAMISH | Santa! |
| LAIRD | Thank you for shopping at the Drive-Thru Distillery. Have a nice day. Goodbye. |
| HAMISH | Dougal, do you not think that voice sounded very like the Laird? |
| DOUGAL | Oh, now you come to mention it … |
| HAMISH | You don't think …? |
| DOUGAL | Dooh, Hamish, as if the Laird would have the gall to sell us all that whisky for his own party … |
| HAMISH | No, of course not. |
| DOUGAL | Right, Hamish, you load that 100 cases of whisky on to the bus while I gaze into the distance. |
| HAMISH | Right you are. Hup! One. Hup! Two. Hup … |
| DOUGAL | This is no time to be doing press-ups. Shift those cases. |
| HAMISH | Hup! One. |
| | ***Case clatters after each hup*** |
| HAMISH | Hup two. Hup three. Hup four … |
| ***Band plays*** | ***Link*** |
| | ***Case clatters after each hup*** |
| HAMISH | Hup 98 hup 99 hup 100! |
| DOUGAL | Well done! If only the bus had waited … |
| | ***Approaching vehicle*** |
| HAMISH | Look, why don't we stop this vehicle? |
| DOUGAL | Good thinking. Stop! |
| | ***Screech of brakes*** |
| DOUGAL | Good morning. I wonder if you could drop us off with these cases of whisky at the Big Hoose? |
| HAMISH | He's nodding his head. |

# HAGGIS SOUFFLÉ

No book of Scottish culinary specialities would be complete without inclusion of what has been humbly referred to as my signature dish: haggis soufflé. This is the delicacy they said couldn't be cooked, couldn't be welcomed to the table, couldn't even be eaten! Well time and again, how wrong have they failed to be proved to be?!

INGREDIENTS: 1 freshly plucked haggis, quartered, 1 egg, another egg, 8oz of good quality dark chocolate, 1 carton of triple cream essence of Aston Vanilla.

METHOD: Combine the ingredients into a soufflé and … voila! (Traditionally the haggis is 'piped' to the table, but if you have no pipeline from the kitchen, it may be carried in by hand.) Bring to the table in the soufflé dish then turn out anyone who passes comment.

| | |
|---|---|
| DOUGAL | Thank you. Shall we load them up? |
| HAMISH | He's nodding his head again, and indicating the back of the vehicle. |
| DOUGAL | Very kind of you, sir. |
| HAMISH | He's smiling now and giving the thumbs-up. |
| DOUGAL | Right, let's get these cases loaded. |
| | ***Hup hup huh hup hup*** |
| | ***Cases clatter*** |
| HAMISH | There's plenty of room in the back. |
| DOUGAL | Aye, move those flowers and there's space for more on top of the big box. |
| | ***Cases clatter*** |
| HAMISH | Right, in we get. |
| | ***Door slam. Drives off*** |
| DOUGAL | Here we are driving along in comfort. |
| HAMISH | Preceded by a wee band. |
| | ***Dead march … link*** |
| DOUGAL | Well, thank you very much, you got us here quicker than the bus. |
| HAMISH | He's nodding and winking as if to say 'don't mention it, only too pleased to help. Any time you need a hand I'm your man. Just ring the Happy Endings Funeral Parlour and ask for Jolly Mick. See you soon, have a nice day. Bye bye.' |
| DOUGAL | All that with a nod and a wink, eh? |
| HAMISH | I was paraphrasing. |
| DOUGAL | Well, we can't stand here chatting with Jolly Mick all day. Ring the Laird's doorbell. |
| | ***Doorbell. Door creaks open*** |
| HAMISH | Mrs Naughtie! What are you doing here? |
| MRS NAUGHTIE | Oh, I'm so glad to see the pair of you. |
| DOUGAL | Whatever's the matter? |
| MRS NAUGHTIE | Come with me to the kitchen and all will be revealed. |
| DOUGAL | Very kind, but let's deal with your problem first. |
| MRS NAUGHTIE | My problem is in the kitchen! |
| DOUGAL | Then let's have a look! |
| | ***Door flung open. Hot sizzling bubbling splattering noises …*** |
| DOUGAL | Oh sorry, your Lairdship. I thought it was the kitchen. |
| LAIRD | Pass me that rubber duck before you close the door. |
| | ***Quack! Door slam*** |
| MRS NAUGHTIE | Here we are, gentlemen, this is the kitchen. |

*Door flung open. Hot sizzling bubbling splattering noises …*

DOUGAL — What on earth have you been doing in here, woman?

MRS NAUGHTIE — I've been cooking.

HAMISH — We can see that. But what is it?

MRS NAUGHTIE — It's the catering for Burns Night.

DOUGAL — Well, I can see the tatties bubbling merrily in the pot here …

HAMISH — And I recognise the neeps waiting to be mashed …

*Fade up slobbery steps dragging across the floor*

DOUGAL — But help me out here: what is that nine-foot-high steaming mound of pulsating tissue that's edging its way across the floor?

MRS NAUGHTIE — You mean you don't recognise it?

DOUGAL — Good grief, Mrs Naughtie! It's the haggis!

HAMISH — And it's coming towards us!

DOUGAL — It's alive!

HAMISH — Look at the size of it!

DOUGAL — Hamish! There's a time and a place for everything!

HAMISH — No, look at the size of the haggis!

DOUGAL — Do something, Hamish!

HAMISH — Quick, pass me a knife. And a fork.

DOUGAL — Oh, eyes bigger than your stomach as usual.

*More slushing and slurping*

HAMISH — It's got me! It's got me!

DOUGAL — Don't worry, Hamish! I'm off!

MRS NAUGHTIE — Oh, for goodness' sake! That's not a haggis. It's my nephew Kevin from Pitlochry!

DOUGAL — So it is! Of course we remember wee Kevin.

HAMISH — Jings, Dougal, he's let himself go.

MRS NAUGHTIE — He takes after his mother.

HAMISH & DOUGAL — Oh aye mmm aye oh yes aye …

MRS NAUGHTIE — Kevin's kindly offered to play the bagpipes for the Burns Supper. Haven't you, Kevin?

*Bagpipe drones*

DOUGAL — Well, that's very good of you.

*Bagpipe drones*

MRS NAUGHTIE — Don't just stand there moaning, go and get your bagpipes.

*Bagpipe drones*

DOUGAL — And tidy yourself up while you're at it.

*Slobbery steps dragging across the floor – fade*

| | |
|---|---|
| DOUGAL | Dear me, what a sight. Did you notice his flies? |
| HAMISH | Covered in them! |
| DOUGAL | Well, Mrs Naughtie, we'll leave you to get on with cooking that haggis. |
| MRS NAUGHTIE | Well … you promise not to get angry? |
| HAMISH & DOUGAL | Of course. |
| MRS NAUGHTIE | Well … there is no haggis. |
| HAMISH | *[Furious]* You stupid pea-brained apology for a waste of space! |
| DOUGAL | Now now, Hamish. We promised not to get angry. |
| HAMISH | Hmm! |
| DOUGAL | Now, what do you mean by 'no haggis', you stupid pea-brained apology for a waste of space? |
| MRS NAUGHTIE | I called Big Tam the butcher to place my order, but he said there wasn't a haggis to be had, the length and breadth of the Glen. |
| HAMISH | We can't have Burns Night without haggis! That would be like Bonfire Night without a bang! |
| MRS NAUGHTIE | Not to worry! I am proposing to improvise. |
| DOUGAL | But how? |
| MRS NAUGHTIE | What do you think of this? |
| DOUGAL | Oh. It looks like a haggis … |
| HAMISH | *[Tasting]* Mm! It tastes like a haggis. |
| DOUGAL | Oh yes, mmm! But what is it? |
| MRS NAUGHTIE | It's a can of dog food in a condom. |
| HAMISH & DOUGAL | **Splutters!** |
| DOUGAL | Well, I must say, it's an improvement. |
| HAMISH | Aye, and well worth the extra expense. Slips down a treat. |
| DOUGAL | Well done, Mrs Naughtie. |
| MRS NAUGHTIE | And spotted dick to follow. |
| HAMISH | If you're not very careful. |
| DOUGAL | Come along, Hamish, there's work to be done! |
| *Band* | *Link* |
| | *Railway station atmos. Express train up and past …* |
| DOUGAL | Well, here we are at the railway station. |
| HAMISH | If you say that one more time …! |
| DOUGAL | Well, there might be blind people listening. Oh look, there's his Lairdship. |
| LAIRD | Hello you two. Any sign of the train from London? |
| | *Bingbong* |
| TANNOY | *[Distort]* The train from London … xx xx xxxx xx |

Now allotments.
(Broken claymore visible next to shed.)

Sh
ha

# HAIR CUT
# WHILE
# YOU WAIT!

## At SAFT WULLIE'S
### Barbery Saloon

Be the proud owner of
our Social Diary:

## 'OOT AND ABOOT'

40p at the Post Office

Th
HOI

*"Her*
*All y*

You're su
Thistle

delayed xxx xx xxxx and flock of sheep. Xxx xx xxxx inconvenience  xxx xxxxx. Xxx xx xxxxx over on BBC2, xx xxxxx xx xx xxx Matt Lucas and Paris Hilton ... xx xxx xxxxx xxx of the Baskervilles. Xxxx xxx xxxxx xx xxxxx xx Xxx xxx xx xxxx xxxxxx one minute.

*Bingbong*

**LAIRD** Splendid! My guests from London should be here very soon. Now, you two are arranging transport up to the Big Hoose. I should think you'll need a pony and trap.

**HAMISH** No thanks, I've just had one.

**DOUGAL** Don't worry, your Lairdship, we've hired a people carrier.

**HAMISH** That's right – Big Tam's going to carry the people to the bus stop.

**LAIRD** Splendid. And unless I'm very much mistaken, here comes the train now ...

*Stampede of bellowing cattle*

**LAIRD** By God I was mistaken, wasn't I?  What does it say on that board, Dougal?

**DOUGAL** It says 'Here comes the train now!'

*Train whistle, steam train up and stop. Doors open and passengers disembark*

**ALL** *Murmur murmur*

**HAMISH** Jings, that's a lot of people! Are they all coming to the party?

**LAIRD** Oh no, most of them are just extras. I'll point out the real guests. Ah look, there's Girls Aloud with David Walliams. The Archbishop of Canterbury – oh sorry, madam! Ah, Wayne Rooney and Jan Leeming. Hello, spudface! Not you, Jan. Wonder where they're off to. There's lovely Zara Philips ...

*Horse whinnies*

**LAIRD** And she's brought her mother. And there's Nikki off *Big Brother*, and there's Pete Doherty with the lovely Stirling Moss. Renee Zellwegger of course, and there's dear old Lionel Blair ... oh no, it's Lenny Henry. My good friend Chantelle with Brian Sewell – again! It's a pity Jeffrey Archer said he wasn't coming – and here he is.

**ALL** *Murmur murmur*

| | |
|---|---|
| LAIRD | Hello. Hello everyone. How lovely to see you all. Especially you two – without Bono. Now it's a good ten miles from here to the Big Hoose – that's why I came in the car. See you later! |
| | *Car drives off* |
| ALL | *Angry murmuring* |
| QUEEN | My fellow guests and I, from all corners of the Commonwealth … |
| DOUGAL | Not now, dear, we're busy. |
| QUEEN | We are deeply concerned about the lack of transport to convey us to the Big Hice. |
| HAMISH | Oh, there's always one. |
| DOUGAL | Aye, I knew she was trouble the moment she got off that train. |
| QUEEN | At this time of year, one's thoughts often turn to questions such as: what arrangements have you dickheads made to convey one to the party? |
| HAMISH | Why don't you tell her to naff off? |
| DOUGAL | Don't you realise who this is? |
| HAMISH | No I don't. |
| DOUGAL | Does anybody recognise this woman? |
| BIG TAM | Aye! It's Mad Betty the Bus-driver. |
| HAMISH | Bus-driver? We're in luck! And look! She's brought her bus with her! |
| DOUGAL | Fifty-three singles to the Big Hoose please. |
| QUEEN | I name this bus Number 32. God bless all who catch her. Hold tight! |
| | *Ding ding!* |
| | *Bus drives off* |
| *Band* | *Link* |
| | *After dinner murmur. The Laird silences the room by pingng a spoon on a glass* |
| LAIRD | Ladies and gentlemen. I hope you'll join me in congratulating Mrs Naughtie on providing a truly beautiful dinner. Shame it didn't taste as good as it looked. I think we all had very high hopes of that ribbed haggis. But that's neither here nor there, as the man said when he put his truss on upside down. The entertainment will begin shortly, but for the moment, please sit back and enjoy your brandy and liqueurs as I come round to each table to present you with your bills. |

*'Speciality o' the hoose!'*
*Chip shop magnate Willie Lauderdale packing seasonal mail-order treats: deep-fried Easter eggs!*

|  | *Murmur* |
|---|---|
| DOUGAL | Ladies and gentlemen, no evening of this nature would be complete without some Scottish dancing! So who's up for a Highland Reel? |
| CROWD | *Mixture of yes and no* |
| DOUGAL | Oh. Welcome to *Reel or No Reel*. |
|  | *Phone rings* |
| DOUGAL | Hello? The what? Oh banker! What? Noel who? No he isn't here. Well, just our good luck I suppose. Goodbye. |
| HAMISH | Box number seven! |
| DOUGAL | Don't flog it to death. |
| HAMISH | Very well. Now, here by way of a contrast is a demonstration of Highland flamenco dancing. Accompanied by Kevin the piper, welcome our good friend Pepe McDomingo from the Bide-a-wee Tapas Bar and his twinkling feet! |
|  | *Pipe drone accompanied by frantic flamenco steps* |
|  | *Pipes tacet as steps clatter on and on* |
| LAIRD | Come in. |
|  | *Door opens* |
| LAIRD | Ah Mrs Naughtie. You've missed nothing, the flamenco dancer didn't turn up. |
| MRS NAUGHTIE | Oh, I got enough of that flamenco on my holiday in Leith. Now, I've brought you that book of Rabbie Burns poetry you asked for. You'll see from the stickers on the cover it is 'recommended by Richard and Judy'. 'Two for the price of one', as I believe they're known. |
| LAIRD | Thank you, Mrs Naughtie. Ah, I see you've marked the page. |
| MRS NAUGHTIE | Oh, that'll sponge off. |
| LAIRD | Ahem. 'Address to a Haggis' by Rabbie Burns. |
|  | *[Very English]* |
|  | Fair fa' your honest, sonsie face, Great chieftain o' the pudding-race! Aboon them a' yet tak your place, Painch, tripe, or thairm: Weel are ye wordy o' grace As lang's my arm. |
| HAMISH | What's he talking about? |
| MRS NAUGHTIE | Oh, he's pissed. |
| HAMISH | Fair enough. |
| LAIRD | All together now: Auld Scotland wants nae skinking |

|  |  |
|---|---|
|  | ware That jaups in luggies; |
| DOUGAL | Thank you, your Lairdship … |
| LAIRD | But I hadn't finished … |
| DOUGAL | Big hand for his Lairdship! |
| LAIRD | Trenching your gushing entrails bright, Till a' their weel-swall'd kytes belyve, Then auld Guidman, maist like to rive, Bethankit! hums. |
|  | **Under the Laird's recitation:** |
| HAMISH | I've never heard anything like it. |
| MRS NAUGHTIE | That's what I call a recitation! |
| HAMISH | A once-in-a-lifetime experience. |
| DOUGAL | With any luck. |
| MRS NAUGHTIE | The guests are getting restless. I say it's time for some music. Kevin is inflating his bagpipes in anticipation. |
| HAMISH | Oh, you've got to be careful doing that. |
| MRS NAUGHTIE | Why? |
| HAMISH | You can get a very nasty blowback. Jings, that doesn't half make you ankles swell! |
| LAIRD | Well, he did such a good job earlier, piping in the haggis, why doesn't he give us a tune and pipe out the heftovers? |
| ALL | Hurrah! |
| *Pipes* | **Short burst of Scottish tune** |
| LAIRD | Ho ho, the skirl of the pipes! It always makes me feel like dancing! |
| DOUGAL | Let's get everyone on the floor for the competition. |
| HAMISH | Can they not do it standing up? |
| DOUGAL | Of course they can. It's time for *Strictly Come Reeling*! |
| MRS NAUGHTIE | Oh yes! That's where everyone takes part in an eightsome reel, and at the end of every chorus, they've got to let one go. |
| DOUGAL | Well, we can rely on Hamish for that. |
| *Band* | **Short eightsome reel link. End with a flourish. Drum roll under …** |
| DOUGAL | And the winner of *Strictly Come Reeling* is … |
| HAMISH | Mrs McAlister … it's not you. |
| DOUGAL | Tim Henman … it's not you. |
| HAMISH | Anne Widdecombe … it might be you … |
| DOUGAL | But the winner is … with his partner, the lovely Ross Kemp, the winner is his Lairdship the McCoist of McCoist of that ilk. |
| LAIRD | Omigod. Omigod. Omigod, I think I'm going to cry. |

| | |
|---|---|
| **DOUGAL** | No you're not. Let's have a last word from the Judges. |
| **ALL** | Rubbish! Terrible! Rotten! Booo! |
| | *Raspberry* |
| **HAMISH** | Santa! |
| **DOUGAL** | As you all know, it is traditional for everyone to do a party piece on Burns Night. So for my moment of glory, I shall read out some parish announcements. |
| **HAMISH** | Knock 'em dead, tiger! |
| **DOUGAL** | Reverend Hush has asked me to request that church-goers should not park their bicycles up against the vicar's wife. If this doesn't stop, she has threatened to start clamping. Congratulations to Dr McCorgi, who has successfully crossed a lettuce with a caber and got a salad that tosses itself. |
| **HAMISH** | Tell them about last year when he crossed a length of tartan with a bag of flour, and got a self-raising kilt. |
| **DOUGAL** | I was just going to. The Reverend also asked me to remind you all of the appeal for the church spire – as it still hasn't been returned. |
| **HAMISH** | Tell them about my operation! |
| **DOUGAL** | I didn't know you had one. |
| **HAMISH** | I haven't, now. |
| **DOUGAL** | Next up to entertain you, it's your own, your very own Mrs Beyonce Naughtie …! |
| *Clap* | *Solo clapping* |
| **DOUGAL** | And her performing seal! |
| *Seal* | *Clapping and onking* |
| **MRS NAUGHTIE** | Thank you, Archie, have a fish. |
| | *Splat! Munching. Clapping and onking* |
| **MRS NAUGHTIE** | Good boy, Archie. Now sit still while I bring on my performing seal. |
| *Band plays* | *Accordion intro and theme* |
| **HAMISH** | Jings, Mrs Naughtie, that seal can play the accordion all right! |
| **DOUGAL** | Aye! You should take him round the clubs. |
| *Band plays* | *Accordion stops* |
| | *Terrified oinking as flippers run off* |
| **DOUGAL** | Oh dear, I shouldn't have said 'clubs'. |
| **MRS NAUGHTIE** | No you should not! He can't stand golf. |
| **HAMISH** | Can I do my party piece now? |
| **DOUGAL** | Oh very well. |
| **HAMISH** | Ladies and gentlemen: my impression of 'The Stag at |

|                     |                                                                                      |
|---------------------|--------------------------------------------------------------------------------------|
|                     | Bay'!                                                                                 |
|                     | *Pause*                                                                               |
| ALL                 | *Gasp of horror!*                                                                     |
| MRS NAUGHTIE        | Well really!                                                                          |
| DOUGAL              | That was very … ingenious. But I think that bit at the end was quite uncalled for.    |
| HAMISH              | Oh come on, we've all seen stags do that.                                             |
| DOUGAL              | Yes, but there's usually another stag there. I should have sensed trouble when I saw you mounting the podium. |
| MRS NAUGHTIE        | Oh look, here comes Kevin with his bagpipes akimbo.                                   |
|                     | *Drones. Slobbery dragging footsteps*                                                 |
| HAMISH              | He looks very smart in his Highland dress.                                            |
| MRS NAUGHTIE        | One of mine. Slit to the thigh and a hint of cleavage. Mind you, he's got the legs for it. |
| DOUGAL              | Well, we've got the bagpipes, we've got the band: it must be time for a song!         |
| LAIRD               | It certainly is. What do you want me to sing?                                         |
| ALL                 | *Mutter*                                                                              |
| DOUGAL              | We've taken a vote, and we all want you to sing 'Somewhere Over the Rainbow'.         |
| LAIRD               | No, I'm staying right here.                                                           |
| DOUGAL              | Damn!                                                                                 |
| LAIRD               | As you all know, I've always had an ear for a good tune.                              |
| HAMISH              | Pity he hasn't got the voice.                                                         |
| LAIRD               | Why don't I sing a song that we all know?                                             |
| HAMISH              | Why don't you sing a song that you know?                                              |
| LAIRD               | Tell you what, why don't you all join me in a rousing little number made famous by Sir Harry Lauder and his sister Estee, entitled 'Keep Right On to the End of the Road'. I'll do the first verse … |
| DOUGAL              | And we'll do the tune.                                                                |
| HAMISH              | Kevin! Haul out your chanter and hit those pipes!                                     |
| *Band & pipes*      | *'Keep Right On to the End of the Road'*                                              |
| LAIRD               | Ev'ry road thro' life is a long, long road, Fill'd with joys and sorrows too, As you journey on how your heart will yearn For the things most dear to you. With wealth and love, 'tis so, But onward we must go. |
| ALL                 | Keep right on to the end of the road,                                                 |

Keep right on to the end,
Tho' the way be long, let your heart be strong,
Keep right on round the bend.
Tho' you're tired and weary still journey on,
Till you come to your happy abode,
Where all you love you've been dreaming of
Will be there at the end of the road.
*Repeat with the aid of song sheet*

ALL + AUDIENCE   Keep right on to the end of the road,
Keep right on to the end,
Tho' the way be long, let your heart be strong,
Keep right on round the bend.
Tho' you're tired and weary still journey on,
Till you come to your happy abode,
Where all you love you've been dreaming of
Will be there at the end of the road.

ALL   *Happy Burns Night everybody!*

*THE END*

# CULLEN SKINK

CRAZY NAME – CRAZY RECIPE!

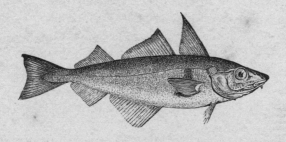

INGREDIENTS: A large smoked haddock (about 2 lb), 1 medium onion, finely chopped, 1½ pints milk, 2 oz butter, 8 oz mashed potato, Salt and pepper, Chopped parsley, Water and Toast

METHOD: Lay the smoked haddock in a shallow pan, skin side down, and cover with water. Bring to the boil and simmer for 4/5 minutes, turning once. Take the haddock from the pan, remove the skin and bones, and break up the fish into flakes. Return the flaked haddock to the stock, adding the chopped onion, salt and pepper. Simmer for another 15 minutes. Strain but retain the stock and fish. Add the milk to the fish stock and bring back to the boil then add mashed potato to create a rich creamy consistency. Add the fish and reheat, seasoning to taste. Just before serving, dot with small pieces of butter. Serve sprinkled with chopped parsley, accompanied by toast.

# PICTURE CREDITS